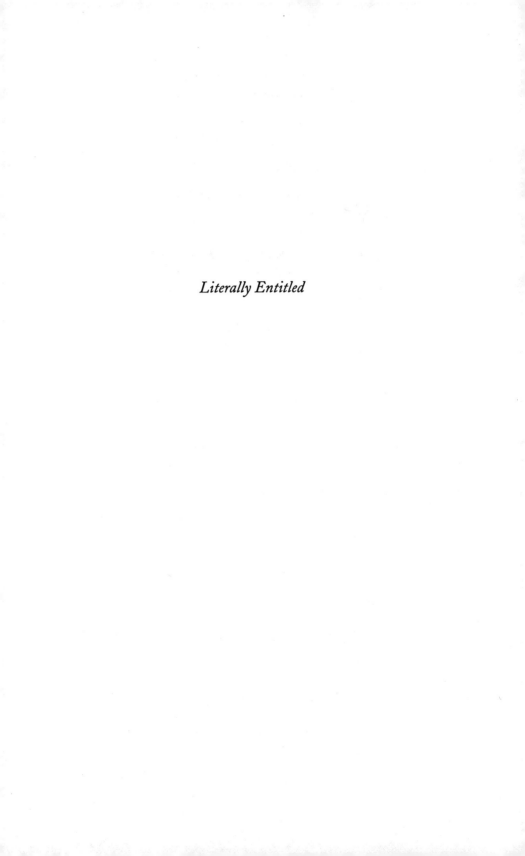

Literally Entitled

Literally Entitled

*A Dictionary of the Origins of the
Titles of Over 1300 Major Literary Works
of the Nineteenth and Twentieth Centuries*

by
ADRIAN ROOM

McFarland & Company, Inc., Publishers
Jefferson, North Carolina, and London

For John and Gwen, and long-shared literary loves

The note prefacing item 704's *London Fields* (by Martin Amis) is reprinted by permission of the Peters Fraser & Dunlop Group Ltd.

British Library Cataloguing-in-Publication data are available

Library of Congress Cataloguing-in-Publication Data

Room, Adrian.
   Literally entitled : a dictionary of the origins of the titles of
over 1300 major literary works of the nineteenth and twentieth
centuries / by Adrian Room.
      p.   cm.
   Includes bibliographical references and index. ∞
   ISBN 0-7864-0110-9 (lib. bdg. : 50# alk. paper)
   1. English literature—19th century—Dictionaries.   2. English
literature—20th century—Dictionaries.   3. American
literature—19th century—Dictionaries.   4. American
literature—20th century—Dictionaries.   5. Titles of books—
Dictionaries.   I. Title.
PR451.R66   1996
820.9'008'03—dc20   95-38299
                                                                  CIP

Manufactured in the United States of America

McFarland & Company, Inc., Publishers
  Box 611, Jefferson, North Carolina 28640

CONTENTS

Of all my verse, like not a single line;
But like my title, for it is not mine.
That title from a better man I stole;
Ah, how much better, had I stol'n the whole!

INTRODUCTION

I. The State of Play

Almost every literary work (with the exception of some shorter poems) has a title, serving both to identify it and in some way encapsulate it, either directly or allusively. As such, the title is part of the work itself, and is as creative or original as the work's author chooses to make it. However, titles are curious things, and are likely to linger imperfectly remembered in the mind. One English novelist has a theory that titles mean perhaps more to authors than readers, since the latter, "as every writer knows, frequently forget or garble the names of books they claim to admire" (David Lodge, *The Art of Fiction*, 1992). His theory is supported by evidence from booksellers and librarians, who have many a tale to tell of imperfectly recalled titles by would-be customers or readers. Garbled titles recorded in a British anthology of such things include *Roger the Taurus* for Roget's *Thesaurus*, *Tess of the Dormobiles* (a make of camper) for Hardy's *Tess of the d'Urbervilles*, *James Joyce Is Useless*, for James Joyce's *Ulysses*, *Jude the Obstreculous* for Hardy's *Jude the Obscure*, *Catch 66* for Heller's *Catch-22*, *Up Dee's Back* for Updike's *Bech*, *Lionel Richie and the Wardrobe* for C. S. Lewis's children's classic, *The Lion, The Witch and the Wardrobe*, *Donkey's Oats* for Cervantes' *Don Quixote*, and many more (Shaun Tyas, ed., *More Bookworm Droppings*, 1990).

The present book considers the different types of title that exist in 19th- and 20th-century literary works (mainly, though not quite exclusively, fiction), and aims to explain or elucidate where possible the more elusive (as well as allusive) titles, with particular reference to those found in American literature.

Some titles seem straightforward enough. In the present century, most readers have become familiar with titles such as Jack London's *The Call of the Wild* (about a dog called back to the wild), E. M. Forster's *The Longest Journey* (about a long journey), Edith Wharton's *Ethan Frome* (with a central character

1

of that name), Sinclair Lewis's *Babbitt* (with a protagonist of *that* name), Theodore Dreiser's *An American Tragedy* (about an American tragedy), William Faulkner's *As I Lay Dying* (about someone who is dying), Ernest Hemingway's *The Green Hills of Africa* (set in Africa), George Orwell's *Animal Farm* (about animals on a farm), John Updike's *Bech: A Book* (a book about Bech), and Vance Bourjaily's *Old Soldier* (about an old soldier).

But such titles are not necessarily what they seem. And how about Henry James's *The Wings of the Dove*, for example, or Ezra Pound's collection of poems *Lustra*? What is one to make of William Faulkner's *The Sound and the Fury*, T. S. Eliot's *Burnt Norton*, Iris Murdoch's *An Unofficial Rose*, or Armistead Maupin's *Maybe the Moon*? Titles like these must surely have more to them than meets the eye.

Such reservations are right, of course. It would be naive to suppose that a fictional work should have a title that works on one level only. Purely descriptive titles characteristic of 19th-century novels, such as *The Adventures of Huckleberry Finn* or *The Tenant of Wildfell Hall* are now largely a thing of the past. In the 20th century, one has come to expect something more original.

Allusive titles tend to be associated with particular authors and particular types of literature. Eugene O'Neill is one writer whose titles stay long in the mind, even when one has merely heard them and has not read the works they name: *The Moon of the Caribbees, Beyond the Horizon, The Hairy Ape, All God's Chillun Got Wings, Desire Under the Elms, Mourning Becomes Electra, The Iceman Cometh, Long Day's Journey into Night*. These are pure poetry (though they are actually plays). But what do they *mean*, and what is their particular relevance or significance?

Another writer very much in the same category is Tennessee Williams. It is not easy to banish from the mind such resonant titles as *A Streetcar Named Desire, The Rose Tattoo, Cat on a Hot Tin Roof, Suddenly Last Summer* or *The Night of the Iguana*. Like O'Neill's titles, they are meaningful in themselves, in the way that the title of a painting might be, but they clearly demand some kind of gloss or explanation. On the British side of the Atlantic one finds similar enigmas in the titles of Aldous Huxley. Typical of him are *Antic Hay, Point Counter Point, Eyeless in Gaza*, and *After Many a Summer*.

More recent fiction than this sometimes yields titles that are elusive to the point of being surreal. One thinks of Thomas Pynchon's *Gravity's Rainbow*, Anthony Burgess's *A Clockwork Orange*, Martin Amis's *Dead Babies*, or Paul Theroux's *O-Zone*. One expects such titles in science fiction or fantasy fiction, but how should they be handled in mainstream novels? Some titles, again, have a peculiar ability to bemuse, such as the alliterative artifacts of J. P. Donleavy: *Meet My Maker, the Mad Molecule, The Saddest Summer of Samuel S., The Beastly Beatitudes of Balthazar B.*, and *The Destinies of Darcy Dancer, Gentleman*. Some writers go further, and incorporate bogus titles in their fiction. The British novelist Anthony Powell has a publisher's literary adviser reflecting on a novel he has been offered: *The Pistons of Our Locomotives Sing the Song of the Workers*. He decides this is too cumbersome, and it is reduced to *Engine Melody*. Another of Powell's characters, a publisher's secretary, has written three novels: *I Stopped at a Chemist*, *Bedsores*, and *The Bitch Pack Meets on Wednesday*. A third is the author of *Camel Ride to the Tomb* and *Dogs Have No Uncles*. These last two have something of the same esoteric flavor as Powell's own *Books Do Furnish a Room*.

The titles of poetical works are also frequently allusive. In short, they are "poetic," since that is what poetry is about. One is not too surprised when poets such as Robert Bly, Galway Kinnell, and Charles Simic come up respectively with titles such as *The Man in the Black Coat Turns*, *Body Rags*, and *Weather Forecast for Utopia and Vicinity*. (They are Surrealist poets, after all!) But, although poetry is usually a more esoteric literary form than fictional prose, the titles cry out for an interpretation.

How is one to discover the meaning or origin of all these titles? The obvious method is to read the work concerned, when all should be revealed. It may not be, however, and it could well be that the author has deliberately devised an allusive or elusive title, and prefers it to stay that way.

Another recourse is to study the text with the aid of a commentary or set of explanatory notes, rather in the manner of a college student. But even this may not work, since the writers of such commentaries frequently devote such detailed attention to an explication of the plot, the characters, and the style of the work, that they often overlook the significance of the title altogether. Perhaps they simply regard it as a designation, and outside their area of interest, much as a travel writer will describe Boston or Barbados in detail but will not bother to explain the name.

A third way is to use such a book as this. They are rarely found, which is why this particular work came into being. It may be a "test run," or what is sometimes known in the literary world as a *ballon d'essai*, but at least it is a start.

II. The Rules of the Game

Although literary titles are a complex matter, it is possible to distinguish certain types of title and so to determine something about their origins and their significance. There are basically seven categories, according to their composition and reference. The first six categories involve individual words or phrases. The seventh comprises whole sentences. They are as follows:

1. Titles that consist of a noun or a noun phrase, with or without a preceding article. They relate to the general theme or nature of the work, or less often, to its climax or dénouement, and can be directly descriptive or allusive. Examples are Arthur Conan Doyle's *The Lost World*,

E. M. Forster's *A Passage to India*, William Faulkner's *Sanctuary*, Alison Lurie's *The War Between the Tates*, James Baldwin's *The Fire Next Time*, and Kurt Vonnegut's *Cat's Cradle*.

2. Titles that relate to the protagonist or to a particular character without actually naming him or her (or them). Examples are Henry James's *The Ambassadors*, Baroness Orczy's *The Scarlet Pimpernel*, Arnold Bennett's *The Card*, William Saroyan's *The Daring Young Man on the Flying Trapeze*, Graham Green's *The Quiet American*, and Eugene O'Neill's *The Hairy Ape*.

3. Titles that actually name the character(s), with or without an accompanying word such as an adjective or noun. Examples are Eugene O'Neill's *The Emperor Jones*, G. B. Shaw's *Saint Joan*, F. Scott Fitzgerald's *The Great Gatsby*, Sinclair Lewis's *Elmer Gantry*, Samuel Beckett's *Watt*, Saul Bellow's *Herzog*, and Philip Roth's *Portnoy's Complaint*.

4. Titles naming the setting or location of the narrative. Among them are E. M. Forster's *Howards End*, Aldous Huxley's *Crome Yellow*, John Dos Passos's *Manhattan Transfer*, G. B. Shaw's *Heartbreak House*, John Irving's *The Hotel New Hampshire*, and Grace Metalious' *Peyton Place*.

5. Titles consisting of an adjectival or adverbial phrase. Examples include Erich Maria Remarque's *All Quiet on the Western Front*, Iain Banks's *Against a Dark Background*, F. Scott Fitzgerald's *This Side of Paradise*, and V. S. Naipaul's *In a Free State*.

6. Titles consisting of a verbal phrase or simply a single verb. They include Harper Lee's *To Kill a Mockingbird*, Ernest Hemingway's *For Whom the Bell Tolls*, Dorothy Simpson's *The Night She Died*, Kingsley Amis's *Ending Up*, Garrison Keillor's *Leaving Home*, and Margaret Mitchell's *Gone with the Wind*.

7. Titles comprising a complete sentence. Examples are Ursula Le Guin's *The Word for World Is Forest*, Brian Moore's *I Am Mary Dunne*, John Wain's *Hurry On Down*, Ken Kesey's *One Flew Over the Cuckoo's Nest*, and Norman Mailer's *Tough Guys Don't Dance*.

Within these categories, the first (1 through 3) are more likely to be the author's own creation. The last (4 through 7) may also be the writer's own words, but may equally be a quotation. Looked at another way, a short title is likely to be the author's own and may be prosaic. A longer title frequently represents a quoted text, or an adapted form of a quoted text, and will often be more colorful and evocative.

Whatever a title's length, if it is indeed what the writer regards as an apt quotation, it may be very familiar or entirely obscure. A quotation-title can be borrowed, in whole or in part, from a common idiom, phrase, or proverb, such as Mike Nicol's *The Powers That Be*, a text from a familiar literary source such as the Bible or Shakespeare, such as Pearl Buck's *A House Divided* and R. C.

Sherriff's *Journey's End*, or words from a popular rhyme or song, such as Robert Penn Warren's *All the King's Men* and Malcolm Bradbury's *Eating People Is Wrong*.

How important is it in such cases to know the source of the quotation? Perhaps ultimately not all that important. But many writers choose such a title under the assumption that the reader will be able to supply the rest of the relevant passage, and so make it fully significant. Thus Warren's *All the King's Men*, just quoted, is a title that is not particularly relevant as it stands. But the novel charts the rise and fall of a demagogue, and the reader is expected to supply the missing words of the quote to allude to this. In other words, the writer assumes that the reader will recall the nursery rhyme lines about the fate of Humpty Dumpty after he "had a great fall":

> All the king's horses,
> And all the king's men,
> Couldn't put Humpty together again.

Sometimes the reader is required to make a fairly sophisticated or subtle deduction by this method. The title of Thomas Dixon's novel *The Leopard's Spots*, published at the turn of the 20th century, was intended to suggest in the reader's mind the first half of the biblical passage: "Can the Ethiopian change his skin, or the leopard his spots?" The unreconstructed Southerner's book aimed to show what fearful consequences would ensue if the black American were raised above his station, and its title was intended to posit the writer's views on this.

Thus although it is not necessary to pin down chapter and verse of a biblical quotation, or act and scene of a Shakespearean one, it certainly helps to be familiar with the original words, and not merely those used in the title, but those which surround it or support it in the original.

Fairly frequently, a writer will take a well-known phrase or quote and adapt it, often punningly, to his or her own end. The result may be corny or embarrassingly contrived, but the reader is still expected to recognize the source, *and* appreciate the point of the alteration or adaption. Examples are Tom Sharpe's *Ancestral Vices* (for Coleridge's "ancestral voices"), Len Deighton's *Twinkle, Twinkle, Little Spy* (for Jane Taylor's "Twinkle, twinkle, little star"), and Samuel Beckett's *More Pricks than Kicks* (for the biblical "kick against the pricks"). In a surprisingly large number of cases, such punning quotation-titles are based on existing titles, with which the reader is expected to be equally familiar. Examples are Dylan Thomas's *Portrait of the Artist as a Young Dog* (for James Joyce's *Portrait of the Artist as a Young Man*, itself suggesting a painted portrait title), Nicholas Blake's novel *Malice in Wonderland* (for Lewis Carroll's *Alice in Wonderland*), and Stuart Berg Flexner's study of the American language, *I Hear America Talking* (for Walt Whitman's poem *I Hear America Singing*).

Many quotation-titles that are not punning alterations of the original are nevertheless intended punningly, even wittily, or as a double entendre. Thus Conrad Hilton's *Be My Guest*, about his experiences as a hotelier, takes the familiar invitation to "feel free," and William Golding's *Free Fall* sets a deeper meaning to the term for an aspect of a parachute jump. When not intended punningly, too, a quotation-title (and even an original one) may be employed ironically. This is a favorite device with thriller writers, who frequently have recourse to a pleasant-sounding title for a tale that is anything but pleasant. Raymond Chandler alone offers several examples of the genre in *Farewell, My Lovely*, *The Big Sleep*, *The Little Sister*, and *The Lady in the Lake*. The last title here is both ironic and punning, and refers to the "Lady of the Lake" in the Arthurian legends as well as a murder victim who has been deep-sixed. (But perhaps Chandler is being subtler than he seems, since this original lady is involved in a death and is herself killed.) Many of Angela Carter's novels, too, have titles that belie their dark and sinister content. Among them are *The Magic Toyshop*, *Love*, *Nights at the Circus*, and *Wise Children*. Not much magic, love, amusing entertainment, or innocent wisdom here, at any rate in the normal sense of these words.

The precise identification of a quotation-title's origin is the business of the present book. In some cases, however, the book itself may identify the source of its quotation in an epigraph. The identification may be precise, as in C. S. Lewis's *That Hideous Strength*, or only approximate, as in John Wain's *Hurry on Down*, which simply has "Old Song" as the source. Many novels in fact have one or more epigraphs entirely unrelated to the title. (Lee Harper's *To Kill a Mockingbird* has a six-word sentence from Charles Lamb.)

More complex than these are the titles that appear to be quotations but that as far as one can tell are not. This is true of the more evocative titles, such as Barbara Taylor Bradford's *Hold the Dream* or Raymond Chandler's *Farewell, My Lovely*, already mentioned. Of course, they may be quotations from somewhere or somebody, but if they are, Bradford, Chandler et al. are not revealing the source.

On a more practical note, it should be mentioned that novels and other literary works are sometimes given new or modified titles when reissued in a new edition. This is most likely when an American work comes out in a British edition, or vice versa. John Wain's *Hurry on Down*, already mentioned, was titled *Born in Captivity* in its first American edition, this despite the fact that Nellie Lutcher, who wrote the song from which the British title is taken, was an American. On the other hand, Margaret Miller's thriller *Rose's Last Summer*, first published in the United States, kept this title in its British edition, but was subsequently retitled *The Lively Corpse* in a new American edition. (The first of these two titles is surely the better.) Some title alterations are so slight as to appear unnecessary. Two novels by the British writer Anita Brookner, *A Start in Life* and *A Misalliance*, were respectively retitled *The Debut* and *The Misalliance* in their American editions. But some titles with specific American allusions have remained unchanged in British editions, as have British allusions in novels appearing in the United States. Examples are Kurt Vonnegut's *Breakfast of Champions* (from a slogan for an American breakfast cereal), Paul Theroux's *O-Zone* (for the Ozark region), and Paule Marshall's *Brown Girl, Brownstones*. British readers may have become familiar with a "brown girl" through pop music (Boney M, back in the 1970s), but few even now will know what "brownstone" implies. The converse applies for Anthony Burgess's *Any Old Iron* (from a turn-of-the-century music hall song about a scrap metal merchant) or David Benedictus' *Fourth of June* (about Eton College, and named for that school's speech day).

The Bible and Shakespeare have undoubtedly proved the richest source of literary quotation-titles, and there are dozens of examples of each in the present book. Poets of all ages, too, from Spenser in the 16th century and Milton in the 17th to Keats in the 19th and Wallace Stevens in the 20th have also proved a fruitful hunting ground for this purpose. And certain titles themselves have become part and parcel of the language, either because they introduced a particular phrase or concept or because they widely popularized it. Among them are J. K. Galbraith's *The Affluent Society* (1958), Nigel Balchin's *The Small Back Room* (1943), Evan Hunter's *The Blackboard Jungle* (1954), W. Somerset Maugham's *Creatures of Circumstance* (1947), C. P. Snow's *Corridors of Power* (1964), S. J. Perelman's *Crazy Like a Fox* (1944), Walter Greenwood's *Love on the Dole* (1933), Damon Runyon's *Guys and Dolls* (1931), T. C. Worsley's *Flannelled Fool* (1967), Albert Bigelow Paine's *The Great White Way* (1901), Vance Packard's *The Hidden Persuaders* (1957), Upton Sinclair's *The Jungle* (1906), Nathanael West's *Miss Lonelyhearts* (1933), Charles Jackson's *The Lost Weekend* (1944), Marshall McLuhan's *The Medium Is the Message* (1967), Desmond Morris's *The Naked Ape* (1967), Frederic Raphael's *The Glittering Prizes* (1976), Ernst Friedrich Schumacher's *Small Is Beautiful* (1973), Robert Graves's *Goodbye to All That* (1929), and John Braine's *Life at the Top* (1962). These, and others, have gained an equally firm place in dictionaries of quotations.

Something must now be said about the content and arrangement of the present book, which in its way is also such a dictionary.

III. Totaling the Titles

The main section of this book contains over 1300 titles. They are all from the 19th and 20th centuries. They almost all originate in the English language, and the majority are American. Several later became movie titles, and won new popularity.

They come mainly from well-known authors of fiction, although a very few titles are of nonfiction works and some are from the pens of less familiar writers. In general, titles of science fiction, crime novels, and romantic novels are in the minority, not because they are any the less valid, but because they are mostly stereotyped and will be known to a more specialized readership. Titles of dime and pulp novels are altogether absent for the same reason. On the other hand, titles of some stories are included, especially collections of short stories for the title story, as are the titles of some plays and works of poetry.

Writers who have created some particularly interesting or unusual titles are usually more generously represented than others, or may have more detailed entries. Examples are Ernest Hemingway, Eugene O'Neill, and Vladimir Nabokov in the United States, and Anthony Powell in the United Kingdom. For such writers, specialist works were consulted. They are not listed in the Select Bibliography, but typical of them are Arthur and Barbara Gelb's *O'Neill* (New York: Harper & Row, 1962), and James Tucker's *The Novels of Anthony Powell* (London: Macmillan, 1976).

The heading for each entry is composed of these elements: title, author, year of publication. Titles run alphabetically (by the second word if they begin with *A, An,* or *The*). Authors are given their usual or familiar name, even if a pseudonym, although real names are supplied in parentheses for authors using an occasional pseudonym for a given title.

The entry itself usually opens with the nationality of the author and, for novelists or playwrights, frequently gives the publication order of the title. A typical entry might thus start: "The American author's first novel..." or "The British dramatist's third play..."

The rest of the entry does its best to reconcile the theme or plot of the book with the source and significance of its title. This frequently proved something of a juggling act, balancing a succinct summary of the former against an elaborated elucidation of the latter. In a few instances, where hard facts were difficult to come by, it was necessary to propose a reason for the choice of a particular title rather than categorically state one, but I hope that in such cases the judgment is fair and reasonable. Where a quotation-title is involved, the source is usually cited and identified in full, with the name of its author and the year of its publication, as for the titles themselves. Shakespeare's plays are not given a date, however, partly because it is still not certain when many of them were written or first performed (they date from the late 16th or very early 17th century), and partly because they are so well known that such information adds little that is meaningful for the purposes of this book. Literary passages that have yielded titles are usually displayed separately, especially if they are lines of verse, although short quotations can appear in the main text.

The alphabetical arrangement of the entries conceals the tendency that certain authors have to favor particular types of titles. Mention has been made of the striking and colorful titles of writers such as Eugene O'Neill and Tennessee Williams. The American writer Howard Fast, under the pen name E. V. Cunningham, wrote 12 novels between 1960 and 1973 that were each simply titled with a woman's name (*Sylvia, Phyllis, Alice, Lydia,* and others). All of the novels by the British writer Frederick Forsyth begin with *The* (*The Day of the Jackal, The Odessa File, The Dogs of War, The Shepherd,* etc.), and it is true to say that the definite article does lend weight and authority to a title. (Compare Chaucer's *The Knight's Tale, The Miller's Tale, The Reeve's Tale,* and others in *The Canterbury Tales.*) The British writer Dick Francis favors brief titles of an equine flavor for his own adventure stories, as befits a former jockey. The first six were *Dead Cert, Nerve, For Kicks, Odds Against, Flying Finish,* and *Blood Sport.* Half of his 30 novels to date have a title of a single word. Arthur Hailey has also shown the strength of a one-word title: *Hotel, Airport, Wheels* are three such. The American writer Ronald Sukenick's first three novels had the briefest of titles: *Up, Out,* and *98.6.* But his fourth went (deliberately, no doubt) to the other extreme: *Long Talking Bad Conditions Blues.* Most authors deploy a mix of long and short titles, however, though not everyone manages a display as impressive as that of the prolific novelist Joyce Carol Oates, whose titles range from the one-word (and uncapitalized) *them* to the ten-word quotation-title *Because It Is Bitter, and Because It Is My Heart.*

Not all these titles appear among in this book, but they deserve a mention here as being typical of their creators.

A survey of the 6600 or so titles listed in Lesley Henderson's *Contemporary Novelists* (see Select Bibliography, page 232), which includes not only novels but collected short stories and plays, shows that certain words are favored more frequently than others to begin a title. First words (other than *A, An,* or *The*) of more than 10 occurrences are as follows (frequency in parentheses): *All* (18), *At* (11), *Big* (13), *Black* (31), *Blood* (12), *City* (18), *Dark* (20), *Day* (16), *Death* (31), *End* (13), *Family* (12), *Far* (11), *Girl* (11), *Going* (13), *Golden* (15), *Great* (20), *Green* (11), *High* (12), *House* (14), *How* (13), *I* (29), *In* (57, of which 26 are *In the*), *King* (11), *Last* (37), *Life* (13), *Little* (11), *Long* (25), *Love* (30), *Magic* (11), *Man* (42, of which 14 are *The Man Who*), *Mr.* (17), *Murder* (16), *My* (36), *New* (25), *Night* (24), *No* (23), *Old* (21), *On* (20, of which 13 are *On the*), *One* (25), *Other* (13), *Season* (11), *Second* (18), *Summer* (11), *Tales* (16), *This* (14), *Three* (13), *Time* (17), *To* (18; followed by verb or noun), *Two* (25), *What* (11; mostly not interrogative), *Where* (12; also mostly not interrogative), *White* (13), *Who* (11; all interrogative), *Winter* (11), *Woman* (17), *World* (11), *Year* (12; mostly *The Year of*), *Young* (11).

These no doubt say something about human preoccupations or, more precisely, human apprehensions, since the only words scoring over 30 occurrences (apart from *In* and *My*) are *Man* (42), *Last* (37), *Black* (31), and *Death* (31). Crime fiction, although included, is not solely responsible for the high number of such words.

Adrian Room
September 1995

THE TITLES

1 A Lume Spento (Ezra Pound, 1908)
The American poet's first volume of poetry was privately printed in Venice and has an Italian title translating as "By extinguished light."

2 Aaron's Rod (D. H. Lawrence, 1922)
The title of the British writer's novel, ostensibly of biblical origin, refers to the central character of the novel, Aaron Sisson, an amateur flautist. The "rod" is his flute, which at the end of the novel is symbolically destroyed. In the Bible, Aaron, brother of Moses, had a rod (the "rod of Levi") which was made to blossom by God as a sign of his spiritual authority.

3 Aberration of Starlight (Gilbert Sorrentino, 1980)
The American writer's sixth novel, like his earlier works, is realized from a spatial perspective rather than a temporal. It is arranged in four separate narratives and recounts the events of a single summer at a New Jersey vacation lodge. The multiple points of view from which the narrative is presented are alluded to in the title, which is based on the astronomical term for the apparent displacement of stars due to the combined effects of the motion of light and the motion of the observer.

4 Abie's Irish Rose (Anne Nichols, 1924)
The American writer's play is a comedy about a Jewish boy (Abie) and an Irish girl (the "Irish Rose" of the title) who fall in love, so leading to a clash between their families.

5 Abinger Harvest (E. M. Forster, 1936)
The work by the British writer contains a collection or "harvest" of the author's essays, reviews, poems and the like. Its title refers to the village of Abinger Hammer, near Dorking, Surrey, with which Forster's family had long been connected and in which he was then living.

6 Absalom, Absalom! (William Faulkner, 1936)

The American writer's novel concerns the attempts of Thomas Sutpen, son of a poor, white, West Virginia family, to fulfill his "grand design" and gain acceptance as a Southern aristocrat and founder of a wealthy family. He achieves his rise to fame and recognition, but then, through a series of deaths and disasters, ultimately falls from grace, his dream shattered. The title refers to the biblical Absalom, son of David, king of Israel, who plotted to become king in place of his father but who was killed by one of King David's soldiers. The precise reference is to David's lament for his son: "O my son Absalom, my son, my son Absalom! would God I had died for thee, O Absalom, my son, my son!" (2 Samuel 18:33).

7 Absolute Beginners (Colin MacInnes, 1959)

The British writer's novel is a study of "new Britain" in the late 1950s, when youth culture was born, and passed from a brief period of innocence to worldly maturity. It was this book that inspired the 1986 movie of the same title.

8 The Acceptance World (Anthony Powell, 1955)

The British writer's third novel in the series **A Dance to the Music of Time** centers on an ageing novelist and his secretary who strive to be accepted wherever it "matters," whether in upper-class society or in extreme left-wing circles. The title thus takes *acceptance* in its commercial sense, as in "acceptance house" (a British banking institution), and applies it to to the "world" or life in general.

9 Accident (Nicholas Mosley, 1965)

The British author's novel is perhaps his best known, from the fine 1967 movie made of it by the American director Joseph Losey (from a screenplay by Harold Pinter). It opens with the accident of the title, an automobile smash involving two students tutored by the narrator, Stephen Jervis, an Oxford philosophy lecturer. More broadly, the title alludes to the accidents or chance occurrences that can radically alter people's lives in their personal and professional environment, the latter in this case being the academic world.

10 The Accidental Tourist (Anne Tyler, 1985)

The American author's tenth novel has love and the family as its theme. It tells the story of Macon Leary, who writes travel books for businesspeople and "accidental tourists," people who would rather not be traveling but who need to make their way across alien terrain. When his wife Sarah leaves him, he tries to apply the same technique to his existence at home, where he is now a sort of "accidental tourist." He is eventually reunited with her, but his involvement with another woman meanwhile has taught him that there is much more to life than emotional "accidental tourism."

11 Across the Black Waters (M. R. Anand, 1940)

The novel is the second in the Indian writer's trilogy about a rebellious and independent young Sikh peasant who fights for the British army in World War I. "Black water" is an expression used by Indians, especially Hindus, for the sea, translating Hindi *kālā pānī*. The other two novels in the trilogy are *The Village* (1939) and *The Sword and the Sickle* (1942).

12   Across the Common   (Elizabeth Berridge, 1964)

The English writer's novel centers on a Victorian villa beside a common, a refuge from the world for the family who live in it. The youngest member is Louise, who leaves it to marry, but returns to it as her original home when the marriage fails. Now the only inhabitants are her old aunts. While there, she unravels a past tale of rape, murder, and suicide. At the same time, the house is still secure, and she fears to leave it for the equally sinister and frightening outside world that the common represents. Berridge was raised near Wandsworth Common, London, and had this in mind when writing the book.

13   Across the River and into the Trees   (Ernest Hemingway, 1950)

The American writer's novel has as its central character a middle-aged battered war veteran, Colonel Cantwell, sick, tired, disillusioned and in the throes of a final love affair. The title refers to the last words of the Confederate general "Stonewall" Jackson after being accidentally shot down by his own men when at the point of victory (May 1863) in the Civil War: "Let us cross over the river, and rest under the trees."

14   Across the Wide Missouri   (Bernard De Voto, 1947)

The American writer's book tells the story of the mountain men who from 1832 to 1838 penetrated the unknown land between the Missouri River and the Rocky Mountains. The title quotes from the familiar (anonymous) shanty:

> Oh, Shenandoah, I long to hear you,
> Ha-ha, we're bound away,
> 'Cross the wide Missouri!

15   Act of Darkness   (Francis King, 1983)

The British writer based his novel on the famous case of Constance Kent, which has long intrigued writers from Dickens onwards. The book is divided into five sections: "Omens," before the murder takes place, "Act," when the mother's young child is discovered murdered, "Darkness," when investigations take place and the murder confesses, an "Interlude," and finally "Illuminations," when the circumstances behind the murder are elucidated. The titles of the second and third sections reflect the novel's title, which itself comes from Shakespeare's *King Lear:* "A serving-man, proud in heart and mind: that curled my hair, wore gloves in my cap, served the lust of my mistress's heart and did the act of darkness with her" (III.iv.84).

16   The Adding Machine   (Elmer Rice, 1923)

The play by the American writer tells how its protagonist, Mr. Zero, a slave to routine, murders his boss when the latter tells him he has been replaced by an adding machine in the department store where he works. Zero is condemned to death and executed, but is unable to work in his new celestial surroundings until he is set to operate a giant adding machine. He is eventually sent back to earth, where he works an even bigger and better machine. The play is a satire on the "half-humans" produced by the machine age.

17   The Admirable Crichton   (J. M. Barrie, 1902)
The title of the Scottish writer's play refers to its central character, Bill Crichton, butler to Lord Loam, who demonstrates his superiority to the aristocrats with whom he is shipwrecked on a desert island but who reverts to his subservient role when the party is rescued. The nickname "Admirable Crichton" was already established for the Scottish traveler and scholar, James Crichton (1560–1585), who is so called by Sir Thomas Urquhart in his account of Crichton's colourful career in "Vindication of the Honour of Scotland" in *The Jewel* (1651). Harrison Ainsworth's historical novel *The Admirable Crichton* (1837) was based on Urquhart's story. The term survives as a nickname for an enterprising or highly talented person.

18   Adonaïs   (P. B. Shelley, 1821)
The poet's work is an elegy on the death of Keats, whom he laments under a form of the name Adonis, that of the Greek god of beauty and fertility. He perhaps chose this form of the name to suggest the related Adonai, a Hebrew name of God, itself from a word meaning "lord."

19   Adventures in the Skin Trade   (Dylan Thomas, 1955)
The Welsh writer's collections of short stories takes its title from its main (unfinished) story, about the experiences of a young poet in London. The "skin trade" is the world of tricks and subterfuge.

20   The Adventures of God in His Search for the Black Girl   (Brigid Brophy, 1973)
The British writer's book has the subtitle *A Novel and Some Fables*. It takes its main title from the "novel," in essence a philosophical dialogue in the manner of Lucian or Shaw, in which the central character, God, strives to establish once and for all that he is a fictitious creation of man. The title inverts that of Shaw's own sociopolitical parable, *The Adventures of the Black Girl in Her Search for God* (1932).

21   Advise and Consent   (Allen Drury, 1959)
The American writer's novel about Washington politics takes its title from Senate Rule 38: "The final question on every nomination shall be, 'Will the Senate advise and consent to this nomination?'" In the U.S. Constitution (1787) itself, the verbs are nouns, "advice and consent": "He [the President] shall have Power, by and with the Advice and Consent of the Senate, to make Treaties, provided two thirds of the Senators concur" (Article II, section 2, clause 2).

22   The Affair   (C. P. Snow, 1960)
The British writer's eighth novel in the sequence of 11 entitled **Strangers and Brothers** is the last to be set in Cambridge. It concerns a young research fellow who

is accused of a scientific fraud and deprived of his fellowship. The narrative tells how his case is twice reopened so that he is eventually reinstated. This is the "affair," which Snow later stated he had based on the notorious Dreyfus affair of 1894, in which the French Jew Alfred Dreyfus was falsely imprisoned for treason.

23   The African Queen   (C. S. Forester, 1935)
The "African Queen" of the British writer's title is the launch that sets off down a river in Africa with the aim of destroying a German gunboat in World War I.

24   After Many a Summer   (Aldous Huxley, 1939)
The British writer's novel centers on a Californian oil magnate, Jo Stoyte, who experiments with a rejuvenating system. A researcher, Jeremy Pordage, discovers that an 18th-century earl used the same system. The two go to England and find the earl, over 200 years old, living as a filthy ape. The title is a quotation from Tennyson's *Tithonus* (1860):

> The woods decay, the woods decay and fall,
> The vapours weep their burthen to the ground,
> Man comes and tills the fields and lies beneath,
> And after many a summer dies the swan.

25   After Strange Gods   (T. S. Eliot, 1934)
The Anglo-American writer's volume contains the author's Page-Barbour Lectures, given at the University of Virginia the previous year. In the autumn 1985 issue of the literary quarterly, *The Southern Review*, the title was pondered by the American critic Cleanth Brooks:

> The phrase *After Strange Gods* is itself provocative. It has a definitely biblical ring, though I have not been able to find this exact phrasing in either the Old Testament or the New. The phrase would seem to be an amalgam of a number of texts found in the Scriptures, texts which reproach various persons or peoples for going "a whoring after" gods other than the true God, and of several other texts which carry a similar reproach for seeking after "strange gods." I expect that the phrasings "after other gods" and seeking "strange gods" simply fused in Eliot's memory. The amalgamation probably sounded so right that he didn't take the trouble to look it up. I, for example, was so certain that "after strange gods" was an exact quotation that I was shocked when I couldn't find it listed in Cruden's *Concordance*.

The title actually comes from Rudyard Kipling, and is found in his story "On the City Wall" in *In Black and White* (1888):

> "He is an Interesting Survival," said Wali Dad, pulling at the *huqa*. "He returns to a country now full of educational and political reform, but, as the Pearl says, there are many who remember him. He was once a great man. There will never be any more great men in India. They will all, when they are boys, go whoring after strange gods, and they will become citizens—'fellow citizens'—'illustrious fellow-citizens.' What is it that the native papers call them?"

Eliot in Virginia in 1933 had himself returned to a country full of educational and political reform, and he was also concerned with what it was to be a fellow citizen, especially among mixed races. He might even have thought of himself as an "Interesting Survival." So the phrase would have seemed apt, and he appropriated it accordingly.

26 After the Last Sky   (Edward W. Said, 1986)
The Palestinian-born American writer's book, illustrated with photographs by Jean Mohr, is effectively a commentary on everyday life and people in the West Bank and Gaza Strip, and especially in Damascus and Nazareth. The title is from a poem by the contemporary Palestinian writer Mahmoud Darwish:

> Where should we go after the last frontiers?
> Where should the birds fly after the last sky?

27 Afternoon Men   (Anthony Powell, 1931)
The British writer's first novel, recounting the social and sexual lives of a group of young people at a fairly unremarkable level of London society in the interwar years, takes its title from Robert Burton's *The Anatomy of Melancholy* (1621): "They are a company of a giddy-heads, afternoon men."

28 The Age of Innocence   (Edith Wharton, 1920)
The American writer's novel, a satirical picture of New York society in the 1870s, tells how a married man falls in love with his wife's unconventional cousin but is unable to derive satisfaction from the relationship because he defers to convention. The title puns on *age* in the sense "era" (as in "Age of Reason") and "year of life" (as in "age of consent").

29 Age of Iron   (J. M. Coetzee, 1990)
The South African writer's sixth novel opens with its central character, the white woman Elizabeth Curran, arriving home after a doctor has diagnosed cancer to find a black vagrant living rough in her garden. The two form an unlikely alliance and companionship, which endures other experiences and relationships, most of them bitter and harrowing. The novel ends with Elizabeth mourning the turmoil and loss of life in South Africa's "age of iron," otherwise the years of apartheid. South Africa's future looks almost as bleak as Elizabeth's own, with the age of iron followed by an age of bronze. She muses: "How long, how long before the softer ages return in their cycle, the age of clay, the age of earth?"

30 Aged 26   (Anne Crawford Flexner, 1937)
The play by the American playwright is based on the life of John Keats. Hence the title, referring to the age at which the English poet died.

31 Agents and Patients   (Anthony Powell, 1936)
The British writer's fourth novel concerns two young men who seek to advance themselves in a tough and competitive society by obtaining easy money from the well-off. That way they can gain their independence. The title uses *patient* as the opposite to *agent* in the sense of a person to whom actions are done as distinct from

the person who does the actions. The allusion is to a sentence from John Wesley's *Sermons* (1791): "He that is not free is not an Agent, but a Patient."

32   Ah, Wilderness!   (Eugene O'Neill, 1933)

The title of the American playwright's only pure comedy, a light-hearted story of a middle-class American adolescent, alludes to the "wilderness" of youth from which the protagonist makes his way into the adult world in 1906, aged 17.

33   The Air-Conditioned Nightmare   (Henry Miller, 1945)

The "air-conditioned nightmare" of the American writer's title is the United States, to which the author returned after long expatriation in Europe and which he found altered for the worse during his absence, with evidence of soulless materialism everywhere.

34   An Air That Kills   (Francis King, 1948)

The British writer's lyrical tale of childhood gain and loss takes its title from a line in A. E. Housman's poem *A Shropshire Lad* (1896):

> Into my heart an air that kills
> From yon far country blows:
> What are those blue remembered hills,
> What spires, what farms are those?

The same title was used by the Canadian writer Margaret Millar for a mystery novel published in 1957.

35   Alastor   (P. B. Shelley, 1816)

The poet's visionary work, subtitled *The Spirit of Solitude*, has a title representing the Greek name of the Avenging Deity, literally "he who forgets not." In Shelley's eyes, this evil spirit pursues the poet to his death because he is not satisfied by domestic affections and "human sympathy."

36   Alexander's Bridge   (Willa Cather, 1912)

As often, the bridge serves symbolically in this novel by the American author. The story is that of Bartley Alexander, an American engineer, who encounters an actress, a former flame, on a visit to London. He is torn between his attraction to her and his loyalty to his wife, but his conflict is unresolved when a bridge on which he is working crashes and kills him.

37   The Alexandria Quartet   (Lawrence Durrell, 1957–60)

The British writer's work comprises four novels set in the Egyptian city of Alexandria: *Justine* (1957), *Balthazar* (1958), *Mountolive* (1958), and *Clea* (1960). Each novel presents a different point of view and and different truths about the same characters. Justine is the Jewish wife of the banker Nessim Hosnani, Balthazar is a Jewish doctor and mystic, Mountolive is a British diplomat, and Clea is a painter.

38   All God's Chillun Got Wings   (Eugene O'Neill, 1924)
The play by the American playwright concerns the tensions of a mixed marriage, that between a black man, Jim Harris, and a white girl, Ella Downey. The strain of the marriage gradually affects Ella's mind, so that she finally loses her reason and believes that she and Jim are children again. They may thus be "God's chillun" but as adults their "wings" have been clipped. O'Neill took the title from an old Negro spiritual:

> I got wings
> You got wings
> All God's chillun' got wings.
>
> When I get to Heav'n
> Gonna put on my wings
> Gonna fly all over God's Heav'n.

39   All My Pretty Ones   (Anne Sexton, 1962)
The collection of poems by the American poet deals with the intimate pains and losses of daily life that the author felt as daughter, wife, and mother, with constant intimations of death. (She suffered from depression and committed suicide at the age of 45.) The title refers to the deaths of both the poet's parents in their fifties within three months of each other. It comes from Shakespeare's *Macbeth*, from the tragic reaction of Macduff when he learns that his wife and children have been slaughtered by Malcolm:

> All my pretty ones?
> Did you say all? O hell-kite! All?
> What! All my pretty chickens and their dam,
> At one fell swoop?   [IV.iii.216]

40   All Our Tomorrows   (Douglas Reed, 1942)
The British writer's book about World War II and its possible consequences for the British has a title based on that of H. M. Tomlinson's **All Our Yesterdays**, as he explains in an "Author's Note":

> This book was first called *The Critic on the Hearth*, but I am told this title has been used before. So I call it *All our To-morrows*. After the last war, a famous book was written, by H. M. Tomlinson, called *All Our Yesterdays*. He took the words from Macbeth. [...] This book still pursues the hope that the people of this country [...] may yet use the light that comes to them from all our yesteryears to show them the way to something better than dusty death. That is why I call it *All our To-morrows*.

41   All Our Yesterdays   (H. M. Tomlinson, 1930)
The British writer's novel, one of the best known about World War I, is a quasi-historical view of British affairs from 1900, when the Boer War was in progress, to the Armistice in 1919. The title is from Shakespeare's *Macbeth*:

> All our yesterdays have lighted fools
> The way to dusty death.   [V.v.22–3]

42   All Passion Spent   (Vita Sackville-West, 1931)
The British writer's novel is the study of an elderly widow who has abandoned her artistic passion in a wealthy marriage. The title comes from the final words of Milton's *Samson Agonistes* (1671):

> His servants he with new acquist
> Of true experience from this great event
> With peace and consolation hath dismiss'd,
> And calm of mind all passion spent.

43   All Quiet on the Western Front   (Erich Maria Remarque, 1929)
The German-born American writer's antiwar novel, originally written in German, has as its title an ironic reproduction of a phrase used in official communiqués regarding operations in France and Flanders. The original German title was *Im Westen Nichts Neues*, "Nothing New in the West."

44   All the King's Men   (Robert Penn Warren, 1946)
The American writer's novel tells the story of the rise and fall of Willie Stark, a Southern demagogue modeled on Huey Long. Stark is finally assassinated by Adam Stanton, a famous surgeon. The title is from the familiar nursery rhyme about Humpty Dumpty, who "had a great fall":

> All the king's horses
> And all the king's men
> Couldn't put Humpty together again.

No doubt Warren intended that Adam Stanton's biblical name should be reflected in the title, with its suggestion of "fallenness."

45   All the President's Men   (Carl Bernstein and Bob Woodward, 1974)
The American writers' first book on Watergate took its title from a line in a speech by Henry Kissinger at the time of the Cambodia invasion of 1970: "We are all the President's men and we must behave accordingly."

46   All This, and Heaven Too   (Rachel Field, 1938)
As the American author herself acknowledges in her popular novel, set in New England, the title comes from a remark attributed by the English Bible commentator, Matthew Henry (1662–1714), to his minister father in his *Life of Mr. Philip Henry* (1698).

47   All We Need of Hell   (Harry Crews, 1987)
The American writer's ninth novel is a satire examining the folkways of modern marriage. It takes its title from Emily Dickinson's *Complete Poems* (No. 1732, n.d.):

> So huge, so hopeless to conceive
> As these that twice befell.
> Parting is all we know of heaven,
> And all we need of hell.

48 Alms for Oblivion (Simon Raven, 1976)
The title is the overall one for the British writer's sequence of ten volumes, picturing high and low life in the postwar years 1945 through 1973. Raven himself comments, "If there is one theme that dominates the series, it is that human effort and goodwill are persistently vulnerable to the malice of time, chance, and the rest of the human race." The title comes from a speech by Ulysses in Shakespeare's *Troilus and Cressida* in response to Achilles' question, "What! are my deeds forgot?":

> Time hath, my lord, a wallet at his back,
> Wherein he puts alms for oblivion,
> A great-siz'd monster of ingratitudes:
> Those scraps are good deeds past; which are devour'd
> As fast as they are made, forgot as soon
> As done.   [III.iii.145]

49 Alphabetical Africa (Walter Abish, 1974)
The Viennese-born American author's first novel is a linguistic tour de force. The first of its 52 chapters is entitled "A" and has every word in it beginning with that letter ("Ages ago, Alex, Allen and Alva arrived at Antibes, and Alva allowing all, allowing anyone, against Alex's admonition, against Allen's angry assertion: another African amusement" etc.). The second is called "B" and adds words beginning with that letter. The chapters progress in this way to "Z." Another chapter "Z" follows, after which the chapters wind back with a now contracting alphabet through "Y," "X," and so on to finish with "A" again. Hence the title.

50 Altered States (Paddy Chayefsky, 1978)
The American writer's novel is a science fiction tale about genetic experimentation, in which a psychophysiologist hallucinates himself back into the primitive states of human evolution, and in this "altered state" is ready to kill. The title obviously alludes to this, and also presumably to the modern "altered states" of consciousness or awareness that hallucinatory drugs can induce.

51 Amandla (Miriam Tlali, 1980)
The black South African writer's novel, set during the year after the schoolchildren's rebellion in Soweto in 1976, has a title that is a popular African freedom cry meaning "power."

52 The Ambassadors (Henry James, 1903)
The central character of the American writer's novel, Lambert Strether, is sent from America to Paris by a wealthy widow (whom he plans to marry) in order to persuade her son, Chad, involved with a French woman, to come home. Strether is thus the first "ambassador." The second is Chad's sister, Sarah, who comes to Paris on the same errand. In the end Strether, convinced that Chad is better where he is, urges him to stay in Paris.

53 American Appetites (Joyce Carol Oates, 1988)
The American writer's nineteenth novel (apart from two as Rosamond Smith) is set in a research university at Hazelton-on-Hudson, New York, in 1986, and is a story

of domestic violence, culminating in the death of a cookbook writer in the midst of a quarrel with her misunderstood husband. The "appetites" of the title are at one level those for the cookbook dishes. More widely, they are the petty and pretentious maneuverings for power and prestige made by the illustrious members of the American university. The novel is thus both a psychological thriller and a social satire.

54   The American Dream   (Edward Albee, 1961)
The one-act play by the American playwright is a part nonsensical, part ironical study of a middle-class American family, with Mommy, Daddy, and Grandma as leading characters and the Young Man personifying (in his own words) "the American Dream" as a "clean-cut, midwest farm-boy type." The concept of "the American dream" dates from at least the early 19th century, and possibly before that.

55   An American Tragedy   (Theodore Dreiser, 1925)
The American writer's novel is based on an actual New York murder case of 1906, and this is the prime reference of the title. However, the title has a broader application. The author's novel is an indictment of the aggressive materialism that he saw around him, and that, for him, was the real "American tragedy."

56   Amphigorey   (Edward Gorey, 1972)
The American writer's collection of humorous writings bases its title (as a pun on his own name) on *amphigory*, the term for a type of burlesque writing, especially one of nonsensical content. The term itself is said to be devised from Greek *amphi-*, "about," and *-gory* as in *allegory* (in which it means "speaking") or *category* (in which it means "assembly").

57   Amphitryon 38   (S. N. Behrman, 1937)
The American writer's comedy was based on the French play of the same title (1927) by Jean Giraudoux. The story is adapted from the Greek legend telling how Jupiter assumed Amphitryon's shape in order to visit and embrace the latter's wife, Alkmena. Giraudoux gave the title on the ground that the legend had been used 37 times already by earlier playwrights, such as Plautus, Molière, and Dryden.

58   Ancestral Vices   (Tom Sharpe, 1980)
The British writer's ninth novel, a satire on the inherited shortcomings of the English, has a title that either puns on that of James Lees-Milne's *Ancestral Voices* (1975), the first volume of the architectural historian's diaries, or else on the words that gave that work's own title. They come from Samuel Taylor Coleridge's poem *Kubla Khan* (1798):

> And 'midst this tumult Kubla heard from far
> Ancestral voices prophesying war!

59   The Angel That Troubled the Waters   (Thornton Wilder, 1928)
The title play of the collection by the American writer dramatizes the urgent wish of the sick to be healed. It tells how a physician arrives at the pool of Bethesda, in

the Holy Land, to be healed of his sin, but is denied a cure by the angel that had "troubled the water." The title refers to Bethesda itself as it is described in the Bible:

> For an angel went down at a certain season into the pool, and troubled the water: whosoever then first after the troubling of the water stepped in was made whole of whatsoever disease he had. [John 5:4]

60 Angels on Toast (Dawn Powell, 1940)

The American writer's comic account of New York City businessmen on the make has a title that puns on *angels on horseback* as a colorful term for a dish of oysters wrapped in bacon and served on toast.

61 Anglo-Saxon Attitudes (Angus Wilson, 1956)

The British author's novel concerns a historian's investigation into a possible archaeological forgery. It takes its title from a remark made by the King to Alice in Lewis Carroll's *Through the Looking Glass* (1872) as the Messenger approaches "skipping up and down, and wriggling like an eel, with his great hands spread out like fans on each side": "He's an Anglo-Saxon Messenger—and those are Anglo-Saxon attitudes."

62 Animal Farm (George Orwell, 1945)

The novel by the British writer is a satirical allegory directed against Stalin's Russia, and describes how the animals on Mr. Jones's farm rise up against their human masters, expel them, and run the farm themselves. It seems likely that Orwell implied a reference to a Soviet collective farm, and that "animal" in the title alludes to a human being who is little better than a brute.

63 Anna and the King of Siam (Margaret Landon, 1937)

While living in Thailand (then Siam) in the 1920s and 1930s, the British author read about Anna Leonowens, a Welsh widow who was secretary to King Monghur of Siam and governess to his many children in the 1860s. This book was the result, and became the basis of the 1946 movie of the same name and of the 1951 Rodgers and Hammerstein musical and 1956 movie *The King and I*.

64 Anna of the Five Towns (Arnold Bennett, 1902)

The title of the British writer's novel refers to its central character, Anna Tellwright, eldest daughter of the miser, Ephraim Tellright. She lives in Bursley, the fictional name of the Potteries town of Burslem, where this and other of Bennett's novels were set. The four other towns are Turnhill (really Tunstall), Hanbridge (Hanley), Knype (Stoke-on-Trent) and Longshaw (Longton). The "Five Towns" actually represent the six towns that form the modern borough of Stoke-on-Trent, the sixth being Fenton. Bennett himself was born in Hanley.

65 Anne of Green Gables (L. M. Montgomery, 1908)

The Canadian writer's story for girls tells how 11-year-old Anne Shirley is sent by mistake (instead of a boy) from an orphanage to help an elderly brother and sister on their Canadian farm, Green Gables. Hence the title.

66   Another Country (James Baldwin, 1962)
The black American writer's novel has as its theme the self-discovery of its main characters, both black and white, amidst interracial and sexual tension in Harlem and elsewhere. The author had originally planned a novel provisionally titled *Ignorant Armies*, but later realized that he was actually writing two separate novels. One of these became *Giovanni's Room* (1956), and the other eventually *Another Country*. Like its predecessor, it was to have been set in Paris, where Baldwin had lived, but he finally came to set it in in America, as seen from outside. Hence the title, which comes from Sir Cecil Spring-Rice's patriotic poem *I Vow to Thee My Country* (1918), in which "another country" is Heaven:

> And there's another country, I've heard of long ago—
> Most dear to them that love her, most great to them that know.

67   Another Country (Julian Mitchell, 1981)
The British writer's play, which tells how the seeds of defection to Soviet Russia were sown in a group of English public school boys, takes its title from the same lines as for James Baldwin's novel (*above*).

68   Another Part of the Forest (Lillian Hellman, 1946)
The play by the American playwright deals with the same characters as those in **The Little Foxes** (which see), only twenty years younger. The title indicates a shift of focus, and quotes a stage direction heading various scenes in Shakespeare's *As You Like It* (where the forest is the Forest of Arden). A similar title is that of the British writer Beryl Bainbridge's second novel, *Another Part of the Wood* (1968), set in an actual campsite. This is also a Shakespearean stage direction, but from *A Midsummer Night's Dream*.

69   Another Roadside Attraction (Tom Robbins, 1973)
The American author's bizarre first novel centers on a renegade football player, Plucky Purcell, who becomes involved with a secret order of monks in Italy and during an earthquake discovers the mummified body of Jesus in the Vatican. He brings his grotesque find to the "roadside attraction" of the title, a huge West Coast hot-dog stand. The novel continues in similar fantastic manner.

70   Antic Hay (Aldous Huxley, 1923)
The British writer's satirical novel has as its subject the aimless behavior of intellectuals in London society. The title is a quotation from Marlowe's *Edward II* (1593):

> My men, like satyrs grazing on the lawns,
> Shall with their goat feet dance an antic hay.

(An "antic hay" is a grotesque country dance.)

71   Any Minute I Can Split (Judith Rossner, 1972)
The American author's third novel tells the story of Margaret, who flees her husband (splits) when she is about to give birth (split) and who bears his children in a hippie commune.

72 Any Old Iron (Anthony Burgess, 1989)

The British author's novel is an examination of the bloody history of the 20th century as seen through King Arthur's magic sword, Excalibur. The question is whether the sword still has power today or is just "any old iron." The title quotes from a 1911 music hall song, based on the cry of an itinerant scrap iron merchant, which opens:

> Any old iron, any old iron,
> Any any any old iron?

73 The Apes of God (Percy Wyndham Lewis, 1930)

The novel, regarded by many as the Anglo-American author's best work, is a satire mocking the fashionable racket of art and literature in 1920s London. It takes its title from the colloquial phrase ("God's ape") for a fool.

74 The Apple Cart (G. B. Shaw, 1929)

The Irish writer's play has the British Labour Party and its leader, Ramsay MacDonald, then Prime Minister, as its subject, with MacDonald represented by the character Proteus. The Socialist government is upset by the criticisms of King Magnus, a British monarch supposedly reigning in the last quarter of the 20th century, who threatens to abdicate (and so "upset the apple cart") in order to stand as candidate for the Royal Borough of Windsor. The familiar phrase from which the title is adopted occurs in the dialogue itself:

> *Crassus* A king cannot resign. [...]
> *Magnus* [...] I cannot resign, but I can abdicate. [...]
> *Crassus* You can't upset the apple cart like this. [Act II]

75 Appointment in Samarra (John O'Hara, 1934)

The American author's first successful novel is an ironic picture of the members of a country club in a fictional Pennsylvania town. To have an "appointment in Samarra" is to expect one's death. The expression seems to have originated in W. Somerset Maugham's play *Sheppey* (1933), in which the servant to a merchant meets Death in the market place at Baghdad, and flees to Samarra (a town now in northern Iraq) to escape him. When questioned by the merchant, Death explains: "I was astonished to see him in Bagdad, for I had an appointment with him tonight in Samarra."

76 April, June and November (Frederick Forsyth, 1972)

The title of the British writer's novel represents the younger (April) and older (November) women with whom the central character, a man approaching middle age (June), has an affair when he suspects that his true self has been lost in the glitter and glamor of his youth. The use of names of the month for the different ages of human life is a popular poetic convention, partly prompted by the association of May with a young woman who is "blooming" in her early summer. The title also evokes the *September Song* from Maxwell Anderson and Kurt Weill's musical *Knickerbocker Holiday* (1938):

> Oh, it's a long, long while
> From May to December,
> But the days grow short,
> When you reach September.

77   The Armies of the Night   (Norman Mailer, 1968)

The American writer's autobiographical account of the Peace March on the Pentagon in October, 1967, a peaceful rally that turned violent, takes its title from Matthew Arnold's poem *Dover Beach* (1867):

> And we are here as on a darkling plain
> Swept with confused alarms of struggle and flight,
> Where ignorant armies clash by night.

78   The Arrow and the Song   (H. W. Longfellow, 1845)

The American poet, in three quatrains, likens his art to the shooting of arrows into the air. He finds an arrow imbedded in an oak long after losing it, and relates this to his song, which "from beginning to end" he "found again in the heart of a friend."

79   The Arrow of Gold   (Joseph Conrad, 1919)

The Polish-born British writer's novel centers on the relationship between a Basque peasant girl and the young Frenchman that she eventually marries. He is wounded in a duel and cared for by the girl, who then goes out of his life, leaving him only the jeweled arrow of gold that she wore in her hair. An "arrow of gold" (or "golden arrow") is one sought by a pair of lovers in their dreams.

80   Arsenic and Old Lace   (Joseph Kesselring, 1941)

The American writer's satirical play concerns two apparently well-meaning old ladies (the "old lace" of the title) who invite derelicts to their Brooklyn home and kill them for their own good by poisoning them with elderberry wine (the "arsenic"). The title was suggested by that of Myrtle Reed's *Lavender and Old Lace* (1902), a novel criticized by reviewers of the day for its saccharine sentimentality.

81   An Artist of the Floating World   (Kazuo Ishiguro, 1986)

The Japanese-born British writer's second novel is set in 1948 and concerns a painter, Masuji Ono, who is reconsidering his past in the light of the present. His "floating world" is "the night-time world of pleasure, entertainment and drink" that is frequented by his fellow artists.

82   Arundel   (Kenneth Roberts, 1930)

The American writer's historical novel, telling of the expedition against Quebec led by Benedict Arnold, takes its title from the original name of Kennebunkport, Maine.

83   As for Me and My House   (Sinclair Ross, 1941)
The Canadian author's first novel portrays the repressive nature of prairie life from the point of view of a minister's wife in a small Saskatchewan town. The title is biblical in origin:

> Choose you this day whom ye will serve; whether the gods which your fathers served that were on the other side of the flood, or the gods of the Amorites, in whose land ye dwell: but as for me and my house, we will serve the Lord. [Joshua 24:15]

The minister chooses the "Amorite" life, and is a failure.

84   As I Lay Dying   (William Faulkner, 1930)
The American writer's experimental novel concerns the events that surround the illness, death, and burial of its central character, the Mississippi farmwoman Addie Bundren.

85   The Ascent of F6   (W. H. Auden and Christopher Isherwood, 1936)
The play by the two British writers is a tragedy symbolizing and allegorizing the political problems of the 1930s. F6 is the reputedly haunted mountain on the frontier between the fictional countries of British Sudoland and Ostrian Sudoland. Both nations claim the mountain, and local people believe that "the white man who first reaches the summit of F6 will be lord over *both* the Sudolands." The British send an expedition to climb it, but are killed by an avalanche.

86   Ask the Fellows Who Cut the Hay   (George Ewart Evans, 1956)
The British writer's novel, a study of rural life in an English village, with the old ways slowly giving way to new, takes its title from a line by the American poet Ezra Pound.

87   Asolando   (Robert Browning, 1889)
The title of the poet's last volume of poems derives from an invented Italian verb *asolare*, "to disport in the open air," derived from Pietro Bembo's dialogue on love, *Gl'Asolani* ("The residents of Asolo") (1505). *Asolando* would thus mean "sporting in the open," or in the poet's other definition, "amusing oneself at random."

88   The Aspern Papers   (Henry James, 1888)
The American writer's novel concerns an editor who is enthusiastic about the works of Jeffrey Aspern, an early 19th-century romantic poet, and who goes to Venice to acquire the letters (the "papers" of the title) that Aspern wrote to his mistress. He eventually discovers that they have been destroyed.

89   The Asphalt Jungle   (W. R. Burnett, 1949)
The American writer's novel tells how an elderly crook comes out of jail and gathers a gang for just one final robbery. The title is the descriptive phrase for a city setting, where the paving is asphalt and the "law of the jungle" prevails.

90 At Swim-Two-Birds (Flann O'Brien, 1930)
The Irish writer's best-known novel is a surreal story which includes a description of his daily life by the narrator, a Dublin student, an account of the Irish folk hero Finn MacCool in a novel-within-a-novel by "Dermot Trellis," and a bizarre treatment of Irish folklore. The title is a typical literal English rendering of an Irish placename.

91 At the Bottom of the River (Jamaica Kincaid, 1983)
The book by the Antiguan-born American writer comprises ten episodic and meditative sections ("stories") narrated by a young girl, talking either to herself or to a perceived listener. Much of what she narrates is visionary and contemplative, but deep down in the flow of her consciousness, as the title implies, truth and reality appear, as cold and hard as the rocks on the river bed.

92 At the Jerusalem (Paul Bailey, 1967)
The British writer's first novel depicts life in an old people's home, the "Jerusalem" of the title.

93 Attachments (Judith Rossner, 1977)
The title of the American writer's novel puns on the physical state of the Siamese twins, Amos and Eddie, who are two of the main characters, and on the sexual liaisons formed with them by the two women, Nadine and Dianne, who respectively marry them.

94 The Autobiography of Alice B. Toklas (Gertrude Stein, 1933)
The book is really the American writer's own autobiography, presented as if written by her secretary and longtime companion, Alice Toklas.

95 The Autumn Garden (Lillian Hellman, 1951)
The play by the American dramatist is set in a Gulf Coast resort and is about middle-aged people (in the "autumn" of their lives) trying to recapture a sense of youth.

96 The Autumn of the Patriarch (Gabriel García Márquez, 1975)
The Colombian writer's novel (with an original Spanish title *El otoño del patriarca*) centers on the intense solitude of a single character, an all-powerful and depraved general (the "patriarch") who tyrannizes his people in the course of an impossibly long life (he is in its "autumn"). An English translation was published in 1976.

97 Awake and Sing! (Clifford Odets, 1935)
The play by the American playwright concerns the disasters suffered by the Bergers, a poor lower-class Jewish family in the Bronx. The title is biblical in origin: "Awake and sing, ye that dwell in dust" (Isaiah 26:19).

98 An Awfully Big Adventure (Beryl Bainbridge, 1989)
The British writer's thirteenth novel has as its central character a teenage female assistant stage manager, whose failure to understand the doomed homosexual and

heterosexual loves around her is the catalyst for a killing. The novel is based on an earlier short story, *Clap Hands, Here Comes Charlie*, which concerns a production of the Scottish writer J.M. Barrie's play *Peter Pan* (1928), and the title quotes from this play: "To die will be an awfully big adventure" (Act 3).

99   Axel's Castle   (Edmund Wilson, 1931)
The American writer's volume of critical essays on symbolism considers various authors, including the French writer Villiers de l'Isle-Adam, whose Wagnerian-style drama, *Axel* (1890), gives the work its title. It centers on Count Axel, the young lord of an ancient castle in a German forest, a character and setting that Wilson regarded as typifying the symbolic quality of the literature he was considering.

100   Babycakes   (Armistead Maupin, 1984)
The American author's novel is the fourth in the sequence of six with the overall title of *Tales of the City* (also the title of the first in the series, published in 1978). The city is San Francisco, and the main characters are tenants of a seedy rooming-house. Among them are Mary Ann Singleton, an innocent young woman from Cleveland, Ohio, and Brian Hawkins, formerly a lawyer but now a waiter. A third is the hopelessly romantic Michael Tolliver, eternally seeking Mr. Right. By the time of this novel, Mary Ann and Brian are married, and the title alludes to Brian's desire to have a child. The word is also the the principal term of endearment used by Michael, who is now HIV-positive.

101   Back to Methuselah   (G. B. Shaw, 1922)
The Irish writer's play, in five distinct, individually named parts, has creative evolution as its theme, and ranges in time from the biblical Garden of Eden to the far future. The title refers to the Old Testament patriarch (Genesis 5:21–27) who was said to have lived 969 years and whose name has come to epitomize longevity. Shaw's play saw humans eventually evolving into beings who could similarly live for hundreds of years.

102   The Ballad of the Sad Café   (Carson McCullers, 1951)
The American writer's collection of stories is named for its title novella, concerning a grotesquely tall woman who runs a café for other grotesques, including the dwarfish hunchback she falls in love with. The novella was dramatized under the same title by Edward Albee (1963).

103   Barren Ground   (Ellen Glasgow, 1925)
The title of the American writer's novel refers to the farm owned by the father of the central character, Dorinda Oakley, a country woman who hopes to earn enough money working in a local store to make the farm profitable.

104   The Barretts of Wimpole Street   (Rudolf Besier, 1930)
The play by the British writer is a comedy telling the love story of the two poets Elizabeth Barrett and her husband, Robert Browning. It is set in Elizabeth's one-room apartment at 50, Wimpole Street, London, and introduces many other members of her family.

105   Barriers Burned Away   (E. P. Roe, 1872)
The American writer's novel is a moral tale recounting the love of a poor but well educated man for his employer's daughter. She does not return his affection until he bravely rescues her in the disastrous Chicago fire. The title thus has a fairly transparent literal and figurative allusion.

106   Beast in View   (Margaret Millar, 1955)
The Canadian-born American writer's unusual novel tells the story of Helen Carnoe, a woman terrified as she is pursued by Evelyn Merrick, who is finally shown to be the "bad" half of Carnoe's own split personality. The titles quotes words from Dryden's poem *The Secular Masque* (1700):

> All, all of a piece throughout:
> Thy chase had a beast in view;
> Thy wars brought nothing about;
> Thy lovers were all untrue.

107   Beau Geste   (P. C. Wren, 1924)
The British writer's bestselling novel tells the tale of the high-minded Englishman Beau Geste who serves under this name in the French Foreign Legion in the Sahara. The novel is thus named for him, and the name itself is the French phrase *beau geste* (literally "fine gesture"), adopted in English to denote a display of magnanimity. It also happens to suggest the name of a famous man of fashion, such as Beau Brummel or Beau Nash.

108   The Beautiful and Damned   (F. Scott Fitzgerald, 1922)
The American writer's second novel tells of a rich, aristocratic young artist and his wife (the "beautiful") who condemn themselves (the "damned") to a life of increasing dissipation. The title appears to be the author's original creation.

109   The Beautiful Words   (Mervyn Jones, 1979)
The British writer's novel has as its main character 17-year-old Tommy, a handsome boy with the mind of a very small child. He is shunted from one relative to another, and has many unhappy experiences. During these, when lonely, afraid, or despairing, all he can recall are the "beautiful words" his one kind aunt taught him to remember.

110   The Beautyful Ones Are Not Yet Born   (Ayi Kwei Armah, 1969)
The novel by the Ghanaian writer is set in Accra and is a bitter indictment of President Nkrumah's postcolonial betrayal of Ghana's independence. The title comes from a slogan seen by the author on a local bus.

111   Because It Is Bitter, and Because It Is My Heart   (Joyce Carol Oates, 1990)
The American writer's twenty-second novel tells of love and antagonism among and between various families and races in small-town, upstate New York from the 1950s to the time of the assassination of John F. Kennedy in 1963. The lengthy title is a quotation from Stephen Crane's poem *The Black Riders* (1895):

In the desert
I saw a creature, naked, bestial,
Who squatting upon the ground,
Held his heart in his hands,
And ate of it.
I said, "Is it good, friend?"
"It is bitter—bitter," he answered;
"But I like it
Because it is bitter,
And because it is my heart."

112 Bech: A Book (John Updike, 1970)

The American writer's novel is an examination of the personal and literary life of the Jewish author Henry Bech, in whose person and character Updike parodies his fellow writers (Norman Mailer, Philip Roth, Saul Bellow, among others) as well as himself. A sequel, *Bech Is Back* (1982), has Bech producing a bestseller but finding no greater fulfillment in his personal life.

113 Bedknob and Broomstick (Mary Norton, 1957)

The British writer's novel for children was originally published in two separate parts, the first in the United States (where the author was living at the time) as *The Magic Bedknob* (1943), and the second as *Bonfires and Broomsticks* (1947). The story concerns three children living with a country spinster who is learning to be a witch. Hence the particular objects in the title(s). (The Disney movie of the book was titled *Bedknobs and Broomsticks*, with both objects plural. A *bedknob* is one of the two brass knobs at the head of an old-fashioned bedstead. When rubbed, it can work magic, like Aladdin's lamp.)

114 The Beggar Maid (Alice Munro, 1978)

The collection of interlinked short stories by one of Canada's most respected writers was originally published in her homeland as *Who Do You Think You Are?*, a title her American publishers thought her readers would fail to understand. For the American edition she thus gave it the present title, which relates to Rose, the central character who appears in all the stories, and whose life is charted from her childhood in the 1930s to maturity. "The Beggar Maid" of the title is the nickname given Rose by the man who courts her, Patrick Blatchford, heir to a chain of department stores. It is based on Burne-Jones's famous painting on this theme, *King Cophetua and the Beggar Maid* (1884), and represents Blatchford's casting of himself as a "king" who can rescue the impoverished young woman that Rose was when the two first meet in college.

115 Beggar on Horseback (George S. Kaufman and Marc Connelly, 1924)

The comedy by the American writers is a satire on big business and the way its affects the artist, and takes its title from the old proverb: "Set a beggar on horseback and he will ride a gallop" (or "he will ride to the devil").

116 Bell, Book and Candle (John Van Druten, 1950)

The play by the British-born American writer concerns a publisher who discovers that his girlfriend is a witch. The title appropriately quotes part of a form of excommunication from the Roman Catholic Church, One version dating from 1200 runs: "Do to [close] the book, quench the candle, ring the bell."

117 The Bell Jar (Sylvia Plath, 1963)
The American writer's semiautobiographical novel tells how Esther Greenwood, a Smith College student, undergoes a number of experiences that drive her to a suicide attempt. The title refers to the central image: the way that a person who suffers from mental illness, as Esther does, is apart from the world, as if trapped in a bell jar. After her suicide attempt, Esther responds well to electrotherapy: "The bell jar hung, suspended, a few feet above my head. I was open to the circulating air." At the end of the novel, about to be released from psychiatric treatment, she realizes that even if she returns to the outside world there is no guarantee that "the bell jar, with its stifling distortions, wouldn't descend again." Within a month of the book's publication, Plath herself committed suicide.

118 Bellman and True (Desmond Lowden, 1975)
The British writer's thriller tells how a young burglar in a heist is protected by the computer skills of an older crook. The title comes from a line naming four foxhounds in the song "D'Ye Ken John Peel" (1832) by the British huntsman and songwriter John Woodcock Graves:

> Yes, I ken John Peel, and Ruby too,
> Ranter and Ringwood, Bellman and True.

The next two lines of this gave the title of Anthony Powell's novel, **From a View to a Death**.

119 Bells and Pomegranates (Robert Browning, 1841–6)
The poet's series of plays and collections of shorter dramatic poems had a title that baffled the critics. Browning's wife, Elizabeth Barrett Browning, persuaded her husband to explain it in the last number. He did so by saying that it denoted:

> An alternation, or mixture, of music with discoursing, sound with sense, poetry with thought; which looks too ambitious, thus expressed, so the symbol was preferred.

The "symbol" itself derives from Exodus 28:33, 34, in the description of the ornamentation and embroidery on the High Priest's robe:

> And beneath upon the hem of it thou shalt make pomegranates of blue, and of purple, and of scarlet, round about the hem thereof; and bells of gold between them round about: A golden bell and a pomegranate, a golden bell and a pomegranate, upon the hem of the robe round about.

120 Beloved (Toni Morrison, 1987)
The American writer's novel is a ghost story which explores the psychological effects of murder, grief, and loneliness. It begins with the search by Paul D. for Sethe, the woman he had loved over 18 years before. He finds her living with her daughter, Denver, in a haunted house, where Denver's only companion is the ghost of Beloved, a poltergeist spirit. The arrival of Paul D. appears to exorcise the ghost,

until one day the three return together and find a stranger sitting at the gate. It is Beloved, reborn in the flesh as an 18-year-old girl. The narrative develops from this point, and is itself based on a true story about a woman in the 19th century who murdered her baby to save it from the slavery that she had herself escaped.

121   Ben-Hur   (Lew Wallace, 1880)
Subtitled *A Tale of the Christ*, the American writer's novel centers on the title character, Judah Ben-Hur, a Jewish youth wrongly accused of attempting to kill the Roman governor of Judea. His surname means "son of Hur."

122   A Bend in the River   (V. S. Naipaul, 1979)
The Trinidad-born British writer's novel takes its title from a bend in a fictional African river which has been the site of many civilizations. As Salim, the narrator, tells, it has been a "forest, a meeting place, an Arab settlement, a European outpost, a European suburb, a ruin like the ruin of a dead civilization, the glittering Domain of a new Africa, and now this," "this" being what is apparently the imminent disintegration of the now independent country in which it is located. There is a real town Big Bend in Swaziland, on a broad bend of the Usutu River.

123   Between the Acts   (Virginia Woolf, 1941)
The British writer's last novel centers on the performance in the summer of 1939 of a village pageant, itself a re-enactment of British history and an evocation of rural England. The title appears to refer to the society of the day, caught between the lasting values of English country life on the one hand and the threat of annihilation by a world war on the other.

124   A Bewitched Crossroad   (Bessie Head, 1984)
The black South African writer's novel, the last published in her lifetime, is a historical reconstruction of the past of Southern Africa (not just South Africa). The title refers to the magical possibilities opened up for Africa by Botswanan history.

125   Beyond the Horizon   (Eugene O'Neill, 1920)
The play by the American playwright concerns two brothers, Robert and Andrew Mayo, who work on the same farm and love the same girl. Their personal lives and loves collapse, and as the play ends Robert, dying of consumption, watches the sunrise from a hill: "It isn't the end. It's a free beginning [...] beyond the horizon!"

126   Bid Me to Live   (H. D. [Hilda Doolittle], 1960)
The English writer's novel is effectively a straight autobiography, charting the author's relationships in the last years of World War I both with her husband, Richard Aldington, and with D.H. Lawrence and the composer Cyril Gray. Frederick (Lawrence) "bids her to live," and she responds by living, and writing, on her own terms. The title quotes from Robert Herrick's poem *To Anthea* (1648):

> Bid me to live, and I will live
> Thy Protestant to be:
> Or bid me love, and I will give
> A loving heart to thee.

127   The Big Money   (John Dos Passos, 1936)
The American writer's novel, the second in the trilogy *U.S.A.*, focuses on the pursuit of "big money" (the American dream of riches and fame) in the economic boom of the 1920s that ended in the stock market crash and the Great Depression.

128   The Big Sleep   (Raymond Chandler, 1939)
The American writer's novel, in which the author introduced his famous detective, Philip Marlowe, has a title that is a euphemism for death.

129   Big Sur and the Oranges of Hieronymus Bosch   (Henry Miller, 1957)
The American writer's anecdotal account of his life on the Californian coast is effectively summarized by its title. Big Sur is the resort region where he lived. The Oranges of Hieronymus Bosch are the fruit depicted by that artist as symbolic of a garden of earthly delights.

130   Bijou   (David Madden, 1974)
The American author's fourth novel, autobiographical like many of his others, narrates the early adolescent years of the central character, Lucius Hutchfield, when he becomes an usher in a movie theater. The title is the name of the theater.

131   The Bird of Night   (Susan Hill, 1972)
The British writer's novel centers on Harvey Lawson, who in old age recalls three of the twenty years he spent with Francis Croft, a mentally disturbed poet. Croft drags Lawson from his bed in the small hours and takes him on a walk through the woods. A tawny owl flies past, as an omen of both wisdom and terror, which materialize as the narrative proceeds. The owl is thus the "bird of night" of the title, which itself quotes from Shakespeare's *Julius Caesar*:

> Yesterday the bird of night did sit,
> Even at noon-day, upon the market-place,
> Hooting and shrieking.   [I.iii.26]

132   The Birthday Boys   (Beryl Bainbridge, 1991)
The "boys" of the title are the five members of Robert Falcon Scott's doomed expedition to the South Pole in 1910–12, which the British author re-creates by having each member narrate his version of the journey, each celebrating his birthday on the appropriate date.

133   Black April   (Julia Peterkin, 1927)
The title of the American writer's novel is the name of the central character, the black who dominates a South Carolina plantation. (There are no white characters in the book.)

134   Black Dogs   (Ian McEwan, 1992)
The British writer's novel concerns a man researching the life of his wife's parents. He is keen to discover what the horror was that they found on their honeymoon

trip to France in 1946. He finds that their holiday was ruined when the wife was attacked by two black dogs which, she learns, had been trained by the Nazis to attack prisoners. The experience ("my discovery") takes on religious significance for her, and she separates from her husband, who had not shared it. The dogs' spirits do not disappear, and they are seen as "black stains in the grey of dawn." The title thus alludes both to the phrase *black dog* in its sense of "depression," "melancholy," and also specifically to the evil forces then endemic in Europe.

135   The Black Dwarf   (Walter Scott, 1816)

The title character of the novel is a strong but ugly dwarf who settles in Scotland in the early 18th century and gains a reputation for supernatural powers. His "blackness" relates as much to his dark powers (he was thought to be in league with the Devil) as to his physical appearance. He actually has a beneficent effect on his neighborhood, however.

136   Black Marina   (Emma Tennant, 1985)

The British writer's novel is set on Christmas Eve 1983 in the imaginary island of St. James, near Grenada in the Caribbean, where a Marxist-Leninist coup is expected, similar to the real attempted coup that took place in Grenada earlier that year. The story centers on a daughter's quest for her father, as implied by the title, which alludes not only to Marina, the king's long-lost daughter in Shakespeare's *Pericles*, but to T. S. Eliot's related Ariel poem *Marina*. The title also seems to suggest "Black Maria," a nickname for a police van (patrol wagon): the Englishwoman who is the central character, Holly Baker, has been a virtual prisoner in the island since the 1960s.

137   Black Narcissus   (Rumer Godden, 1939)

The British writer's third novel, known to many through the classic movie (1947) based on it, is set in India, where an Anglo-Catholic order sends a young Sister Superior and five nuns to establish a community. They face many obstacles, not least the temptations offered by the exotic young local man known as Black Narcissus, who is sent to the nuns to be educated. The story ends in tragedy.

138   Black Robe   (Brian Moore, 1985)

The novel by the Northern Ireland-born Canadian writer (living in the United States) is set in 1634 and tells the story of the Jesuit priest Father Laforgue, the "black robe" of the title, and his young companion, Daniel Davost, as they make their way from Quebec through the bleak region of the Great Lakes to relieve a mission in a Huron village and convert the inhabitants.

139   The Blackboard Jungle   (Evan Hunter, 1954)

The American author's first novel, based on personal experience, is a somewhat sensationalized account of an American urban high school where the boys are rough, the headmaster a bully, and the teachers overworked and plagued additionally by personal problems. The term was devised by Hunter to evoke an unruly school, where teachers and taught are "animals," and came to be adopted for any undisciplined school of this type.

140   Blaze of Noon   (Rayner Heppenstall, 1939)

The British writer's first novel has "profane" love as its theme, as experienced by the tactile senses of its blind narrator, who works as a masseur. The title is taken from Milton's *Samson Agonistes* (1671), itself the story of the biblical Samson when he is a prisoner and blind (*cf.* **Darkness at Noon**):

> O dark, dark, dark, amid the blaze of noon,
> Irrecoverably dark, total eclipse
> Without all hope of day!

141   Bleak House   (Charles Dickens, 1852–3)

The title names the house in which the main characters live (John Jarndyce and his ward, Esther Summerson). The name itself is obviously evocative, even directly meaningful, but it seems likely that it was actually derived from a real house, Bleak Hall, in St. Albans, Hertfordshire, which Dickens is said to have visited.

142   The Bleeding Heart   (Marilyn French, 1980)

The American feminist writer's second novel centers on Dolores Durer, a tenured professor and the author of two books. She successfully recovers from a difficult marriage and divorce, but finds life dry and barren and long remains celibate. She is thus the "bleeding heart" of the title.

143   Blind Man's Bluff   (Baynard Kendrick, 1943)

The novel by the American mystery writer has a punning title referring to the *bluff* or subterfuge that involves the central character, the *blind* detective Duncan Maclain.

144   Bliss   (Peter Carey, 1981)

The Australian author's first novel tells how a middle-aged businessman, Harry Joy, experiences clinical death after a heart attack but revives with am entirely different perception of reality. Death enables him to recognize "the worlds of pleasure and pain, bliss and punishment, Heaven and Hell." The title is ironic, since he now has to cope with a world that seems more like Hell than Heaven.

145   Blithe Spirit   (Noël Coward, 1941)

The play by the British writer is a comedy in which an author, Charles Condomine, is obliged to live with his second wife, Ruth, and the ghost of his first, Elvira, whom he alone is capable of hearing. Coward adopted the title from the opening line of Shelley's poem, *Ode to a Skylark*: "Hail to thee, blithe spirit!", with a pun on "spirit" in the sense of "ghost."

146   The Blithedale Romance   (Nathaniel Hawthorne, 1852)

The novel is itself a "romance" in the sense of being a love story. Blithedale Farm was suggested by Brook Farm, the cooperative community that existed in the 1840s near West Roxbury, Massachusetts, to which Hawthorne and other writers belonged. The character of Zenobia represents the writer Margaret Fuller, a fellow member, while Miles Coverdale (in reality the name of a medieval English translator of the Bible) is Hawthorne himself.

147 Blix (Frank Norris, 1899)
The title of the American writer's novel is the pet name of one of its two central characters. She is Travis Bessemer, the daughter of a socially prominent family who is the close friend, and subsequently lover, of Condy, otherwise Condé Rivers, a San Francisco journalist.

148 Blott on the Landscape (Tom Sharpe, 1975)
The British author's fourth novel, like others a satire on the English upper classes, recounts the transformation of a country house to a theme park. The title puns on the name of the central character, the handyman Blott, who falls for the haughty and homicidal owner, Maude Lynchwood.

149 The Blue Guitar (Nicholas Hasluck, 1980)
The Australian writer's second novel concerns the quest of the central character, Dyson Garrick, for financial backing for a guitar that will play "automatically." The story symbolizes the two main strands of contemporary Australian society: idealism (represented by the search) on the one hand, but commercialism (represented by the guitar) on the other. The title quotes from the American poet Wallace Stevens's poem *The Man with the Blue Guitar* (1937) (which see separately for its own origin):

> They said, "You have a blue guitar,
> You do not play things as they are."
> The man replied, "Things as they are
> Are changed upon the blue guitar."

150 The Bluest Eye (Toni Morrison, 1970)
The black American author's first novel is the story of a year in the life of an 11-year-old black girl in Ohio. She is incestuously raped by her father and, in her need to be loved, longs to have "the blue eyes of a little white girl," like those of a friend's doll. Her yearning drives her insane, and she comes to believe that she has them, their blue color being that of the sky to which she attempts to fly.

151 The Body (William Sansom, 1949)
The British writer's first and best novel concerns a happily married Londoner who one day observes a neighbor spying on his wife in the bath. He is convinced the two are having an affair, and takes various steps to confirm his suspicions. The story ends when he learns that the neighbor has been critically injured in an automobile accident (a young girl he was with is killed) and that his fears were groundless. The title alludes primarily to his wife's body when bathing, but could also be said to relate to the victims of the car smash.

152 The Bone People (Keri Hulme, 1985)
The New Zealand writer's first novel tells the story of a woman who attempts to "release" an autistic child through her reflections on Maori legend and culture. "The bone people," meaning "the beginning people," are the Maori themselves.

153   The Bonfire of the Vanities   (Tom Wolfe, 1987)

The American writer's first novel contrasts life on Park Avenue, New York, with that in the Bronx ghettoes, and takes its title from the "burning of the vanities" by Savonarola in Florence in 1497. This involved the destruction of such objects of corruption (as he regarded them) as personal ornaments, lewd pictures, cards, and gaming tables.

154   Books Do Furnish a Room   (Anthony Powell, 1971)

The British author's tenth volume in the sequence of 12 entitled **A Dance to the Music of Time** is mainly concerned, as its title implies, with the re-entry of its central character, Nicholas Jenkins, into the London literary world after World War II. The dust jacket of the book's first edition carried the following comment:

> The book's title is taken to some extent from the nickname of one of the characters, Books-do-furnish-a-room Bagshaw, all-purpose journalist and amateur of revolutionary theory, but the phrase also suggests an aspect of the rather bleak post-war period—London's literary world finding its feet again.

The idea of books serving as furniture is not new. In *Love of Fame: The Universal Passion* (1725–8), for example, the poet Edward Young has, "Thy books are furniture," and the clergyman and essayist Sydney Smith (1771–1845) is recorded in Lady Holland's *Memoir* (1855) as writing, "No furniture so charming as books."

155   Born Yesterday   (Garson Kanin, 1946)

The play by the American playwright is a farce about wartime Washington in which an ignorant girl eventually wins out. It takes its title from the expression "I wasn't born yesterday," meaning "I'm not so naive as you think."

156   The Borough   (George Crabbe, 1810)

The work by the English poet, in 24 "letters," describes the life and characters of a town based directly on Aldeburgh, Suffolk, his birthplace. Hence the title.

157   The Borrowers   (Mary Norton, 1952)

The classic English children's book tells the story of a family of tiny people who live beneath the floors of an old country mansion and survive by "borrowing" things from the household above. Hence the title.

158   Both Your Houses   (Maxwell Anderson, 1933)

The play by the American playwright, an exposé of corruption among congressmen, has a title alluding to the two chambers of Congress (the House of Representatives and the Senate). It is itself a quotation from Shakespeare's *Romeo and Juliet* (in which it refers to the two houses of Montague and Capulet):

> A plague o' both your houses!
> They have made worms' meat of me.   [III.i.112]

159   The Box of Delights   (John Masefield, 1935)

The British writer's fantasy novel for children centers on a magic box that can take people into the past. The novel is a sequel to **The Midnight Folk**.

160   Boy   (James Hanley, 1931)
The British author's second novel is based on personal experience, for at the age of 13 he ran away to sea, sailing around the world until he finished up in the Canadian army. The story is that of Arthur Fearon, nearly always referred to impersonally as "the boy," who at the same age stows away in a ship bound for Alexandria, in the innocent belief that he will find a life of romantic adventure. Small, shy, and sensitive, he is cruelly disabused of his dream by the crudeness and hostility of the sailors, who mock the weakness of the new "ship's boy" and sexually abuse him. In Cairo, he attempts to prove his manhood by sleeping with a young prostitute, but contracts syphilis. In his final delirium, he repeats the word "boy" that had taunted and haunted him all his life, and that represents the innocence that he has now irretrievably lost. The book was prosecuted for obscenity even in an early expurgated edition, and republication was banned by Hanley in his lifetime. The first full edition was republished only in 1990.

161   A Boy's Will   (Robert Frost, 1913)
The American poet's first collection of poems takes its title from a line in the refrain of Longfellow's poem *My Lost Youth* (1858):

> A boy's will is the wind's will,
> And the thoughts of youth are long, long thoughts.

162   Brave New World   (Aldous Huxley, 1932)
The British writer's novel is a black comedy on what the future of the world could be, with all individuality suppressed. Huxley ironically adopted the title from Miranda's lines in Shakespeare's *The Tempest*:

> How many goodly creatures are there here!
> How beauteous mankind is! O brave new world,
> That has such people in't!   [V.i.182]

163   Breakfast at Tiffany's   (Truman Capote, 1958)
The American writer's short novel relates the experiences of the free-spirited playgirl Holly Golightly in her quest for the romantic dream of happiness. Her favorite dream is the one of waking up to have "breakfast at Tiffany's." Hence the title.

164   Breakfast of Champions   (Kurt Vonnegut, 1973)
The American writer's most metafictional novel, in which he competes for attention with his character Kilgore Trout, a science fiction writer, takes its title from a slogan used to promote Wheaties breakfast cereal.

165   The Breast   (Philip Roth, 1972)
The American writer's fifth novel tells how a male professor of literature wakes up one morning to find he has been turned into a gigantic breast, as distinct from the beetle of Kafka's *Metamorphosis* or the nose of Gogol's tale. The import is that he has been the victim of too much teaching and "nurturing."

166   Bricks Without Straw   (A.W. Tourgée, 1880)
The American writer intended his novel to demonstrate the fallacy of freedom for
Southern Negroes, who lacked the "straw" of a proper social and economic base for
free development. The title is itself a standard figure of speech deriving from the
biblical story (Exodus 5) of the Israelites who had to build bricks with stubble instead of straw. (Straw was originally the binding agent of sun-dried bricks.)

167   Brideshead Revisited   (Evelyn Waugh, 1945)
The title of the British writer's novel relates to the country house, Brideshead Castle, where its central character, Charles Ryder, is billeted during the war, when he
recalls his past experiences there as the guest of the Roman Catholic family, the
Marchmains. Brideshead itself is thought to be based on Castle Howard, Yorkshire,
which Waugh had visited. The televised version of the novel (1981) was actually
filmed at Castle Howard.

168   The Bridge   (Hart Crane, 1930)
The poem by the American poet, which attempts to create a unity out of American art and technology, ostensibly centers on Brooklyn Bridge, which was visible to
the author from his apartment window as he wrote. Crane saw the arching span of
the bridge as a symbolic search for adequate values through time and space: into the
past and across the nation.

169   A Bridge Too Far   (Cornelius Ryan, 1974)
The book by the Irish writer is about the World War II airborne landings in Holland, which were designed to capture eleven bridges needed for the Allied invasion
of Germany. The plan failed at Arnhem, and the Allies suffered heavy casualties.
Before the action began (in 1944), Lt. Gen. Sir Frederick Browning is said to have
protested to Field Marshal Montgomery, who had masterminded the landings,
"But, sir, we may be going a bridge too far." This gave the title of the book.

170   The Bridges of Madison County   (Robert James Waller, 1992)
This particular Madison County is the one in Iowa, where the American writer's
novel is set. It tells of the intense love affair between two middle-aged people:
Robert Kincaid, a divorced photographer, and Francesca, the unfulfilled wife of a
stolid farmer. The two meet when Kincaid is looking for a particular covered bridge
to photograph. The "bridges" of the title are also symbolic of the close relationship
that develops between the two. When first published in Britain, the novel was given
the prosaic title *Love in Black and White*, presumably with an allusion to photog-
raphy.

171   Brigadoon   (Alan Jay Lerner, 1947)
The title of the American writer's musical fantasy is the name of the vanished but
occasionally reappearing Scottish village in which it is set. The name itself puns on
rigadoon as a type of lively jig-like dance.

172   Bright Lights, Big City   (Jay McInerney, 1984)
The American author's first novel is the story of a disillusioned young man who has
lost mother, wife, and job and who goes from club to club in New York searching

for women and cocaine. The title is thus ironic, and combines those of two vintage movies: Busby Berkeley's *Bright Lights* (1935) and Tod Browning's *Big City* (1927).

173   A Bright Particular Star   (Michael Coveney, 1993)

The British theatre critic's biography of the actress Dame Maggie Smith takes its title from lines in Shakespeare's *All's Well That Ends Well*:

> It were all one
> That I should love a bright particular star
> And think to wed it, he is so above it.   [I.i.97]

The words are apt, but it is odd that the biographer chose them from lines spoken by a woman (Helena) about a man (Bertram).

174   Brighten the Corner Where You Are   (Fred Chappell, 1989)

The American writer's comic yet compassionate novel describes the events of one long day in the life of a North Carolina husband, father, and schoolteacher immediately after World War II. The novel's title comes from an old church hymn.

175   Brill Among the Ruins   (Vance Bourjaily, 1970)

The American writer's novel has as its central character Brill, a middle-aged lawyer from Illinois, who attempts to escape his responsibilities by conducting an archaeological dig in Oaxaca, Mexico. The "ruins" of the title are thus the breakdown of his former ordered life and the archaeological remains themselves. The title echoes that of *Love Among the Ruins*, used for earlier novels by two British writers: Warwick Deeping in 1904 and Evelyn Waugh in 1953.

176   Bring Forth the Body   (Simon Gray, 1974)

The penultimate volume in the British writer's sequence of ten entitled **Alms for Oblivion** is set in 1972 and opens with an investigation into a politician's mysterious suicide. The title clearly alludes to this, and is probably a quotation, although apparently not biblical.

177   Brother to Dragons   (Robert Penn Warren, 1953)

The American writer's narrative poem, which tells of the axe-murder of a black slave by nephews of Thomas Jefferson, takes its title from the Bible: "I am a brother to dragons, and a companion to owls" (Job 30:29).

178   Brown Girl, Brownstones   (Paule Marshall, 1959)

The black American author's first novel is partly autobiographical, and reflects her experiences as a young girl in her mother's Brooklyn brownstone home, as the title implies.

179   Brown on Resolution   (C. S. Forester, 1929)

The British writer's novel is a thriller about a sailor named Brown who is captured by an enemy ship during World War I. He is taken to the remote island of Resolution, in the Galapagos group. He escapes and endeavors to prevent the refitting of the ship before he himself is hunted down and killed.

180   Burnt Norton   (T. S. Eliot, 1936)

The poem that became the first of the Anglo-American author's *Four Quartets* (1943) takes its title from the country house in Gloucestershire, England, that is its subject. The house (near Chipping Camden) presented a scene of settled order and innocence that made it the natural place for the poet's meditation.

181   A Burnt-Out Case   (Graham Greene, 1961)

The title of the British writer's novel alludes to its central character, the architect Querry, a man of arid heart who has lost all motivation for love and work. He finds solace working in a leper hospital, where the physical mutilation of the patients matches his own spiritual degeneration. The title's main reference, however, is to the lepers themselves, as Greene explained in his *Congo Journal* (1959):

> Leprosy cures where disease has been been arrested and cured only after the loss of fingers or toes are known as burnt-out cases.

182   Bury My Heart at Wounded Knee   (Dee Brown, 1970)

The book by the American writer is an account of the thirty fateful years between the outbreak of the Civil War and the massacre of Chief Big Foot's Sioux at Wounded Knee, South Dakota, in 1890. The title quotes a line from Stephen Vincent Benét's poem *American Names* (1927).

183   But Look, the Morn   (MacKinlay Kantor, 1947)

The American newspaperman and columnist tells the story of his childhood ("morn") in this book, which takes its title from Shakespeare's *Hamlet*:

> But, look, the morn in russet mantle clad,
> Walks o'er the dew of yon high eastern hill.   [I.i.166]

Cf. **Russet Mantle.**

184   The Butcher Shop   (Jean Devanny, 1926)

The New Zealand writer's novel is an exposure of farm conditions and tells how the "pure" and equal marriage of Margaret and Barry Messenger is corrupted by social pressure into one of male dominance and female subservience, with the women becoming economically dependent on the man. The title symbolically alludes to the slaughterhouse that society has become.

185   Butterfield 8   (John O'Hara, 1935)

The American writer's novel centers on a Manhattan newspaperman, and is based on the true account of a New York murder. The title (more correctly, *BUtterfield 8*) is the telephone exchange and number that offers access to Gloria Wandrous, a society call girl with a complex love life.

186   By Grand Central Station I Sat Down and Wept   (Elizabeth Smart, 1945)

The Canadian author's first novel is a passionate autobiographical love poem in prose, based on her affair with the poet George Barker and imbued with biblical language and imagery. Hence the title, which plays on the first verse of Psalm 137 in its Prayer Book version: "By the waters of Babylon we sat down and wept: when we remembered thee, O Sion."

187   Cabbages and Kings   (O. Henry, 1904)
The American writer's novel comprises a collection of episodes based on the author's experiences in 1896, when he was indicted for embezzlement and fled to Central and South America before being sentenced to the penitentiary. The title is a quote from the ballad on the Walrus and the Carpenter in Lewis Carroll's *Alice in Wonderland* (1865):

> "The time has come," the Walrus said,
>   "To talk of many things:
> Of shoes—and ships—and sealing wax—
>   And cabbages—and kings—."

Henry was thus announcing his intention "to talk of many things."

188   Cakes and Ale   (W. Somerset Maugham, 1930)
The British writer's satire of English literary life takes its title from a remark by Sir Toby Belch to Malvolio in Shakespeare's *Twelfth Night*:

> Does thou think, because thou art virtuous, there shall be no more cakes and ale? [II.iii.114]

"Cakes and ale" subsequently became a synonym for enjoyment.

189   The Call of the Wild   (Jack London, 1903)
The "hero" of the American writer's story is the dog, Buck, who is kidnapped from a California estate and sold into service as a sledge dog in the Klondike. When his cruel master, to whom he is nevertheless loyal, is killed by Indians, Buck abandons human civilization and returns to "the wild" to be the leader of a wolf pack.

190   Cambridge   (Caryl Phillips, 1991)
The novel by the black British writer tells the story of Cambridge, a christianized plantation slave in the Caribbean, and his tragic struggle with a cruel overseer.

191   Candy   (Maxwell Kenton [Terry Southern] and Mason Hoffenberg, 1958)
The American writer's second novel, a bawdy satire on American institutions, has a title that is the name of its central character, who is herself so called as she is cast in the mold of Voltaire's Candide.

192   The Cannibal Galaxy   (Cynthia Ozick, 1983)
The American writer's second novel has the Holocaust as its theme, as implied by the title, which uses the astronomical image of a black hole sucking in surrounding stars to oblivion. The title also appears to relate to American culture, which has "devoured" Euopean culture in the same way that the Holocaust itself irreparably damaged the high culture of Europe.

193 Caponsacchi (Arthur Goodrich, 1926)
The American writer's play is a dramatization of Robert Browning's long poem *The Ring and the Book* (1868–9). The title represents the name of one that work's main characters, the young priest Caponsacchi.

194 Caprice (Ronald Firbank, 1917)
The British writer's novel is the tale of a country innocent abroad in London. The "caprice" of the title is that of the innocent herself, Sarah Sinquier, a cleric's daughter, who leaves her father's quiet ecclesiastical milieu for a career on the stage.

195 Captains and the Kings (Taylor Caldwell, 1973)
The American writer's novel, about an immigrant orphan boy who founds a political dynasty (based on the Kennedy family), takes its title from Rudyard Kipling's poem *Recessional* (1897):

> The tumult and the shouting dies;
> The Captains and the Kings depart.

196 Captains Courageous (Rudyard Kipling, 1897)
The British writer's novel tells of the adventures of a 15-year-old boy, Harvey Cheyne, the pampered son of a Los Angeles millionaire. When lost overboard from a transatlantic steamer, he is picked up by a fishing schooner and taken on as ship's boy. His experiences transform him from a weak and arrogant youth to a strong and skilled young man. The title comes from the anonymous ballad *Mary Ambree*:

> When captains courageous whom death could not daunt,
> Did march to the siege of the city of Gaunt,
> They mustered their soldiers by two and by three,
> And the foremost in battle was Mary Ambree.

197 The Card (Arnold Bennett, 1911)
The British writer's humorous novel tells of the audacious maneuvering of the businessman and entrepreneur Edward Henry Machin. He is a *card*: "an amusing person: one given to freakish, clownish, or uninhibited behavior" (*Webster's Third New International Dictionary*, 1971).

198 Careless Love (Alice Adams, 1966)
The American writer's first novel tells the story of Daisy Duke, who has rejected her husband and her lover and has finally found fulfillment in a lover with something of the glamor of Rudolf Valentino. The novel was published in Britain in 1967 under the title *The Fall of Daisy Duke*, no doubt as the original title was regarded as too specifically "American." It comes from Robert Lowell's poem *Skunk Hour* (1959):

> My mind's not right.
>
> A car radio bleats,
> "Love, O careless love […]." I hear
> my ill-spirit sob in each blood cell,
> as if my hand were at its throat….

199   Carpenter's Gothic   (William Gaddis, 1985)
The American writer's third novel has a bizarre and complex plot centering on an immoral veteran, Paul Booth, who works as a media consultant for a fundamentalist preacher. Two of the novel's themes are that religious faith has failed and that the modern world has become decayed and violent. Hence the title: the world has turned Gothic, and faith today has become distorted from that of history's first great Carpenter, Jesus.

200   Carrie's War   (Nina Bawden, 1973)
The British writer's novel for children tells the story of a brother and sister evacuated from London to Wales during World War II. The "war" of the title is not only the historic one but the dispute that develops between the Welsh householder, a Bible-thumping local government official, and his relatives, who live in a farmhouse nearby. Sister Carrie tries to heal this breach, with disastrous consequences.

201   Casanova's Chinese Restaurant   (Anthony Powell, 1960)
The British writer's fifth novel in the sequence of 12 entitled **A Dance to the Music of Time** is set in the late 1930s against the background of the Spanish Civil War and the British constitutional crisis over the abdication of King Edward VIII. The story opens three years earlier with a group of acquaintances who consolidate their friendship in the restaurant of the title, whose "recklessly hybrid name" they see as offering "one of those unequivocal blendings of disparate elements of the imagination which suggest a whole new state of mind or way of life." And so it proves, with one of the book's main themes a consideration of the nature of marriage, as illustrated by the terrible relationship that one of the major characters has with his wife. (King Edward's determination to marry the American divorcee Wallis Simpson was the reason for his abdication.)

202   A Case of Knives   (Candia McWilliam, 1988)
The British writer's first novel tells the story of a middle-aged heart surgeon in love with a young male estate agent (realtor). The title alludes not only materially to the surgeon's knife but metaphorically to the hearts that are wounded in the various relationships that combine to form the novel's narrative. The title itself comes from lines in George Herbert's poem *Affliction* (1633):

> My thoughts are all a case of knives
> Wounding my heart
> With scattered smart.

203   Cat on a Hot Tin Roof   (Tennessee Williams, 1955)
The play by the American playwright concerns the maneuverings of two brothers and their wives to gain pride of place in their dying father's will. The "cat" is Maggie, wife of the younger brother, who untruthfully announces that she is pregnant in an attempt to help her husband gain his inheritance. The title, adopted from an old idiom (*cf.* "like a cat on hot bricks"), is alluded to more than once in the play, as in the following two extracts:

What is the victory of a cat on a hot tin roof?—I wish I knew. [...] Just staying on it, I guess, as long as she can.   [Act 1]

Nothing's more determined than a cat on a tin roof—is there? Is there, baby? [Act 3, last line]

204   Cat's Cradle   (Kurt Vonnegut, 1963)

The American writer's fourth novel is a satire on the confused interrelationship between science and religion. There are two stories representing each: that of an eccentric inventor of an atom bomb and a crystal called "ice-nine" which freezes everything it touches, and that of an American dictatorship and its religion of untruth. The two narratives intertwine like the strings of a cat's cradle, and finally combine in a frozen apocalypse. As an exchange between two of the characters runs:

> "A cat's cradle is nothing but a bunch of Xs between somebody's hands, and little kids look and look and look at all those Xs ..."
> "And?"
> "No damn cat, and no damn cradle."

205   Catch-22   (Joseph Heller, 1961)

The American writer's bestselling novel about World War II, set in a U.S. Army Air Force base, has Captain John Yossarian as its protagonist. He hopes to gain a medical discharge by pretending to be insane, but is kept in the war by the "Catch-22" ruling: anyone rational enough to want to be grounded could not possibly be insane, so is capable of returning to flight duty. In the words of the novel itself:

> There was only one catch, and that was Catch-22. [...] If he flew them [more missions] he was crazy and didn't have to; but if he didn't want to he was sane and had to.

The title has now entered the language to describe a "no win" situation. The first chapter of Heller's novel was published in 1955 with the original title *Catch-18*. He was obliged to rename it, however, when Leon Uris's *Mila-18* (1961), also set in World War II, was published shortly before his own novel was due out.

206   The Catcher in the Rye   (J. D. Salinger, 1951)

The American writer's novel centers on the rebellion of 16-year-old Holden Caulfield against middle-class values. Its title echoes the refrain of an anonymous Scottish ballad, "Coming through the Rye," adopted by Robert Burns for his poem of the same name, beginning:

> Gin a body meet a body
> Coming thro' the rye,
> Gin a body kiss a body
> Need a body cry?

When Caulfield is asked by his sister to say what he would like to be, he replies that he imagines himself as the older protector of small children, basing his dream on his misheard words of the poem ("catch" for "kiss"):

> I keep picturing all these little kids playing some game in this big field of rye. [...]
> I mean if they're running and they don't look where they're going I have to come
> out from somewhere and *catch* them. That's all I'd do all day. I'd just be the catcher
> in the rye and all.   [Chapter 22]

207   The Caucasian Chalk Circle   (Bertolt Brecht, 1944)

The German writer's play is based on a 13th-century Chinese play, *The Circle of
Chalk*, from which the title was adopted. The old story concerns the rival claims of
two women to a baby, whom a judge places in a chalk circle, telling the women to
pull him out. One does so, but the other does not, for fear of hurting him. The latter thus wins her claim. The modern play involves a dispute over ownership of a valley in the Caucasus after World War II, but uses the old story as a "play within a
play" for two of its six scenes. The method of judgment is similar to that of the famous "judgment of Solomon" in the Bible (1 Kings 3:16–28), when each of two
harlots claims a baby as her own. Solomon orders the baby to be cut in half and
shared between them. One of the women begs the king to give the child to the
other rather than kill it, thus proving that she is its true mother.

208   Cavalcade   (Noël Coward, 1931)

The British writer's play has as its subject the impact of historical events on an English Edwardian family. The title thus refers to the passage of such events. *Cavalcade*
literally means "ride on horseback," and Coward's adoption of the word for the title
did much to popularize it, as he subsequently acknowledged:

> I was fortunate to be able to administer a little artificial respiration to the word:
> "Cavalcade." Before I wrote the play of that name the word had fallen into disuse.
> [*Australia Visited*, 1941]

209   The Cay   (Theodore Taylor, 1969)

The American writer's novel for children concerns a black adult and a white child
marooned on a desert island (the "cay" of the title), where they become mutually dependent.

210   The Cement Garden   (Ian McEwen, 1978)

The British writer's first novel concerns a teenage brother and sister who are or-
phaned when they murder their unfeeling parents and bury them in a pool of cement in the garden. The "cement garden" itself destroys the surrounding living grass
and plants, and is a symbol of the loss of childhood innocence and of the potential
for death and destruction that adolescence and adulthood can bring.

211   The Centaur   (John Updike, 1963)

The characters of the American writer's third novel undergo experiences that parallel those of Greek myths. The hero, George Caldwell, a high school science
teacher, is thus Chiron, the centaur who was a teacher of heroes. (The characters'
names suggest their mythical counterparts, so that his son, Peter, is Prometheus, his
wife, Cassie, is Ceres, and his father-in-law, Pop Kramer, is Kronos. The novel is set
in Olinger, Pennsylvania, otherwise Olympus.)

212   The Chamber   (John Grisham, 1994)
The American author's thriller centers on an elderly Ku Klux Klansman who has been convicted of the killing of two Jewish children in a 1967 bombing. Now on death row, he has run through nine years of the slow and complex appeals procedure and has only 16 days until the death sentence is carried out. His grandson, a young liberal lawyer, has taken up his case. The title thus alludes both to the courtroom (chamber) where his grandson presents his case and to the gas chamber that the old man is due to enter.

213   Chance   (Joseph Conrad, 1913)
The ironic title of the Polish-born British writer's novel refers to the unhappy youth and marriage of the central character, Flora de Barral, daughter of a corrupt financier.

214   Change Lobsters and Dance   (Lilli Palmer, 1974)
This is the English title of the Austrian movie actress's autobiography, which in the original was called *Dicke Lilli, gutes Kind* ("Big Lilli, Good Child"). It derives from the directions that precede the "Lobster-Quadrille" in Lewis Carroll's *Alice in Wonderland* (1865), although the words do not occur in precisely this form ("'Change lobsters again!' yelled the Gryphon at the top of its voice").

215   Changing Places   (David Lodge, 1975)
The British writer's fifth novel is a comedy based on coincidence. It recounts the parallel experiences of two academics, one British, the other American, who leave their wives behind to embark on a six-month exchange program. The American, Morris Zapp, is ambitious and professional. The Englishman, Philip Swallow, is a gentle dilettante. They each suffer severe culture shock on arrival. The title relates both to the actual exchange and to the relationships that, perhaps inevitably, develop between each man and the other's wife.

216   Chanting the Square Deific   (Walt Whitman, 1865–6)
The American poet's work is an expression of his religious thought, written in four stanzas, each representing an aspect of the "square deific." The first side of the square is Jehovah, or the laws of nature. The second is Christ, the "consolator." The third is Satan, opposed to the first. The fourth is the Santa Spirita, the soul, as a kind of all-pervading female Holy Spirit.

217   Charlotte's Web   (E. B. White, 1952)
The American writer's second and best-known novel for children takes its title from its central character, the spider Charlotte, whose web saves the pig Wilbur from the butcher's knife.

218   The Charm of Birds   (Viscount Grey of Falloden, 1927)
The popular ornithological study by the former British foreign secretary has a straightforward descriptive title. At another level, however, it may well have been intended as a pun on *charm* in its specialized sense of "group of songbirds."

219   Cheaper by the Dozen   (Frank B. Gilbreth, 1948)
The enjoyable family saga tells how the author, an American engineer and efficiency expert, with the help of his wife, Lillian, organizes the lives of his twelve
children on a mathematical basis. The title is a familiar commercial slogan.

220   Cheerful Weather for the Wedding   (Julia Strachey, 1932)
The British writer's novella, her first of two, is in comic mode and describes the
wedding on a windy clifftop in far from cheerful weather between the two main
characters, Dolly Thatchman and Owen Bigham. The wedding is is further spoilt
by bickering and drunkenness, but cheerfulness is provided by the bride's mother,
who is determined that all shall be well despite intimations of disaster. The title is
thus not exactly ironic but at least tongue-in-cheek.

221   Chicago Loop   (Paul Theroux, 1990)
The American author's sixteenth novel, a study in sexual obsession and violence, recounts the mental and spiritual disintegration of Parker Jagoda, a successful entrepreneur who turns serial killer but who is ultimately the victim of his own crime.
He symbolizes the greed and egocentrism of the 1980s, which often came full circle ("looped") to prey on those who sought to prey on others. Hence the title, which
puns on Chicago's "Loop" or downtown area (so nicknamed from the 1890s, when
elevated lines entering it were joined into an overhead network of tracks encircling
several blocks).

222   The Child in Time   (Ian McEwan, 1987)
The British writer's prizewinning novel is about a young couple who are devastated
when their three-year-old daughter is mysteriously abducted in a supermarket. The
action is set two years after the disappearance, when the two have have drifted
apart, so that the little girl is now simply a "child in time" for each of them. Drawn
briefly together again through mutual grief and loneliness, the two make love and
another child is born, which the husband is obliged to deliver himself. The title thus
alludes both to the child who has gone and the one that will come, the latter serving as a symbol of hope and restoring the love of the past.

223   Children of a Lesser God   (Marc Medoff, 1979)
The American writer's play about the relationship between a deaf girl and her
speech therapist takes its title from Tennyson's "The Passing of Arthur" (1869) in
Idylls of the King:

> For why is all around us here
> As if some lesser god had made the world,
> But had not force to shape it as he would.

Medoff is implying that people with a hearing disability are "children of a lesser
god" (instead of the more usual full-blooded "children of God").

224   Chips with Everything   (Arnold Wesker, 1962)
The play by the British playwright attacks the arrogance of the British establishment and the submissiveness to it of the working class, who in a café traditionally

ask for "chips [French fries] with everything." The significance of the phrase is spelled out early in the play:

> And then I saw the menu, stained with tea and beautifully written by a foreign hand, and on top it said [...] "Chips with everything." Chips with every damn thing. You breed babies and you eat chips with everything.   [I. ii]

225   The Chocolate War   (Robert Cormier, 1974)

The American writer's first novel for children tells how one of the brothers in a Catholic boys' school plans to raise funds by getting the boys to sell chocolates in the neighborhood. When one of the boys refuses to participate, he is first a hero, then an outcast, and a target for "war" and destruction.

226   The Choir Invisible   (J. L. Allen, 1897)

The American writer's romance was originally published in 1893 under the title *John Gray*. This is the name of its central character, a young Kentucky schoolmaster, who falls in love with a coquette, Amy Falconer, far inferior to him in will and intelligence. He realizes his mistake, and sees that his ideal lies in Amy's married aunt, Jessica. The title is from George Eliot's poem (1867) beginning:

> Oh may I join the choir invisible
> Of those immortal dead who live again
> In minds made better by their presence.

227   The Cider House Rules   (John Irving, 1985)

The American writer's novel centers on Homer Wells, raised in a rural Maine orphanage and abortion clinic run by the saintly Dr. Larch. He struggles against his destiny, which is to become a gynecologist and take his mentor's place. He runs away and becomes manager of a cider factory, where he falls in love with a young woman who has been to the clinic for an abortion. Each year the cider factory hires a team of black apple-pickers, who are required to observe the (unwritten) rules of the title. As in the various cases of adultery and abortion, the rules are shadowy until they are broken, when their full force becomes apparent.

228   Cider with Rosie   (Laurie Lee, 1959)

The British author's lyrical and nostalgic account of his childhood in rural Gloucestershire has a title that relates to his first drink of cider, and first consequent sexual experience, with Rosie Burdock, a girl slightly older than himself. The event is described in the chapter titled "A First Bite at the Apple."

229   Cigarettes   (Harry Mathews, 1987)

The American writer's fourth novel is a family chronicle set among a group of privileged New Yorkers in the late 1930s and early 1960s. The characters are "cigarettes," in that they burn with elegant passion and are ultimately self-destructive. Hence the title.

230   Cimarron   (Edna Ferber, 1930)

The American writer's novel centers on the land rush of 1889 in Oklahoma, beginning when the country was still Indian territory. The story depicts the degeneration of Yancey Cravat, an editor, lawyer, and wanderer, as contrasted with the gradual elevation of his wife, Sabra, into a shrewd businesswoman and, ultimately, a congresswoman. The title refers both to the Cimarron River, which flows into the Arkansas River in Oklahoma, and to *cimarron* as a term for a fugitive slave, to whom Yancey Cravat is likened.

231   The Circle Home   (Edward Hoagland, 1960)
The American author's second novel tells the story of Denny Kelly, a feckless young man who has failed as both prize fighter and husband. The story ends (rather lamely) with Denny phoning his wife to say that he will return home and be a good family man. The title suggests that he will indeed come home, but that because he has failed before he may well relapse into another cycle of irresponsibility.

232   City of Night   (John Rechy, 1963)
The American writer's first novel is an allegorical account of gay life in New York, where morality is inverted and the only god is that of sexual love. The title is clearly based on that of James Thomson's poem, *The City of Dreadful Night* (1874), although the epithet of "dreadful" is not explicitly realized in the text.

233   City of Spades   (Colin MacInnes, 1957)
The novel is the first of three collectively known as *The London Trilogy*. Their English author was a social journalist with a special empathy for the world of blacks and teenagers, and his novels mirror the youth culture of the 1950s almost in a documentary fashion. The title of this first novel refers to the "spades" (blacks) who make up the African and Caribbean community of London and who are its chief characters. For the other two novels, *see* **Absolute Beginners** and **Mr. Love and Justice**.

234   The Clicking of Cuthbert   (P. G. Wodehouse, 1922)
The story by the British (later American) writer tells how Cuthbert Banks "clicks" with Adeline Smethurst, successfully winning her hand.

235   The Cliff-Dwellers   (H. B. Fuller, 1893)
The American writer's story centers on the activities of the workers in a Chicago skyscraper, the Clifton Building, and this is the "cliff" of the title.

236   Clinging to the Wreckage   (John Mortimer, 1982)
The autobiography of the English writer and lawyer has a title that that he explains in the book itself:

> A [yachts]man with a bristling grey beard [said:] "I made up my mind, when I bought my first boat, never to learn to swim [...]. When you're in a spot of trouble, if you can swim you try to strike out for the shore. You invariably drown. As I can't swim, I cling to the wreckage and they send a helicopter out for me. That's my tip, if you ever find yourself in trouble, cling to the wreckage!"

Sixty-year-old Mortimer commented: "It was advice that I thought I'd been taking for most of my life."

237   A Clockwork Orange   (Anthony Burgess, 1962)

The British writer's bleak novel, a vision of violence, high technology, and despotism, describes an attempt to turn its criminal hero, Alex, into a "mechanical man" by means of therapy and brainwashing. It takes its title from the Cockney expression "queer as a clockwork orange," meaning "homosexual." The relevance of this to the novel or any of its characters is uncertain, although in the story itself it is the title of a book being typed up by a writer whose house Alex and his mates burst into:

> Then I looked at its top sheet, and there was the name—A CLOCKWORK OR-
> ANGE—and I said: "That's a fair gloopy [silly] title. Who ever heard of a clock-
> work orange?" Then I read a malenky [little] bit out loud [...]: "—The attempt to
> impose upon man, a creature of growth and capable of sweetness, to ooze juicily
> at the last round the bearded lips of God, to attempt to impose, I say, laws and
> conditions appropriate to a mechanical creation, against this I raise my sword-
> pen—"

238   The Clockwork Testament   (Anthony Burgess, 1974)

The British writer's novel is the third of the trilogy about the self-indulgent poet F.X. Enderby, the first two being *Inside Mr Enderby* (1963) and *Enderby Outside* (1968). The present volume, in which Enderby goes to Hollywood, has a title based on that of Burgess's well-known earlier work, **A Clockword Orange** (1962), and parodies the author's ordeal at the hands of the media following Stanley Kubrick's 1971 movie version of this, when he had been charged with immorality and obscenity.

239   Cobbers   (Thomas Wood, 1934)

The book is an account by the British composer of his travels in Australia. The title is an Australian colloquial word meaning "friends." (In *Who's Who*, Wood gave one of his recreations as "making and keeping friends.")

240   Cold Comfort Farm   (Stella Gibbons, 1932)

The British writer's novel is a parody of the rural fiction made popular by such writers as Mary Webb. The fictional Cold Comfort Farm is located in the imaginary village of Howling, Sussex. The title was suggested to the author by a fellow journalist, the writer Elizabeth Coxhead, who took the name from a real farm so called near her home at Hinckley, Leicestershire. Farms of the name still exist today elsewhere in England, and "cold comfort" as a phrase for little comfort goes back to medieval times.

241   The Colleen Bawn   (Dion Boucicault, 1860)

Subtitled *The Brides of Garryowen*, the Irish writer's melodrama was adapted from Gerald Griffin's social novel, *The Collegians* (1829). The title, which means "fair girl" (Irish *cailín bán*), relates to the central character, the poor but honest Eily O'Connor, secretly married to Hardress Cregan, who really needs to marry the heiress, Anne Chute, in order to redeem the family fortune. The Anglo-Irish phrase *colleen bawn* was already current for a girl in general when Griffin wrote his novel.

242 The Color Purple (Alice Walker, 1982)

The American writer's third novel covers thirty years in the lives of two Southern black women, sisters separated when young. Celie has been raped by the man she believes is her father, while Nettie has gone to Africa as a missionary. The novel is told through the despairing letters of Celie to Nettie and to God. The novel has many characters, and one of them, Shug Amery, teaches Celie about sexual arousal and maintains that God is not a white male but but someone who is present in all beautiful things, and especially in the color purple:

> I think it pisses God off if you walk by the color purple in a field somewhere and don't notice it [God]. What it do when it pissed off? I ast. Oh, it make something else. People think pleasing God is all God care about. But any fool living in the world can see it always trying to please us back. [p. 167]

243 The Colour of Blood (Brian Moore, 1987)

The novel by the Northern Ireland-born Canadian author is a thriller about Cardinal Stephen Bem, primate of a small Soviet bloc country, who survives an assassination attempt. He sets aside his cardinal's robes (the "colour of blood" of the title) in an attempt to discover who is trying to kill him.

244 Come Hither (Walter de la Mare, 1923)

The British poet's anthology of poems for children has a title that invites the young reader. It quotes from Shakespeare's *As You Like It*, from the song "Under the greenwood tree":

> Come hither, come hither, come hither:
>   Here shall he see
>   No enemy
> But winter and rough weather.

245 Come Like Shadows (Simon Raven, 1972)

The eighth novel in the British writer's sequence entitled **Alms for Oblivion** is set in 1970, with the central character, Fielding Gray, working on a filmscript of *The Odyssey*. He is kidnapped while on location in Greece, and embroiled in a shady plot involving a death, an affair with a starlet, and the selling of secrets to an antifascist organization. Hence the title, which comes from Shakespeare's *Macbeth*:

> Show his eyes, and grieve his heart;
> Come like shadows, so depart!   [IV.i.110]

246 Cometh Up as a Flower (Rhoda Broughton, 1867)

The British author's novel tells of the marriage of convenience with a rich old man that the young heroine is obliged to make as the head of a motherless household. The title is adopted from the first anthem in the Order for the Burial of the Dead in the Book of Common Prayer:

> Man that is born of woman hath but a short time to live, and is full of misery. He cometh up, and is cut down, like a flower.

247   The Comfort of Strangers   (Ian McEwan, 1981)
The British writer's second novel considers the nature of human relationships. It is set in Venice and centers on the encounter between an English couple on holiday and a totally different couple that they meet. (Thomas Mann's *Death in Venice* is a clear influence.) The title evokes a line in Tennessee Williams's play *A Streetcar Named Desire* (1947), Blanche's final words in scene ix:

> Whoever you are—I have always depended on the kindness of strangers.

248   Coming into the End Zone   (Doris Grumbach, 1991)
The American writer's book is a celebration of her 70th year in the form of journal entries. The title takes its metaphor from football (or ice hockey), with the "end zone" of a person's life being that beyond the biblical goal of "three score years and ten."

249   The Common Pursuit   (F. R. Leavis, 1952)
The book of essays by the English literary critic takes its title from a phrase in T. S. Eliot's essay "The Function of Criticism" (1923), in which he states that the critic "must compose his differences with as many of his fellows as possible in the common pursuit of true judgement."

250   The Common Reader   (Virginia Woolf, 1925, 1932)
The title of the English novelist's two volumes of collected essays comes from Dr Samuel Johnson's life of Thomas Gray in *The Lives of the English Poets* (1779–81). Praising Gray's *Elegy Written in a Country Churchyard* (1751), he writes:

> In the character of his Elegy I rejoice to concur with the common reader [...]. The churchyard abounds with images which find a mirror in every mind, and with sentiments to which every bosom returns an echo.

251   A Confederacy of Dunces   (John Kennedy Toole, 1980)
The American author's only novel, published eleven years posthumously, is a comic satire directed against the world in general and New Orleans in particular. Its title comes from Jonathan Swift's *Thoughts on Various Subjects* (1711):

> When a true genius appears in the world, you may know him by this sign, that the dunces are all in confederacy against him.

252   The Confidence-Man   (Herman Melville, 1857)
The title of the American writer's unfinished satirical novel refers not to a crook but to its central character, a deaf-mute on board a Mississippi steamboat, whose innate confidence in his fellow men is replaced by distrust in a series of episodes. Melville's title puns on the more familiar sense of the term, which was beginning to be popularized at the time of his writing the book.

253   Coniston   (Winston Churchill, 1906)
The title of the American writer's novel names the New England town where the novel is set and the central character has his home.

254   The Conscience of the Rich   (C. P. Snow, 1958)
The novel is the seventh in the British author's sequence of 11 novels entitled **Strangers and Brothers**. It centers on Charles March, born into a wealthy Anglo-Jewish family. Rejecting the expectations of his father's world, and tormented by "the conscience of the rich," he becomes a doctor in London's needy East End district. The consequences of his action form the basis of the story.

255   The Conservationist   (Nadine Gordimer, 1974)
The South African writer's sixth novel is a critique of the conservative and capitalist patriarchy that governs South Africa. The title is ironic. It relates to the central character, Mehring, a wealthy white businessman who is concerned with preserving the land on his farm for his own use and enjoyment only, while remaining indifferent to the uprooting and dislocation of whole ethnic groups within South Africa.

256   The Constant Nymph   (Margaret Kennedy, 1924)
The popular novel by the British writer tells the story of the family and friends of an eccentric musician, Albert Sanger, whose talented children, both legitimate and illegitimate, are known as "Sanger's circus." The "constant nymph" and central character of the story is 14-year-old Teresa (Tessa) Sanger, who has to cope with many adult problems of love and fidelity, and who is herself loyal in love from childhood for the young composer, Lewis Dodd. Kennedy may have based the title on that of James Shirley's play *The Constant Maid* (1640), reprinted in 1667 as *Love Will Find Out the Way*.

257   Continent   (Jim Crace, 1986)
The British writer's first (and prize-winning) novel consists of seven short stories linked by the general theme of the "seventh continent," a Third World setting in which ancient taboos conflict with modern commercialism.

258   Continental Drift   (Russell Banks, 1985)
The American writer's fifth novel tells how a young New Hampshire oil-burner repairman, although loving his wife and children, hates his life and vows to start over. He packs up his family and leaves for Florida to work for his brother in a liquor store. His story is paralleled by that of an impoverished Haitian woman, who with her son and nephew leaves for the promise of America. The two characters are united by a common theme: the drifting quality of life in contemporary America, with individual people's lives following a course like that of the tectonic plates of continents. Hence the title of the novel.

259   The Corn King and the Spring Queen   (Naomi Mitchison, 1931)
The historical novel by the Scottish-born writer is set in Greece and the eastern Mediterranean in the 3rd century BC. The heroine is Erif Der, a young witch, who is the Spring Queen of the title, and who partners Tarrik, the Corn King and the country's ruler, in the seasonal fertility rituals.

260   Corridors of Power   (C. P. Snow, 1963)
The British writer's novel has as its theme the conflict between ambition and conscience in the world of politics. The title refers to the corridors of government and political offices such as those in London's Whitehall and Houses of Parliament. These are not only corridors and passages in the physical sense, but pathways to power and promotion. The expression was popularized by Snow's novel, but was already in use when he adopted it as a title.

261   The Cotillion   (John Oliver Killens, 1971)
The black American writer's fifth novel is a satire on black high society, with all its snobbishness and shallowness. "The Cotillion" is the annual dance of the black women's club known as the Femmes Fatales, the word itself being a term for a formal ball.

262   Cotter's England   (Christina Stead, 1966)
The novel by the Australian-born writer, who spent much of her life in Europe and America, was originally published in the United States as *Dark Places of the Heart*, a title that her publisher judged would have greater appeal that side of the Atlantic. (It has a biblical ring, and may have been based on the "dark places of the earth" that are "full of the habitations of cruelty" in Psalm 74:20.) The novel was published in Britain the following year under Stead's preferred title, which alludes to its central characters, the working-class Cotter family in the fictional northern town of Bridgehead.

263   Couples   (John Updike, 1968)
The title of the American writer's fifth novel refers to its subjects: the young married couples in Tarbox, Massachusetts, who are searching for their own identities, mostly through liaisons with partners of other couples.

264   Cover Her Face   (P. D. James, 1962)
The British writer's first crime novel takes its title from the words spoken by Ferdinand to Bosola after he has strangled the Duchess in John Webster's tragedy *The Duchess of Malfi* (1623): "Cover her face; mine eyes dazzle: she died young" (IV.ii.267).

265   The Cradle Will Rock   (Marc Blitzstein, 1937)
The musical drama or "opera" by the American musician and writer is an attack on the evils of capitalism, with its social injustice but labor unity. The title, intended prophetically, is taken from the well-known lines attributed to Charles Dupee Blake:

> Rock-a-bye-baby on the tree top,
> When the wind blows the cradle will rock,
> When the bough breaks the cradle will fall,
> And down will come baby, cradle and all.

266   The Cream of the Jest   (James Branch Cabell, 1917)
The American writer's novel relates how the author Felix Kennaston, tired of his marriage, discovers a hieroglyphic disk that enables him to escape into a dream

world of the past, in which, as Horvendile, he had loved Ettarre, an "ageless, lovable and loving woman." He yearns for her again, but wakes to find that the disk is the cover of his wife's cold cream jar. The discovery enables him to return to real life and to find in his wife an ideal Ettarre, the "cream" of all women.

267   The Cricket on the Hearth   (Charles Dickens, 1846)

The Christmas book centers on a carrier, John Peerybingle, and his younger wife, Dot. An eccentric old stranger arrives at their house, and is one day discovered by Peerybingle to be a young man engaged in intimate conversation with Dot. Perrybingle becomes jealous of his wife, but the influence of the "Cricket on the Hearth in Faery Shape" prevents him from wreaking revenge.

268   A Critical Fable   (Amy Lowell, 1922)

The American writer's discussion of her fellow poets is an imitation of her kinsman James Russell Lowell's *Fable for Critics* (1848). Her title thus plays on that of the earlier work.

269   Crome Yellow   (Aldous Huxley, 1921)

The British author's first novel is a satire on the literary salon kept by Lady Ottoline Morrell. It centers on an apparently endless house party at the mansion of Crome, where the "bright young things" fill their days with endless witty talk. "Yellow" refers to *The Yellow Book* (1894–7), a notorious publication on literature and art, while the title as a whole puns on *chrome yellow* as a pigment used in painting.

270   Crossing the River   (Caryl Phillips, 1993)

The author was born (in 1958) in the West Indies, raised in Britain, and became a college teacher in the United States. His book is a complex narrative in the form of loosely connected stories about the descendants of an 18th-century man who sold his three children into slavery. His message is that all black people have an unbroken continuity with their African home, even when they have "crossed the river" to the West. As Phillips puts it: "On the far bank of the river a drum continues to be beaten."

271   Crow   (Ted Hughes, 1970)

The British poet's volume of poems is subtitled *From the Life and Songs of the Crow* and represents his identification with the bird community as a metaphor for the human situation.

272   The Crucible   (Arthur Miller, 1953)

The play by the American dramatist is set in Salem in 1692 and is a graphic enactment of the witch-trials held there. The work offered a clear parallel to the "witch-hunt" of McCarthyism (the persecution of Communist or "leftwing" officials) current at the time of its first performance. "Crucible" (a word related to *cross*) has its metaphorical sense of "severe trial."

273   Cry, the Beloved Country   (Alan Paton, 1948)

The South African writer's first novel, a plea for racial understanding and cooperation, tells how a black priest, Stephen Kumalo, sets off to Johannesburg in search of his sister, Gertrude, and son, Absalom. He finds that Gertrude has turned to prostitution and that Absalom has murdered the son of a white farmer, James Jarvis. Absalom is convicted and executed, and Kumalo returns with Gertrude's son and Absalom's pregnant wife. The novel ends with a reconciliation between Kumalo and the farmer. The title is extracted from Kumalo's anguished plea at the end of the novel, which is a "cry" not only for his own son but also for Jarvis's, as well as ultimately for all the sons of Africa: "Cry, the beloved country, for the unborn child that is the inheritor of our fear." The words have a biblical ring, as in "Cry, O city" (Isaiah 14:31), but are Paton's own.

274   A Cry in the Jungle Bar   (Robert Drewe, 1979)

The Australian writer's second novel tells of the experiences of a beefy, ex-footballer Australian, Dick Cullen, while working in Manila as an agricultural scientist. He typifies the blundering Australian caught in an Asian environment he cannot understand. The "jungle bar" is an attraction of the Eden Hotel where he is staying. The "cry" of the title is Cullen's utterance of frustration when faced with the complexities of Asian life.

275   A Cry of Absence   (Madison Jones, 1972)

The American author's fifth novel centers on a middle-aged gentlewoman of the 1960s, whose self-protective devotion to her family is in part responsible for her son's sadistic murder of a black agitator. Filled with despair at the failure she has been as wife, mother, and person, she kills herself. The title quotes from the American poet John Crowe Ransom's poem *Winter Remembered* (1945):

> Two evils, monstrous either one apart,
> Possessed me, and were long and loath at going:
> A cry of Absence, Absence from the heart,
> And in the wood the furious winter blowing.

276   The Crying of Lot 49   (Thomas Pynchon, 1967)

The plot of the American writer's second novel concerns a married woman who learns that her former lover has appointed her an executor of his estate. She leaves her husband to investigate the property, and on her journey meets a number of curious people in many odd places. She eventually hears of a mysterious bidder eager to buy her lover's stamp collection, but the novel closes while she awaits the crying (calling) at the auction of the crucial lot numbered 49.

277   The Custom of the Country   (Edith Wharton, 1913)

The American writer's novel tells the story of the social climber Undine Spragg, who achieves the pleasures of money and aristocratic titles through a series of marriages and divorces. The tale is thus a satire on the vulgar lifestyle (the "custom") of the nouveaux riches in the Midwest (the "country"). The title is adopted from that of John Fletcher and Philip Massinger's play *The Custom of the Country* (c. 1622), in which Count Clodio, an Italian governor, claims his *droit de seigneur* ("the custom of the country") from Zenocia on her marriage to Arnoldo.

278 Cuts (Malcolm Bradbury, 1987)
The British writer's brief fifth novel, a portrait of Britain under Conservative rule in the 1980s, recounts the collision of aims and ideals that occurs between an academic and a woman television executive. The title refers on the one hand to the cuts in funding that the university experiences and on the other to film cutting.

279 Daddy Long-legs (Jean Webster, 1912)
The American writer's popular novel for children tells how a girl in an orphanage is selected to be sent to college, with her fees paid by one of the trustees, who chooses to remain anonymous. She catches sight of him one day, not knowing he is her benefactor, and nicknames him "Daddy Long-legs" for his appearance. She writes letters to him and eventually meets him and falls in love with him, only finally discovering his act of kindness. Her nickname is apt for someone who is in effect her "daddy" and whose "long legs" symbolize the extending of his generosity to her.

280 Daddyji (Ved Mehta, 1972)
The book by the Indian-born American writer is a study of his father. Hence the title, with the Hindi honorific suffix *-ji* (roughly meaning "sir") added incongruously to the English "Daddy." In 1979 he published a similar account of his mother, entitled *Mamaji*.

281 Daddy's Gone A-Hunting (Zoë Akins, 1921)
The American writer's second novel tells the story of a man who leaves his wife for a career in painting. The title quotes from the well-known (anonymous) nursery rhyme:

> Bye baby bunting,
> Daddy's gone a-hunting.
> Gone to get a rabbit skin
> To wrap the baby bunting in.

282 Damballah (John Edgar Wideman, 1981)
The black American writer's first collection of short stories takes its title from the name of the *loa* or voodoo god venerated on Haiti, whose symbolic creature is a snake.

283 Dance and Skylark (John Moore, 1951)
The novel by the former British naval officer, a tale of life at sea, takes its title from the naval command "All hands to dance and skylark," permitting a crew to relax after a heavy period of duty.

284 A Dance to the Music of Time (Anthony Powell, 1951–75)
The British writer's sequence of twelve novels, representing a history of 20th-century English life, is named after the title given by Giovanni Pietro Bellori to a painting by Poussin: *Le quatro stagioni che ballano al suono del tempo*, "The four seasons that danced to the music of time." In his memoirs, *To Keep the Ball Rolling* (1976–82), Powell tells how the picture inspired him:

I found myself in the Wallace Collection, standing in front of Nicolas Poussin's picture there given the title *A Dance to the Music of Time*. An almost hypnotic spell seems cast by this masterpiece on the beholder. I knew at once that Poussin had expressed at least one important aspect of what the novel must be.

At the start of the first novel of the series, *A Question of Upbringing* (1951), the protagonist, Nicholas Jenkins, muses on "Poussin's scene in which the Seasons, hand in hand, facing outward, tread in rhythm to the notes of the lyre that the winged and naked greybeard plays":

> The image of Time brought thoughts of mortality: of human beings, facing outwards like the Seasons, moving hand in hand in intricate measure: stepping slowly, methodically, sometimes a trifle awkwardly, in evolutions that take recognisable shape: or breaking into seemingly meaningless gyrations, while partners disappear only to reappear again, once more giving pattern to the spectacle: unable to control the melody, unable, perhaps, to control the steps of the dance.

Throughout the course of the twelve novels, Nicholas Jenkins thus watches the many other characters in their "dance" through life, over a period extending from the 1920s to the 1970s. It seems that Powell does not intend the word "dance" to have its normal associations of rhythm, harmony, and gaiety, but uses it ironically or even derisively, as in "He led me a proper dance."

285   The Dancer from the Dance   (Janet Burroway, 1965)
The American writer's second novel tells how the central character, the young and innocent (yet wise) Prytania, naively brings about the destruction and downfall of the older and wiser people who are irresistibly drawn to her. The title comes from W. B. Yeats's poem *The Tower (Among School Children)* (1928):

> O body swayed to music, O brightening glance,
> How can we know the dancer from the dance?

286   The Dancers at the End of Time   (Michael Moorcock, 1976)
The British writer's comic science fantasy is a trilogy, comprising *An Alien Heat* (1972), *The Hollow Lands* (1974), and *The End of All Songs* (1976). It is set in a world millennia away from the present, when its inhabitants can change appearance and resurrect each other at will. Even so, the end of the universe is at hand. Hence the title, which mirrors that of Anthony Powell's sequence, **A Dance to the Music of Time**.

287   The Danger Tree   (Olivia Manning, 1977)
The British writer's novel is the first volume in *The Levant Trilogy*, a sequel to *The Balkan Trilogy* (see **The Great Fortune**). The "danger tree" of the title is the mango, a specimen of which shades the room that its two main characters, husband and wife, share in their apartment in Egypt. The two are separated by circumstances, and the novel recounts the experiences encountered, both personal and professional, on the perilous path taken by each.

288   Dangling Man   (Saul Bellow, 1944)
The American writer's first novel centers on a young Chicagoan named Joseph who spends days alone in his room in keen self-analysis, his one goal being "I must know

what I myself am." Failing to find an answer, he enlists for the Army to fight in World War II, and while awaiting the draft again tries to solve his dilemma. Finally called up, he realizes he is simply a "dangling man," unable to find any sense of purpose or commitment in life.

289 The Daring Young Man on the Flying Trapeze (William Saroyan, 1934)
The American writer's short story, a mixture of fantasy and realism that established his reputation, concerns an aspiring but jobless young writer who dreams of a "flight with grace" to "some sort of eternity." Its title comes from a popular song (1860) by George Leybourne:

> He flies through the air with the greatest of ease,
> The daring young man on the flying trapeze.

290 Dark as the Grave Wherein My Friend Is Laid (Malcolm Lowry, 1968)
The British writer's novel is based on a journey he made to Mexico in 1945–6 and was published posthumously. It takes its title from Abraham Cowley's elegy, *On the Death of Mr. William Harvey* (1656).

291 Dark Laughter (Sherwood Anderson, 1925)
The American writer's novel seeks to show that the white man has been corrupted by civilization and that only the black American, with his "dark laughter," has escaped.

292 Darkness at Noon (Arthur Koestler, 1940)
The Hungarian-born British writer's novel, based on the Russian purges of the 1930s, has a title that evokes lines from Milton's *Samson Agonistes* (1671) relating to Samson's blindness:

> O dark, dark, dark, amid the blaze of noon,
> Irrecoverably dark, total eclipse
> Without all hope of day! [l. 80]

There was, however, an anonymous booklet of 1806 published in Boston titled *Darkness at Noon, or the Great Solar Eclipse of the 16th June 1806*, and it is possible Koestler was aware of this.

293 Darkness Visible (William Golding, 1979)
The British writer's novel has as its theme the "spark of the divine" as it manifests itself in human nature, and opens with its central character, Matty, as a tiny child staggering symbolically from the heart of a wartime fire. The narrative charts his life through images of alternating light and dark, so that the reader is left wondering whether Matty is a modern-day Christ or simply a deluded simpleton. The paradoxes of the novel are reflected in its title, which comes from Milton's *Paradise Lost* (1667), in which the poet describes the gloom wherein the fallen angels dwell:

> A dungeon horrible, on all sides round
> As one great furnace flam'd; yet from those flames
> No light, but rather darkness visible

Serv'd only to discover sights of woe,
Regions of sorrow, doleful shades, where peace
And rest can never dwell.

294   Darkness Visible   (William Styron, 1990)

The American writer's brief autobiographical book, subtitled *A Memoir of Madness*, is an essay describing his battle against mental depression and his eventual victory over what he calls his "disorder of mood." The title comes from Milton's *Paradise Lost* (1667):

> A dungeon horrible, on all sides round
> As one great furnace flam'd; yet from those flames
> No light, but rather darkness visible
> Serv'd only to discover sights of woe.   [Book I, lines 61–64]

295   The Darling Buds of May   (H. E. Bates, 1958)

The British writer's novel is the first of five recounting the comic adventures of the Larkin family, and opens with its head, Pop Larkin, surveying his ramshackle farm in the May sunshine and pronouncing it "perfick." His buxom wife, Ma, has borne him six children: Mariette, Zinnia, Petunia, Primrose, Victoria, and Montgomery. These, with their flowery names, are the "darling buds" of the title, which itself comes from Shakespeare's *Sonnets (XIX)*:

> Rough winds do shake the darling buds of May,
> And summer's lease hath all too short a date.

296   The Darling of the Gods   (David Belasco and John Luther Long, 1902)

The romantic tragedy by the two American writers is based on an incident in Japanese history. It tells how the Princess Yo-San, engaged to a man she does not love, sets him the impossible task of capturing an infamous outlaw, Prince Kara, who had once saved her life without revealing himself. She now tries to save him, but he returns to his men and dies with honor. The title is a term for any specially favored person, especially one who dies a noble death, and ultimately derives from the opening line of Lucretius's *De Rerum Natura*:

> Mother of Aeneas and his race, darling of men and gods, nurturing Venus.

297   The Day of the Jackal   (Frederick Forsyth, 1971)

The British writer's first novel tells how a group of veterans of the Algerian war hire a professional assassin from England, code-named "The Jackal," to kill President de Gaulle for betraying the French cause in North Africa. Hence the title.

298   The Day of the Locust   (Nathanael West, 1939)

The American author's last novel has the glittering but meretricious life of Hollywood as its general theme. It centers on a character, Homer Simpson, who like hundreds of others has been brought up on the cinema and has saved up to go to California in search of sun and fame but instead finds boredom and monotony. The book culminates in a surrealist riot as crowds of people ("locusts") attend a movie premiere. The title and theme of the book evoke a biblical apocalypse: "And there came out of the smoke locusts upon the earth" (Revelation 9:3).

299   The Day of the Scorpion   (Paul Scott, 1968)

The novel is the second in the British writer's four volumes that together make up *The Raj Quartet* and that cover the five years 1942 to 1947, the years leading up to the independence of India and the departure from that country of the British. When an Indian friend asked Scott to explain the title, he replied that it referred to the old belief that scorpions sting themselves to death if surrounded by a ring of fire. He continued:

> But actually they are shrivelled by the heat and when they dart their tails they're not committing suicide but trying to attack. Well, that's what so much of the British in India was all about. They were driven out of their places in the end by a number of pressures—and were scorched by fires they had really set light to themselves.

300   The Day of the Triffids   (John Wyndham, 1951)

The British writer's bestselling science fiction novel involves fearsome plants that threaten to overrun the world. They grow to a great size and can move about and kill people. Wyndham himself invented the word *triffid* for them, apparently basing it on the adjective *trifid*, "divided into three parts," since he describes the plants as being supported on "three bluntly-tapered projections extending from the lower part" (of their bodies).

301   Days Without End   (Eugene O'Neill, 1934)

The play by the American playwright concerns the irresistible attraction of the central character to Catholicism. Its title echoes the final words of the Christian doxology: "As it was in the beginning, is now, and ever shall be, world without end."

302   De Profundis   (Oscar Wilde, 1905)

The Latin title is that of the Irish writer's letter of bitter reproach to his friend Lord Alfred Douglas, in the form of a personal essay of confession and reminiscence written in prison. The title, meaning "out of the depths," is taken from the opening words of Psalm 130 in the Latin version. (The whole verse is: "Out of the depths have I cried unto thee, O Lord.") The letter was so titled by Wilde's editor, Robert Ross, and Wilde himself had called it *Epistola: in Carcere et Vinculis* ("A Letter: in Prison and Chains"). The "depths" are not those of Wilde's penitence but of his feelings of bitterness that Douglas had encouraged him in dissipation and had distracted him from his work. The significance of "Lord" in the full verse should not be missed.

303   Dead Babies   (Martin Amis, 1975)

The title of the British writer's second novel is meant to shock, and the text itself is shocking. (The paperback edition, however, had the altered title *Dark Secrets*.) It centers on a country house party at the home of the main character, Quentin, with the participants a group of English and American eccentrics. They indulge in an (asexual) orgy and destroy themselves. As the spokesman for the American trio comments:

> "We've agreed that life is a rat's ass and it's no fun being yourself at the time. [...] Fuck all this dead babies about love, understanding, compassion [...] we have drugs to make you euphoric, sad, horny, lucid, tender."

304   Dead End   (Sidney Kingsley, 1936)

The American writer's play is set on a dead-end street leading to the East River in New York City, a region where luxury apartments overlook poor tenements. The story centers on five children who live "dead-end" lives in these slums and who hate people and the law. A local young woman tries to help them but with little success. The title thus has a literal and a metaphorical reference. (The play was turned into a movie the following year, with the children played by the same young actors. They went on to appear in later movies and became known as the Dead End Kids.)

305   The Dead Father   (Donald Barthelme, 1975)

The "Dead Father" of the American writer's fantasy novel is about one mile long and as the story opens is being hauled across an unnamed country by a team of men under the supervision of Thomas and Julie towards the golden fleece. The Father is not actually dead, but decaying, and he believes the fleece will rejuvenate him. There is no golden fleece, only Julie's pubic hair, which the Father pleads to be allowed to touch. Permission is refused, and instead he is buried alive in a huge grave. His last words are: "One moment more!" The novel is part parody on Greek myth, part parable about the decline and fall of man, as personalized in the figure of the Father.

306   A Dead Man in Deptford   (Anthony Burgess, 1993)

The British writer's last book tells the story of the life (as a spy) and death (in a Deptford inn) of the Elizabethan dramatist Christopher Marlowe, as seen through the eyes of a boy actor. The alliterative title echoes that of *A Chaste Mayd in Cheap-Side*, a play by another Elizabethan playwright, Thomas Middleton.

307   The Dean's December   (Saul Bellow, 1982)

The title of the American writer's eighth novel refers to the central character, Albert Corde, dean of a Chicago college, who accompanies his wife to Bucharest to visit her dying mother. Once there, he compares communism and capitalism, and senses portents that each system is nearing its "December," or end. This foreknowledge is symbolized by the freezing December weather in which he makes the visit.

308   Dear Octopus   (Dodie Smith, 1938)

The British writer's popular play is a comedy concerning the presiding of a matriarch, Dora Randolph, over a reunion of her family. It is the latter that is the "octopus" of the title: "The family—that dear octopus from whose tentacles we never quite escape."

309   Death Comes for the Archbishop   (Willa Cather, 1927)

The American writer's novel, based on true events, tells the story of two Catholic missionaries to New Mexico in the second half of the 19th century and concerns their relationships with each other and with their "primitive" flock. The title seems to suggest a murder story, but was actually adopted by Cather from that of a painting by Holbein, and was designed to evoke the "frozen moment" that she aimed to re-create in her written work.

310   Death Goes Better with Coca Cola   (Dave Godfrey, 1967)

The Canadian author's first collection of short stories explores the connection between American Coca-Cola culture and death. Hence the title.

311   Death Kit   (Susan Sontag, 1967)

The American author's second novel concerns the failure of a man who has no real self. He believes he has committed a murder, and to resolve the situation attempts to assemble a "death kit" out of the materials of his life.

312   Death of a Hero   (Richard Aldington, 1929)

The title of the British writer's novel, one of the angriest to emerge from World War I, is ironic. The story is that of George Winterbourne, who is driven by his family and mistress to join up and commit "suicide" (by exposing himself deliberately to enemy fire) in the last week of the War because his life had become intolerable.

313   Death of a Salesman   (Arthur Miller, 1949)

The play by the American playwright concerns a commercial traveler (the "salesman" of the title), Willy Loman, who gradually realizes that his life has been a complete failure, and who thus commits suicide. The original title of the play was *The Inside of His Head*, hinting at its expressionist techniques.

314   Death of the Fox   (George Garrett, 1971)

The American writer's first historical novel recounts the last days of Sir Walter Raleigh [Ralegh], the "Fox" of the title. (He was executed on a charge of treason.)

315   The Death of William Posters   (Alan Sillitoe, 1965)

The British writer's fourth novel chronicles the movement of Frank Dawley, an archetypal working-class man, away from his native Nottingham, where he feels stifled and hounded. "William Posters" is his *alter ego*, whom he vainly attempts to leave behind. The name is derived from the public notices on walls and elsewhere that read "Bill posters will be prosecuted."

316   Decline and Fall   (Evelyn Waugh, 1928)

The British author's first novel recounts the "decline and fall" of Paul Pennyfeather, an Oxford student who become a schoolmaster at an outrageous boarding school but who become embroiled in the nefarious activities of his aristocratic girlfriend and is sentenced to seven years in prison. The title comes from Gibbon's *Decline and Fall of the Roman Empire* (1776–88).

317   Delusions of Grandma   (Carrie Fisher, 1993)
The American writer's novel recounts the stormy affair between the central character, Cora, a Hollywood scriptwriter, and Ray, a lawyer. The title obviously puns on
the phrase "delusions of grandeur," but is rather more subtle than that. It is coined
by Cora's writing partner, Bud, when Cora's eccentric mother predicts that her
daughter may be one of the "few first-world women to die in childbirth," the delu-
sion of a grandma. (The novel has other punning names and titles of this kind. Ray
and Cora's first date is at an ethnic restaurant called Thai Me Up, and Cora and
Bud work on a romantic thriller titled *Dead and Married*.)

318   Dem   (William Melvin Kelley, 1967)
The black American writer's third novel begins: "Lemme tellya how dem folks live."
It sets out to show how "dem" white folks live out their myths of white (and white
male) superiority and indulge in superficial forms of escapism.

319   The Demon   (Hubert Selby, Jr., 1976)
The "demon" of the title of the American author's third novel is sexual obsession
and its permutations. The central character, Harry White, begins as an impulsive
womanizer and ends as a murderer, passing through debauchery and theft on the
way.

320   Design for Living   (Noël Coward, 1933)
The British writer's comedy tells how two friends, a painter and a playwright, fall
in love with Gilda, an interior decorator. She loves them alternately, then escapes to
New York where she marries an art dealer who is a friend of all three. The title puns
on Gilda's occupation. Coward himself described the title as "ironic rather than
dogmatic."

321   Desire Under the Elms   (Eugene O'Neill, 1924)
The "elms" of the title of the American dramatist's tragedy are those around the
New England farmhouse of the central character, Ephraim Cabot, who acquired
the farm from his dead second wife, mother of his son Eben. The "desire" is not sexual but that greedily expressed by his third wife, Abbie Putnam, for his wealth: she
seduces Eben so that the young man will inherit it. The title is apparently O'Neill's
own creation, though it to some extent evokes that of Thomas Hardy's rustic idyll
of young love, *Under the Greenwood Tree* (1872), itself a quotation from Shakespeare.

322   Devices and Desires   (P. D. James, 1989)
The thriller by Britain's "mistress of crime" takes its title from the Book of Common Prayer: "We have followed too much the devices and desires of our own
hearts" (Morning Prayer: General Confession).

323   The Devil Finds Work   (James Baldwin, 1976)
The American writer's book-length essay about American movies, as seen through
the eyes of a black American as he grows up, has a title that puns on the proverb:
"The devil finds work for idle hands to do."

324   The Devil's Disciple   (G. B. Shaw, 1900)
The play by the Irish writer is set in a New Hampshire farmhouse at the time of the American Revolution. The story involves a widow, Mrs. Dudgeon, whose recently dead husband has left nearly everything to his son, Richard, a smuggler who lives with gypsies and is known as the Devil's Disciple. Richard is nearly hanged as a rebel, but is saved at the last moment by a safe-conduct.

325   The Dharma Bums   (Jack Kerouac, 1959)
The title of the American writer's beatnik novel has *dharma* as the term for the sacred law of society in Hinduism (literally meaning "that which binds") and *bums* in the usual American sense of "hobos," "travelers."

326   Diamond Lil   (Mae West, 1928)
The play by the American actress (who took the main role in it) tells the story of the mistress of Gus Jordan, a Bowery saloonkeeper who is also a pimp. The heroine is so named because of the "ice" (diamonds) Gus has lavished on her.

327   Diamonds Are Forever   (Ian Fleming, 1956)
The British writer's popular James Bond novel takes its title from the advertising slogan "A diamond is forever." This was devised in 1939 by copywriter B.J. Kidd, of the N.W. Ayer agency of Chicago, for the South African-based De Beers Consolidated Mines, on the launch of their campaign to promote diamond engagement rings.

328   The Diary of a Nobody   (George and Weedon Grossmith, 1892)
The British writers' comic novel centers on the diary written by the socially and physically accident-prone city clerk, Charles Pooter, who sees no reason why he should not publish his diary "because I do not happen to be 'Somebody'."

329   The Dick   (Bruce Jay Friedman, 1970)
The title of the American writer's third novel is intended to suggest its parallel themes, treated humorously: sexuality and crime-fighting. This same dualism is implied in the name of its central character, LePeters.

330   A Different Drummer   (William Melvin Kelley, 1962)
The American writer's first novel, about a black American sharecropper, is a plea for nonviolence as a way of lessening racial tension. It takes its title from Thoreau's *Walden* (1854):

> If a man does not keep pace with his companions, perhaps it is because he hears a different drummer. Let him step to the music which he hears, however measured or far away.

331   Difficulties with Girls   (Kingsley Amis, 1988)
The British writer's novel, set in 1967, is a sequel to **Take a Girl Like You** (1970). The susceptible hero, Patrick Standish, is no longer able to "take" girls but has

difficulties with them. Amis had originally planned a novel of this title about a gay couple, with a sympathetic homosexual protagonist. He abandoned this in 1982, however, when the plot for *Stanley and the Women* (1984) occurred to him instead.

332   Dinner at the Homesick Restaurant   (Anne Tyler, 1982)

The American author's ninth novel takes its title from an idea that one of the characters has to run a restaurant in the manner of a family home, where the waiters "mother" you and where you can eat food you are homesick for. This is his response to his own background, in which his father deserted him and his mother was hardhearted and distant. By creating new "families" at such a restaurant, he can fulfill his own family needs.

333   A Diversity of Creatures   (Rudyard Kipling, 1917)

The British writer's collection of 14 short stories and 14 poems, originally published in magazine form, takes its title from a line in the *Arabian Nights*: "Praised be Allah for the diversity of His creatures."

334   Dr. Jekyll and Mr. Hyde   (R. L. Stevenson, 1886)

The novel, whose full title is *The Strange Case of Dr. Jekyll and Mr. Hyde*, has given the phrase "Jekyll-and-Hyde" to the English language. Its central character, Dr. Jekyll, is aware of the duality of his own nature, and its two sides of good and evil. He discovers a drug that enables the evil side of him to assume a separate personality. This is Mr. Hyde. The evil side gradually takes over, so that Hyde commits a murder and, finally, Jekyll takes his own life. The rather unusual names may not have been consciously chosen by Stevenson for their suggestiveness, but *Jekyll* (pronounced "Jee-kill") certainly conjures up "kill" and *Hyde* obviously evokes "hide." The whole story is about the hidden nature of human beings, and the latent force in a person that can lead to a killing.

335   The Doctor's Dilemma   (G. B. Shaw, 1906)

The Irish writer's play, a satire on the medical profession, concerns the dilemma faced by a distinguished surgeon when he has to decide whether he should operate on the amoral artist Louis Dubedat or on an old colleague.

336   The Dog Beneath the Skin   (W. H. Auden and Christopher Isherwood, 1935)

The play by the two British writers is a metaphysical satirical extravaganza in verse and pantomime doggerel. Its appropriately metaphysical title was apparently suggested by the play's producer, Rupert Doone, and is said to be an allusion to a phrase from T. S. Eliot's poem *Whispers of Immortality* (1919):

> Webster was much possessed by death
> And saw the skull beneath the skin.

Cf. The Skull Beneath the Skin.

337   A Dog So Small   (Philippa Pearce, 1962)

The British writer's fifth novel for children tells the story of a lonely London boy who longs for a dog as a companion. His grandfather promises him one, but instead sends a picture of a chihuahua. The boy despises the picture, but is gradually drawn to it so that it becomes the center of his fantasy world: "a dog so small you could see it only with your eyes shut." Hence the title.

338   Dog Soldiers   (Robert Stone, 1974)
The American author's second novel centers on the flight of Ray Hicks, an ex-marine, with the wife of his friend, John Converse, a journalist on assignment in Vietnam (where the story opens), to escape the narcotics agents who are after the heroin Hicks smuggled into California from Vietnam. The title puns on the slang term for a U.S. army soldier.

339   The Doors of Perception   (Aldous Huxley, 1954)
In his book, the British writer tells of his experiences under the influence of mescalin. The title was adopted from words from William Blake's prose work *The Marriage of Heaven and Hell: A Memorable Fancy* (1790): "If the doors of perception were cleansed everything would appear as it is, infinite."

340   Double Honeymoon   (Evan S. Connell, Jr., 1976)
The American writer's sixth novel concerns a New York insurance executive, Muhlbach, who becomes obsessed with a young woman named Lambeth. Her erratic behavior eventually results in suicide after she appears in the porno movie that gives the novel its title.

341   The Double Helix   (James D. Watson, 1968)
The book is the Chicago-born scientist's personal account of the discovery by himself and his British partner, Francis Crick, of the structure of DNA, the "double helix" of the title. The molecular structure of DNA consists of two helical chains linked by hydrogen bonds and coiled around the same axis.

342   Down the Long Table   (Earle Birney, 1955)
The Canadian author's second novel tells how professor Gordon Saunders, a Canadian teaching in the United States, is brought before a committee investigating Communist affiliations. They sit at a long table, and he recognizes one of their number as a face from the past, an ex–Communist turned informer. This provokes the chain of memories ("down the long table") that forms the book.

343   Dred   (Harriet Beecher Stowe, 1856)
Subtitled *A Tale of the Great Dismal Swamp*, the American writer's novel complements her better known *Uncle Tom's Cabin* (1852) by showing the demoralizing effect of slavery on whites. The title is the name of a central character, a Negro religious fanatic. Dred is said to be modeled on the Negro slave leader Nat Turner, but he is probably named after the slave Dred Scott, whose U.S. Supreme Court case in 1856 hastened the Civil War.

344   The Dry Salvages   (T. S. Eliot, 1941)
The poem which became the third of the Anglo-American writer's *Four Quartets* (1943) takes its title from "a small group of rocks, with a beacon, off the N.E. coast of Cape Ann, Massachusetts."

345 The Dud Avocado (Elaine Dundy, 1958)
The American writer's first novel tells the story of Sally Jay, an American innocent abroad, who is attracted to the glamor and romantic debauchery of Paris Left Bank life but who comes to realize that the glitz is pretentious and grotesque. She also discovers that her would-be lover is a pimp, and that her life in Paris has exposed her to "too much prostitution." She declares herself to be a "dud avocado," a seed with no life potential.

346 Dusty Answer (Rosamond Lehmann, 1927)
The British author's first novel, which brought her fame at the age of 26, has a romantic young heroine in the figure of Judith Earle, the daughter of wealthy but mainly absent parents. The plot centers on her amorous relationships with various cousins, none of which bears fruit. She finally realizes that her youth is over, and this is the "dusty answer" towards which the plot itself has been moving. The title comes from George Meredith's poem *Modern Love* (1862) (*cf.* **In This Our Life**):

> Ah, what a dusty answer gets the soul
> When hot for certainties in this our life!

347 The Eagle Has Landed (Jack Higgins, 1975)
The British writer's novel about a German invasion of England in World War II has an author's note to the effect that "The Eagle has landed" was the message passed to Heinrich Himmler in 1943, when a small force of German paratroops landed in England with the aim of kidnapping Winston Churchill. However, the phrase is more familiar from the words spoken by Neil Armstrong in 1969 when his lunar module touched down on the Moon: "Tranquillity Base here—the Eagle has landed." ("Eagle" was the craft's name, for the United States' national symbol.)

348 The Eagle of the Ninth (Rosemary Sutcliff, 1954)
The British writer's first historical novel for children centers on the fate of *Legio IX Hispana*, the Ninth Legion based in Roman Britain, whose ultimate fate is uncertain after they marched to quell some trouble among the Picts. The story tells how the son of one of the missing legionaries determines to discover the fate of his father and, if possible, recover his legion's eagle, its principal standard.

349 Earthly Powers (Anthony Burgess, 1990)
The British writer's novel, regarded by many as his most ambitious, is essentially a moral panorama of the 20th century, as seen through the eyes of its central character and narrator, an aged homosexual writer. Burgess views the world not as a universe, but as a "duoverse," locked in a struggle between good and evil. Hence the title, which alludes both to the earth (the world) and more generally to the earthly or baser powers that are opposed to the more exalted or heavenly powers.

350 East Coker (T. S. Eliot, 1940)
The poem that became the second of the Anglo-American writer's *Four Quartets* (1943) takes its title from the village in Somerset, England, where his ancestors came from and where at Easter 1965 his ashes were buried, in St. Michael's Church.

351   East of Eden   (John Steinbeck, 1952)
The American writer's novel is a loose reconstruction of the biblical story of Cain and Abel, in which God cursed Cain after he had murdered his brother, so that he "went out from the presence of the Lord, and dwelt in the land of Nod, on the east of Eden." (Genesis 4:16.) The novel centers on Adam Trask, who marries and moves west to California with his twin sons Caleb and Aron, only to be abandoned there by his sinister wife.

352   Eating People Is Wrong   (Malcolm Bradbury, 1959)
The British writer's first novel relates the amorous and academic adventures of an ageing professor in a second-rate provincial English university. The title is a quote from the humorous song "The Reluctant Cannibal" (1956) by Michael Flanders and Donald Swann.

353   The Edible Woman   (Margaret Atwood, 1969)
The Canadian author's first novel has emotional cannibalism as its theme. Its title names the central image. The "edible woman" is a cake shaped like a woman which the main character, Marian McAlpin, eats at the key point of the novel, when she is released from the suffocating life she has been leading, engaged to be married to a young man who drains or "eats" her emotionally.

354   The Education of Hyman Kaplan   (Leonard Q. Ross [Leo Rosten], 1937)
The American writer's first novel, a collection of humorous sketches, centers on the well-meant efforts of the European immigrant title character to learn "good English" in night school and so succeed in America. The title itself is a deliberate parody of Henry Adams's autobiography, *The Education of Henry Adams* (1918), in which he maintains that he has failed to educate himself. (Rosten's title usually appears with stars between the letters of Kaplan's name, since that is the way Kaplan himself signs it.)

355   The Egg and I   (Betty MacDonald, 1945)
The American writer's bestseller is a comic autobiography recounting her experiences as a chicker farmer in the primitive Olympic Mountains. Hence the title.

356   The Eighth of January   (R. P. Smith, 1829)
The American writer's play centers on Andrew Jackson's victory a New Orleans on January 8, 1815, and celebrates the success of popular government through his election (1828). Hence the title. G.W.P. Custis wrote a play on the same theme with an identical title (1834).

357   Eimi   (E. E. Cummings, 1933)
The book by the American writer is a tale of travel in Russia, with the author describing what he himself saw, heard, and felt. The title is Greek for "I am."

358   The Elected Member   (Bernice Rubens, 1969)
The British writer's novel centers on a rabbi's son who, as a drug addict, is committed by his distresed parents to a mental institution in an attempt to recover his

normality. While so interned, he becomes convinced that he has been betrayed by his family and is absorbed by the notion that he has taken the entire suffering of the Jews on himself. He is thus the scapegoat, the "elected member" of the family, and following the death of his father he finally realizes that he and his companions in suffering are "the cold and chosen ones." Hence the novel's title, and also that under which it was published in the USA, *The Chosen People*.

359   The Electric Kool-Aid Acid Test   (Tom Wolfe, 1968)

The American writer's second book, as its hallucinogenically-inspired title implies, is am account of the wild lifestyle of fellow author Ken Kesey's rock group The Merry Pranksters. It centers on a huge hippie gathering, which begins as a ban-the-bomb protest meeting but turns into a drug-induced "happening."

360   Electricity   (Victoria Glendinning, 1995)

The British biographer's first novel is the story of a spirited and sensual young woman's adventures in the 1880s. The title alludes to the connections, contacts, and shocks that she experiences, whether emotional, sexual, or intellectual.

361   The Eleven Million Mile High Dancer   (Carol Hill, 1985)

The American writer's fourth novel is a comic fantasy, with a heroine in the person of Amanda Jaworski, America's leading lady astronaut. The story tells how she is selected to make an eighteen-month journey to Mars, but is diverted from this mission by the Great Cosmic Brain, who kidnaps her cat, Schrodinger. The narrative culminates in a dizzy spin through space with the dancer of the title. The novel was published in Britain in 1988 with the expanded title of *Amanda and the Eleven Million Mile High Dancer*.

362   The Emperor Jones   (Eugene O'Neill, 1921)

The play by the American playwright is set on an island in the West Indies where a former Pullman car porter, Brutus Jones, has made himself "emperor." His status retrogresses until he is reduced to a crawling savage and is killed by his rebellious "subjects." The title is thus part ironic. For a similar title by the same writer, *cf.* **The Great God Brown**.

363   The End of the Road   (John Barth, 1958)

The American writer's second novel has the same protagonist as his first, **The Floating Opera**, in which he was contemplating suicide. The title initially suggests that he will reverse his earlier decision not to proceed, but as the novel concludes he appears to be taking the opposite course. This device is typical of Barth, who in the second of a pair of novels often refutes the position he has taken in the first.

364   The End of the World News   (Anthony Burgess, 1982)

The British writer's experimental novel, blending the lives of Freud and Trotsky with a science fiction narrative, takes its title from the final sentence spoken by radio newsreaders on the BBC World Service: "That is the end of the world news." No doubt Burgess also intended that the title should suggest news of the end of the world.

365   Endgame   (Samuel Beckett, 1957)
The Irish-born French writer's play, whose characters are the sole survivors of a world disaster, takes its title from the term for the closing stages of a game of chess, when there are only a few players left on the board. The play was originally staged in French with the title *Fin de partie*, having the same sense.

366   Ending Up   (Kingsley Amis, 1974)
The British writer's thirteenth novel, a consideration of ageing and death, centers on five septuagenarians who share the same house, where they are sad, lonely, and bored at the end of their lives, and where they all die.

367   The Enigma of Arrival   (V. S. Naipaul, 1987)
The novel by the Trinidad-born writer of Indian descent is based on his experiences when making the transition from his homeland to England. As the narrative progresses, subtle links emerge between life in the English countryside and strains of Caribbean and Indian cultures. By coming to terms with the changes and rhythms of life in rural England, the narrator comes to understand his own ambiguous identity: his journey through time and space involves "the enigma of arrival." The title itself comes from the painting of the same name by the Italian metaphysical artist Giorgio de Chirico.

368   The Enormous Egg   (Oliver Butterworth, 1956)
The American writer's novel for children, a satire on contemporary American life, tells how a hen owned by a New Hampshire family lays an enormous egg, from which there hatches a triceratops, or three-horned dinosaur.

369   The Enormous Room   (E. E. Cummings, 1922)
The title of the American writer's book refers to the vast central room of the French concentration camp in which the author spent six months on a (false) charge of "treasonable correspondence" when working as an ambulance driver in World War I. The prisoners waited in the room to be called before the dreaded commission.

370   Enough Rope   (Dorothy Parker, 1926)
The American writer's collection of witty poems takes its sardonic title from the proverb "Give a man enough rope and he'll hang himself."

371   Epipsychidion   (P. B. Shelley, 1821)
The poet's autobiographical work celebrated the writer's endless search for the eternal image of beauty. The Greek title can be understood two ways. It is either an ironic allusion to the *epithalamium*, the song sung before the bridal chamber to celebrate a marriage (from *epithalamios*, "before the chamber"), or it is a combination of *epi*, "over," and *psukhe*, "soul," as if meaning "soul over soul," that is, "beloved one." Possibly it is a blend of both.

372   Erewhon   (Samuel Butler, 1872)
The British writer's satirical writer takes its title (an anagram or near-reversal of *Nowhere*) from the name of the undiscovered country visited by the narrator.

373   Every Good Boy Deserves Favour   (Tom Stoppard, 1977)
The British writer's play for speaker and orchestra takes its title from the mnemonic for remembering the musical notes that fall in the five lines of the treble stave in ascending order: E, G, B, D, and F. (The spaces between the lines represent the notes F, A, C, E, which hardly need a mnemonic.)

374   Evidence of Things Not Seen   (James Baldwin, 1985)
The black American author's book deals with racism as it applies to a series of child murders in Atlanta. Its title is biblical in origin: "Faith is the substance of things hoped for, the evidence of things not seen" (Hebrews 11:1).

375   Excellent Women   (Barbara Pym, 1952)
The British writer's novel is a gentle comedy of manners centering on Miss Lathbury, "an unmarried woman, just over thirty, who lives alone and has no apparent ties." Her "empty" spinster's life becomes a full life when she is acknowledged as one of those "excellent women" of the title who are capable, reliable, and supportive of men who could not manage their lives without them.

376   The Excursion   (William Wordsworth, 1814)
The poet's work in nine books was planned as early as 1798, and the writer tells in the Preface how he had envisioned a "philosophical poem, containing views of man, nature, and society, and to be entitled *The Recluse*, as having for its principal subject the sensations and opinions of a poet living in retirement." In the event, the work is ambulatory rather than sedentary, and the poet travels with a Wanderer, through whom he meets other characters, such as the Solitary and the Pastor. The title thus relates to the traveling rather than to the "discourse" that the poem undoubtedly is.

377   The Eye   (Vladimir Nabokov, 1965)
The Russian-born American writer's short novel deals with the tension between the inner and outer life of the central character, a Russian named Smurov. Its theme, according to the Foreword, is "the pursuit of an investigation which leads the protagonist through a hell of mirrors and ends in the merging of twin images." The author explains the evolution of the title at the beginning of the same Foreword:

> The Russian title of this little novel is SOGLYADATAY [...], pronounced phonetically 'Sugly-dart-eye', with the accent on the penultimate. It is an ancient military term meaning 'spy' or 'watcher', neither of which extends as flexibly as the Russian word. After toying with 'emissary' and 'gladiator', I gave up trying to blend sound and sense, and contented myself with matching the 'eye' at the end of the long stalk.

378   Eyeless in Gaza   (Aldous Huxley, 1936)
The British writer's novel centers on the emotional and spiritual experiences of the profligate Anthony Beavis, and describes his gradual realization of the futility and meaninglessness of life and his subsequent conversion (like that of Huxley himself) to mysticism and pacifism. The title is a quotation from Milton's *Samson Agonistes* (1671), referring to Samson's blindness:

> Ask for this great deliverer now, and find him
> Eyeless in Gaza, at the mill with slaves.

379 Eyes (Janet Burroway, 1966)
The American writer's third novel tackles the problems of race prejudice and of ethics in medicine and journalism, as portrayed through the perspectives of its four main characters. These are (significantly) an eye surgeon, his wife, their somewhat alienated son, and their son's fiancée.

380 Fade Out (Douglas Woolf, 1959)
The American writer's second novel concerns an elderly man, Mr. Twombly, who finds that now he is retired he is a nuisance to his family. Fearing he may end up in an old people's home, he takes his fate in his own hands and "fades out" to find a new life in an Arizona ghost town.

381 Fahrenheit 451 (Ray Bradbury, 1953)
The American science fiction writer's best-known novel is a fantasy about the future in which books are banned and burned in case they spark off political unrest. The title represents the temperature at which books are said to burn.

382 Fair Stood the Wind for France (H. E. Bates, 1944)
The antiwar novel by the former British airforce officer concerns a similar officer who after a bombing mission is forced to crashland his aircraft in France. Injured, he is helped by his crew to an isolated farmhouse where he is tended by the farmer's daughter, with whom he falls in love. Despairing of life in occupied France, the two set off on bicycles for Marseilles and then board a train for Spain. The title is from Michael Drayton's poem *To the Cambro-Britons* ("Agincourt") (1619):

> Fair stood the wind for France
> When we our sails advance,
> Nor now to prove our chance
> Longer will tarry.

383 A Fairly Good Time (Mavis Gallant, 1970)
The Canadian writer's second novel tells how a well-off young Canadian woman grows gradually insane as her second marriage disintegrates. The title quotes words from Edith Wharton, and forms part of the novel's epigraph: "If you make up your mind not to be happy, there's no reason why you shouldn't have a fairly good time."

384 A Fairly Honourable Defeat (Iris Murdoch, 1970)
The British writer's complex novel concerns a Jewish-American biologist, Julius King, who apparently without any motive exploits and manipulates the weakness and vanity of those around him. He represents the forces of evil, which are counterbalanced by the good but weak qualities of Tallis, the former husband of his (King's) former lover, Morgan Browne. The moral of the story is that goodness survives against the odds, even if it does not entirely prevail against evil, and this is the "fairly honourable defeat" of the title.

385   Faithful Are the Wounds (May Sarton, 1955)
The American writer's fifth novel, set against a background of anti-communist witch hunts, centers on the suicide of the central character, the homosexual professor Edward Cavan, and its effect on his friends. The title quotes words from the Bible: "Faithful are the wounds of a friend; but the kisses of an enemy are deceitful" (Proverbs 27:6).

386   Falling (Susan Fromberg Schaeffer, 1973)
The American writer's first novel tells the story of Elizabeth Kamen, a graduate-school Jewish intellectual whose life is apparently a failure on several levels. The various episodes of her life are recounted in sessions with her psychiatrist. He aims to stop her falling, and allow her to gain control of her life. But (implies Schaeffer) the human condition is to fall. As Elizabeth's mother says to her in a dream: "There is no bottom, there is only this falling." Hence the title.

387   Falling (Colin Thubron, 1989)
The British writer's fourth novel is narrated by Mark, a man in love with two women, Clara, a circus artiste, and Katherine, a stained glass window artist. The title works on several levels. Clara falls during one of her acts and is killed, because she won't use a safety net. Katherine makes a stained glass window of the Fall from heaven. All three fall in love (without a safety net). And over all there is the general metaphor of the Fall itself.

388   Falling in Place (Ann Beattie, 1980)
The American writer's second novel, set in Connecticut and New York in the summer of 1979, uses the falling from space of Skylab as a metaphor for characters "falling" in their lives. The plot focuses on the emotional relationships that build up in the John Knapp family. The climax involves the son's (supposedly) accidental shooting of his sister and a final confrontation of all the family members. Things at last fall into place.

389   Fame Is the Spur (Howard Spring, 1940)
The British writer's story of a Labour politician's rise to power takes its title from Milton's *Lycidas* (1637):

> Fame is the spur that the clear spirit doth raise
> (That last infirmity of noble mind)
> To scorn delights, and live laborious days.

(Note that "laborious.")

390   A Fan's Notes (Frederick Exley, 1968)
The American writer's first novel, subtitled "A Fictional Memoir," was hailed as a minor classic. Its central character is an alcoholic English lecturer who is a fanatical devotee of the New York Giants football team and in particular of running back Frank Gifford, whose career he follows eagerly. Despite many relationships with women and friendships with men, he comes to realize that it is his destiny "to sit in

the stands with most men and acclaim others," that it was his fate "to be a fan."
Hence the title.

391   The Far Pavilions   (M. M. Kaye, 1978)

The British writer's romantic novel of the British Raj in India, described by one reviewer as "a *Gone with the Wind* of the North-West Frontier," has a title that the author seems to have devised expressly. However, it echoes a phrase in James Hilton's
Lost Horizon (1933):

> The austere serenity of Shangri-La. Its forsaken courts and pale pavilions shim-
> mered in repose.

392   Far from the Madding Crowd   (Thomas Hardy, 1874)

The novel, in its quintessentially rural setting, tells of the contrast between a patient
love and an overbrimming passion. The title, in its original context, alludes to both
setting and subject:

> Far from the madding crowd's ignoble strife
> Their sober wishes never learned to stray.

In these lines from Thomas Gray's *Elegy Written in a Country Churchyard* (1751),
"madding" means "frenzied," "mad," not "maddening," as sometimes popularly supposed.

393   Farewell, My Lovely   (Raymond Chandler, 1940)

The story tells how the American author's private-eye hero, Philip Marlowe, sets
about tracking down the missing girlfriend of Moose Malloy, an ex-convict. The
title was apparently Chandler's own, although it echoes Franz Lehar and Reginald
Arkell's popular song *Farewell My Love, Farewell* (1925), also known as the *Sere-
nade Frasquita*. The original title was to have been *The Second Murderer*, derived (as
Chandler explained to his publisher) from one of the characters in Shakespeare's
Richard III.

394   Farewell the Trumpets   (Jan Morris, 1978)

The third volume of the English writer's autobiographical trilogy, overall titled *Pax
Britannica*, has a title that is something of a spoof. It suggests a phrase from some
poem. It in fact comes from a poem that the author herself wrote to quote it from.
The poem is the book's epigraph:

> Say farewell to the trumpets!
> You will hear them no more.
> But their sweet and silvery echoes
> Will call to you still
> Through the half-closed door.

395   A Farewell to Arms   (Ernest Hemingway, 1929)

The American writer's novel, set in World War I, tells how a young American is
caught up in the Caporetto disaster in Italy in 1917, deserts (thus bidding "farewell
to arms"), and finally escapes with an English nurse into neutral Switzerland. *Cf.*
Goodbye to All That.

396   Fear and Loathing in Las Vegas   (Hunter S. Thompson, 1971)
The American writer's bizarre and picaresque novel, a semi-fictionalized account of a district attorneys' drugs convention, has a title that first appeared as that of two articles in *Rolling Stone* for November 11 and 25, 1971. Thompson wrote these under the pseudonym "Raoul Duke," the name of the novel's central character.

397   Fear of Flying   (Erica Jong, 1973)
The American writer's first novel deals with the insatiable sexual appetite of its central character, Isadora Wing, and opens with her reluctance to board a Pan Am flight for fear of flying. The title works on a deeper level, however, since although sex for Isadora is a means of "flying," it is an illusory escape from reality and an illusory freedom, and one that she fears.

398   Feasting with Panthers   (Peter Coe, 1981)
The title is that of the British writer's play about the trials of Oscar Wilde. It comes from Wilde's *De Profundis* (1905), in a passage about his life before he was sent to Reading Gaol for homosexual offences:

> People thought it dreadful of me to have entertained at dinner the evil things of life and to have found pleasure in their company. But then, from the point of view through which I, as an artist in life, approach them they were delightfully suggestive and stimulating. It was like feasting with panthers; the danger was half the excitement.

399   The Fermata   (Nicholson Baker, 1994)
The American writer's novel concerns the ability of its antihero, Arno Strine, to freeze time. While people around him are in a state of suspended consciousness, he uses the opportunity to act out his fantasies, taking women's clothes off, watching them in the bedroom and bathroom, and the like. The title refers to the musical sign for a pause. This is in the form of a dot in a semicircle, suggesting the upper half of a breast, and is printed at the head of each chapter.

400   A Few Figs from Thistles   (Edna St. Vincent Millay, 1920)
The American writer's collection of poems takes its title from the Bible:

> Ye shall know them by their fruits. Do men gather grapes of thorns, or figs of thistles? [Matthew 7:16]

Fiesta *see* **The Sun Also Rises**

401   Fifteen   (Beverly Cleary, 1956)
The American writer's seventh novel for children tells the story of 15-year-old Jane, her first boyfriend, and her first dating.

402   The Fifth Column   (Ernest Hemingway, 1938)
The American writer's only play, about espionage in the Spanish Civil War, takes its title from a radio broadcast in 1936 by the nationalist general Emilio Mola after

the fall of Toledo: "We have four columns advancing upon Madrid. The fifth column will rise at the proper time." The "fifth column" is a reference to Franco sympathizers within the city. The phrase later became generally adopted as a term for enemy supporters in one's own country (or one's own supporters in an enemy country), possibly as a result of this very play.

403 Fifty-Four Forty or Fight! (Emerson Hough, 1909)
The American writer's novel deals with the controversy over the boundary line between Oregon and Canada. Its title quotes words from William Allen's 1844 speech in the Senate, adopted as the slogan of the expansionist Democrats in the presidential campaign that year. (On his election, President James K. Polk effected a compromise by which the disputed territory was divided at the 49th parallel, not at 54° 40'.)

404 The Figure in the Carpet (Henry James, 1896)
The American writer's tale is the story of an earnest young critic's study of the works of a brilliant novelist, Hugh Vereker, who tells him that the key to an appreciation of his books is "the figure in the carpet," which no one has yet understood. The young man tells his friend, the experienced critic Corvick, of this, and the latter devotes his time to discovering the "figure." He claims to have done so when he marries Gwendolyn Erme, a woman who had also been searching for the key. The mystery is never satisfactorily solved.

405 Final Payments (Mary Gordon, 1978)
The American writer's first novel tells how a single Catholic woman of Irish descent gives up eleven years of her life to nurse her invalid father, only to find after his death that her religious upbringing is of little use in helping her adjust to the modern world. She eventually breaks free, having made her "final payments," to her father and her faith.

406 A Fine and Private Place (Morley Callaghan, 1975)
The Canadian writer's novel, which includes characters from his own works as well as from those of his long-time admirer Edmund Wilson, takes its title from Andrew Marvell's poem *To His Coy Mistress* (1681):

> The grave's a fine and private place,
> But none, I think, do there embrace.

407 A Fine Madness (Elliott Baker, 1964)
The American writer's first novel depicts the victory of an artist over the forces of conformity. The working-class hero, Samson Shillitoe, is seized by a group of psychiatrists and put through a number of tests and tortures. He emerges intact, his imagination and creativeness triumphing over death and destruction. The title is a quotation from Michael Drayton's lines on Marlowe, *To Henry Reynolds, of Poets and Poesy* (1627):

> For that fine madness still he did retain
> Which rightly should possess a poet's brain.

408   Finnegans Wake   (James Joyce, 1939)

The Irish writer's last novel takes the form of the dreams of a Dublin publican, H. C. Earwicker, and his wife, Anna Livia Plurabelle. The title of the book is typical of the author's surreal yet specifically allusive style of writing. "Finnegan's Wake" is the name of a New York Irish ballad in which a bricklayer falls drunk from his ladder and dies but is revived with whiskey. The title of Joyce's novel thus refers primarily to the song. It also, however, refers to Finn, the chief hero of Irish legend, better known as Fingal, who died then woke again. The different components of the title have thus been interpreted as representing French *fin*, "end," Latin *negans*, "denying," and English *wake*, "resurrection," referring both to Finn's return to life after death and to the recurring cycles of world history which the novel itself is believed to have as its main theme. (The cyclic theme is further spelled out in the work by its closing words, "A way a lone a last a loved a long the," with no period, which continue in its opening words, "riverrun past Eve and Adam's," with no initial capital.) Joyce's provisional title for the novel as he was writing it was *Work in Progress*.

409   Fire Down Below   (William Golding, 1989)

The final novel of the British author's trilogy that began with **Rites of Passage** concerns a ship that is crippled by a loose foremast. To effect a repair, red-hot irons are inserted, but these eventually set the core of the timber alight. The fire that ensues is the novel's most powerful image. As one character says: "Imagine our caravan, we, a fire down here below—spark of the Absolute—matching the fire up there—out there!"

410   Fire in the Morning   (Elizabeth Spencer, 1948)

The American writer's first novel centers on the Gerrard family, who move into Tarsus following Civil War disruptions and become prominent citizens by means of perjury and blackmail. Their schemes, however, result in the destruction of almost everyone, except one Gerrard son and a former school friend. The title is taken from Djuna Barnes's *Nightwood* (1936).

411   The Fire Next Time   (James Baldwin, 1963)

The American author's famous study of Black Muslims, incorporating a recollection of his experiences as a preacher, has a title that is partly explicated in its final words: "If we do not now dare everything, the fulfillment of that prophecy, re-created from the Bible in song by a slave, is upon us:

> *God gave Noah the rainbow sign,*
> *No more water, the fire next time!*

This comes from a spiritual which remembers God's covenant with Noah (Genesis 9:8–17) but which also portends judgment. It runs more fully:

> God gave Noah de Rainbow sign,
> Don't you see?
> God gave Noah de Rainbow sign,
> No more water but fire next time,

> Better get a home in dat rock,
> Don't you see?

412   The First Casualty   (Phillip Knightley, 1975)

The Australian-born British journalist's book about the role of propaganda in wartime takes its title from a saying of the US senator Hiram W. Johnson in 1917: "The first casualty when war comes is truth."

413   The Fist of God   (Frederick Forsyth, 1994)

The British thriller writer's novel is set against the background of the Iraqi invasion of Kuweit. It premises that Dr. Gerald Bull, by inventing the "supergun" in 1990, provided Saddam Hussein with the means to launch his doomsday weapon and so had to be eliminated by the Iraqis. The weapon is the "fist of God" of the title, as a translation of its Arabic name.

414   Five Children and It   (E. Nesbit, 1902)

The children's fantasy novel by the British writer recounts the adventures of five children and "it," a sand-fairy known as the Psammead that reluctantly grants their wishes.

415   The Fixer   (Bernard Malamud, 1966)

The title of the American writer's novel refers to the central character, the Jew Yakov Bok, who as the narrative opens is earning a meager living as a "fixer" or repairman in early 20th-century Russia. In the end he also "fixes" his own identity as Yakov and as a Jew, in the sense that he mends it and also plants it in the mind.

416   Flagons and Apples   (Robinson Jeffers, 1912)

The American writer's first (and self-published) book of poems, mainly on bohemian themes, has a title that alludes to a biblical verse: "Stay me with flagons, comfort me with apples: for I am sick of love" (Song of Solomon 1:5).

417   Flambards   (K. M. Peyton, 1967)

The children's novel, the first in a series by the British writer, takes its title from the name of the Essex country house where its central character, a 12-year-old orphan girl, is sent to live, its owner being her uncle. (A Flambard's Farm in Essex was recorded in the 15th century as Flambards. The author and her husband made their home in Essex and the name was presumably taken from this.)

418   Flannelled Fool   (T. C. Worsley, 1967)

The British writer's book, which he described as "a slice of life in the 30s," takes its title from Rudyard Kipling's poem *The Islanders* (1902):

> Then ye returned to your trinkets; then ye contented your souls
> With the flannelled fools at the wicket or the muddied oafs at the goals.

The "flannelled fools" are cricketers, wearing white flannel trousers.

419   Flaubert's Parrot   (Julian Barnes, 1984)
The British writer's third novel concerns the career of the French writer Gustave
Flaubert, as studied by a dull and incompetent biographer who is so obsessed with
his subject that he loses his own identity and so becomes a "parrot" of his real self.
His researches include an investigation into the true meaning and identity of the
stuffed parrot that Flaubert kept on his desk while writing *Un Coeur Simple*.

420   The Flight from the Enchanter   (Iris Murdoch, 1956)
The British writer's second novel deals with the various degrees of human freedom.
Some of the characters are able to "enchant," or exercise their power over others,
while others are able to build up a resistance to such "enchantments" in order to pre-
serve their identity, even at a superficial level. The title alludes to a phrase from
Shelley's *Ode to the West Wind* (1819):

> O wild West Wind, thou breath of Autumn's being,
> Thou, from whose unseen presence the leaves dead
> Are driven, like ghosts from an enchanter fleeing.

421   The Floating Opera   (John Barth, 1956)
The American writer's first novel recounts the experiences of a man recalled on the
day in 1937 when he was contemplating suicide. After a day of vacillation, he decides against, and continues in words that explain the title:

> It's a floating opera, friend, chock-full of curiosities, melodrama, spectacle, in-
> struction and entertainment, but it floats willy-nilly on the tide of my vagrant
> prose.

422   The Flower Beneath the Foot   (Ronald Firbank, 1923)
The British writer described his novel as a "Record of the Early Life of St. Laura
De Nazianzi and the Times in Which She Lived," and opens with the young Laura
in her convent wondering what "life in the world" is actually like. The story shows
that it is cruel and treacherous, and that she will be spurned, the "flower beneath
the foot" of society. Hence the title.

423   Flowers in the Attic   (Virginia Andrews, 1980)
The first novel in the American writer's quartet about the unhappy Dollenganger
family tells how a brother and sister are kept prisoners in an attic until an inheritance is claimed. The title thus refers to them.

424   Fludd   (Hilary Mantel, 1989)
The title of the British writer's fourth novel is the name of its central character, who
is apparently a reincarnation of the mystical theosophist and alchemist Robert
Fludd (1574–1637).

425   Flying to Nowhere   (John Fuller, 1983)
The British writer is best known as a poet and author of tales for children, and both
these aspects are present in this novel, an adult fantasy about the soul in its efforts

to escape the confines of the body. It concerns a bishop's emissary, Vane, who is sent to a well in Wales to investigate why pilgrims who visit it never return. He is directed to a cemetery, and while excavating the undergound system he finds there, falls into a corpse pit and drowns. The words of the title are put into the mouth of a farm girl, who as she dreams of escaping from a chrysalis, cries: "I'm flying to nowhere. I'm just becoming myself."

426   The Folding Star   (Alan Hollinghurst, 1994)

The British author's second novel takes as its title a colloquial name for the evening star (itself referring to the star's rising at the time when sheep were put in the fold). The novel centers on and counterpoints two fixations: that of a Flemish artist, Edgard Orst, with a flame-haired actress in the 1890s, and that of a gay English tutor, Edward Manners, with his seventeen-year-old pupil in the 1990s. The title has connotations of a physical embrace and an emotional implosion, and hints at the doomed rapture that awaits the novel's protagonists.

427   The Folks That Live on the Hill   (Kingsley Amis, 1990)

The British author's novel is concerned with the problems of everyday life and tells the story of a retired librarian and the large circle of relations that he has acquired. He lives with his widowed sister and her dog in Shepherd's Hill, a fictional location in north London. The title thus alludes to both people and place, and was itself adopted (and slightly adapted) from the song by Jerome Kern and Oscar Hammerstein II, *The Folks Who Live on the Hill*, which featured in the US movie *High, Wide and Handsome* (1937).

428   Fools of Fortune   (William Trevor, 1983)

The British writer's novel tells of the ill-fated love of the Irishman Willie Quinton for his English cousin, Marianne. Murder, suicide, and madness are part of the plot, as reflected in the title, which is adapted from the proverb "Fortune favors fools."

429   For Whom the Bell Tolls   (Ernest Hemingway, 1939)

The American writer's well-known novel of the Spanish Civil War takes its title from John Donne's "Meditation XVII" in *Devotions upon Emergent Occasions* (1624):

> Any man's death diminishes me, because I am involved in Mankind; And therefore never send to know for whom the bell tolls; it tolls for thee.

Hemingway commented on his choice of title in a letter of April 21, 1940 to his publisher Maxwell Perkins (quoted in Carlos Baker, ed., *Ernest Hemingway: Selected Letters 1917–1961*, 1981):

> I think it has the magic that a title has to have. Maybe it isn't too easy to say. But maybe the book will make it easy. Anyway I have had thirty some titles and they were all possible but this is the first one that has made the bell toll for me. Or do you suppose that people think only of tolls as long distance charges and of Bell as the Bell of the telephone system? If so it is out. The Tolling of the Bell. No. That's not right.

430   Foreign Affairs   (Alison Lurie, 1985)

The American writer's seventh novel concerns the parallel love affairs of two American colleagues, Vinnie Miner and Fred Turner, when in London away from home. Hence the title, which additionally refers to the unlikely lovers that each finds.

431   Forest of the Night   (Madison Jones, 1960)

The American writer's second novel recounts the experiences of Jonathan Cannon, whose time in the Tennessee "outback" disabuses him of his previously held conviction that mankind is inherently good. The title comes from William Blake's poem "The Tyger" in *Songs of Experience* (1794), in which the lamb, representing innocent childhood, is contrasted with the tiger, representing corrupt adulthood:

> Tyger! Tyger! burning bright
> In the forests of the night.

432   Forever Amber   (Kathleen Winsor, 1944)

The American writer's historical bestseller tells of the amours of a beauty (named Amber for the color of her eyes) in Restoration London. The American publisher Harold Latham explained the origin of the title in his memoirs, *My Life in Publishing* (1965):

> The novel was not called *Forever Amber* when first offered to us. [...] One of the publicity staff was discussing the manuscript one day. She said, in effect, "I get a little tired of Amber—it's forever Amber, forever Amber, forever Amber ..." "Wait a minute," one of her listeners exclaimed, "We've been wanting a title. You've given it to us—*Forever Amber*." And it was so agreed.

433   Fortune and Men's Eyes   (John Herbert, 1967)

The play by the Canadian dramatist, with homosexuality as its theme, takes its title from Shakespeare's *Sonnets* (*XXIX*):

> When in disgrace with fortune and men's eyes
> I all alone beweep my outcast state,
> And trouble deaf heaven with my bootless cries,
> And look upon myself, and curse my fate.

434   The Fountain   (Eugene O'Neill, 1926)

The play by the American playwright centers on the Spanish explorer Ponce de Léon, and has him fall in love with a woman much younger than himself. He seeks to win her own love by finding Cathay and the fountain of youth. He and his expedition are guided to a fountain on the Florida coast, where he is wounded and left for dead. In the fountain he sees a vision of beauty and eternal life and hears a song with the words: "Life is a flower Forever blooming; Life is a fountain Forever leaping." He ultimately fails in his search, but dies with an ecstatic vision of eternal youth, saying: "I have found my Fountain! O Fountain of Eternity, take back this drop, my soul!"

435   The Fountain Overflows   (Rebecca West, 1957)

The British author's novel about a family growing up in impoverished eccentricity is told from the viewpoint of the young girl Rose, whose main love is music. At the end of the tale she realizes that although her future in the professional world will be demanding, she can always derive pleasure and inspiration from music, for as she plays it seems to her that "the fountain overflows." The title of these words comes from a line in *Proverbs of Hell* in William Blake's *The Marriage of Heaven and Hell* (1790–93): "The cistern contains: the fountain overflows."

436   The Four Feathers   (A. E. W. Mason, 1902)

The British writer's best known novel is a stirring tale of the recovery of lost honor. The central character is Harry Feversham, a young officer who has been disgraced and as a result lost his fiancée, Ethne Eustace. He resigns his commission, ostensibly because of his engagement to Ethne, but really because he has learnt that his regiment is to be sent on active service to Egypt. When three brother officers discover his motive, they send him three white feathers, as symbols of cowardice, and Ethne adds a fourth. The story tells how Harry redeems himself, persuades each of the four to withdraw the feathers, and happily marries Ethne.

437   The Four Million   (O. Henry, 1906)

The American writer's collection of stories has a preface that explains the title:

> Not very long ago some one invented the assertion that there were only "Four Hundred" people in New York City who were really worth noticing. But a wiser man has arisen—the census taker—and his larger estimate of human interest has been preferred.

The "some one" was the lawyer and social leader Ward McAllister, who in 1888 remarked that there were "only about four hundred people in New York society."

438   Four Quartets   (T. S. Eliot, 1943)

The work, considered to be the Anglo-American writer's finest, comprises four related poems, each of which is in a form analagous to that of the classical sonata, as exemplified in the late string quartets of Beethoven. The "quartet" motif is carried further in that each poem represents one of the four seasons and has as its main theme one of the four elements (air, earth, water, fire). For the origins of the titles of the individual quartets, see respectively **Burnt Norton, East Coker, The Dry Salvages,** and **Little Gidding.**

439   The Fox in the Attic   (Richard Hughes, 1961)

The British writer's novel is set in 1923. Its central character, the young Welsh squire Augustine Penry-Herbert, goes to stay with remote German cousins in a castle in Bavaria, where he falls in love with the owner's young daughter. This part of the story is mainly given through the eyes of a young Nazi, Lothar, whose older brother, the killer Wolff, is hiding in the castle's upper rooms. He is thus the "fox in the attic" of the title.

440   The Foxes of Harrow   (Frank Yerby, 1946)

The title of the American writer's first novel, a historical romance, refers to the family of the gambler Stephen Fox, a plantation owner in Harrow, Louisiana, who is ruined by the Civil War.

441   Foxfire   (Joyce Carol Oates, 1993)

The American writer's novel centers on the five members of a girls' high school gang in the 1950s, with its title the gang's name. "Foxfire" itself is a term for the glow of certain phosphorescent fungi on decaying timber, but the name is given a more specific origin in the book:

Afterwards they asked Legs how had she thought of the name FOXFIRE that lovely perfect name FOXFIRE of which they were already proud FOXFIRE FOXFIRE and Legs said that the initial name for the gang she'd thought of had been "Foxes of Fairfax Avenue" but then in a dream she heard "FOXFIRE."

442　Franny and Zooey　(J. D. Salinger, 1961)
The stories by the American writer originally appeared separately in *The New Yorker*, "Franny" in 1955 and "Zooey" in 1957. The names are those of the actress Franny Glass and her television actor brother Zooey.

443　The French Lieutenant's Woman　(John Fowles, 1969)
The title of the British writer's third novel refers to Sarah Woodruff, the enigmatic, beautiful young woman with whom the novel's central character, Charles Smithson, falls in love. She is known locally as "the French lieutenant's woman" because of an alleged shameful liaison in the past with a French naval officer.

444　Frescoes for Mr. Rockefeller's City　(Archibald MacLeish, 1933)
The poems by the American poet are a celebration of America and her people, arranged in six "frescoes." These are supposedly panels designed to replace those removed from New York's Rockefeller Center because their artist, Diego Rivera, had been too outspoken in his pictorial representation of contemporary American capitalist civilization.

445　Friends in Low Places　(Simon Raven, 1965)
The British writer's second novel in the ten-volume sequence **Alms for Oblivion** is set in 1959 and tells of the attempts of its central character, Mark Lewson, a gigolo and conman, to sell a letter that incriminates several senior members of the government with regard to the Suez Crisis. The people that he meets are the "friends in low places" of the title, itself a comic reversal of the traditional "friends in high places," who here can be regarded as the government ministers.

446　From a View to a Death　(Anthony Powell, 1933)
The British writer's third novel, set against a background of English country gentry in the interwar years, concerns the ambition of its central character, Arthur Zouch, to marry into that society of landowners and huntsmen and so enhance his own standing. However his ambition (the "view" of the title) is never realized because he is accidentally killed (the "death"). The title is directly quoted from the song *John Peel* (1820) by the huntsman John Woodcock Graves:

> Yes, I ken John Peel, and Ruby too,
> Ranter and Ringwood, Bellman and True,
> From a find to a check, from a check to a view,
> From a view to a death in the morning.

(Ruby and the others are hounds, and the nouns relate to their actions: a *find* is their scenting of a fox; a *check* is their loss of the scent or a pause to establish which way to run; a *view* is their sighting of the fox as it breaks cover; a *death* is their killing of the fox.)

447   From Here to Eternity   (James Jones, 1951)
The American writer's bestselling novel about life in the U.S. Army takes its title
from the refrain of Rudyard Kipling's poem *Gentlemen-Rankers* (1892):

> We're poor little lambs who've lost our way,
> Baa! Baa! Baa!
> We're little black sheep who've gone astray,
> Baa-aa-aa!
> Gentlemen-rankers out on the spree,
> Damned from here to Eternity,
> God ha' mercy on such as we,
> Baa! Yah! Baa!

448   From Sea to Shining Sea   (Gavin Young, 1995)
The title of the British travel writer's account of his east-to-west journey across
America comes, aptly if rather obviously, from Katharine Lee Bates's patriotic poem
America the Beautiful (1893), the relevant lines being:

> America! America!
> God shed his grace on thee
> And crown thy good with brotherhood
> From sea to shining sea!

449   From Where the Sun Now Stands   (Will Henry (Henry W. Allen),
      1960)
The novel, reckoned to be the American author's best, is a fictional account of Chief
Joseph's struggle against the white man, as narrated by his nephew. Its title comes
from Chief Joseph's declaration to the Nez Percé tribe after surrendering to General Nelson A. Miles in the Battle of Bear Paw Mountains, Montana, September
30-October 5, 1877:

> Hear me, my chiefs. My heart is sick and sad. From where the sun now stands I
> will fight no more forever.

450   Frost in May   (Antonia White, 1933)
The book is the first of the British writer's four autobiographical novels, and follows the fate and fortunes of a young girl in a Catholic convent school, where she
is subjected to a number of emotionally stultifying rules, such as a ban on individual friendships. These chill her natural warmth and vitality, in one respect physically, since she is required to take cold baths. The title thus alludes to this, and is
apparently drawn from the old weather prophecy, "Fog in March, frost in May."

451   Fun in a Chinese Laundry   (Josef von Sternberg, 1966)
The Austrian-American film director took the title of his autobiography from that
of an early short film made by Thomas Alva Edison. It is typical of the humorless
descriptive titles of early movies, such as *The Great Train Robbery* (1903).

452   G   (John Berger, 1972)
The British writer's third, experimental novel is arranged in "stanzas" that vary in
length from a few pages to a single line. The title is the name (or initial) of its

central character, G, born in 1888 as the son of a wealthy Italian merchant. It is not clear why he bears this particular letter, unless it is intended to represent Berger's own name.

453   Gabriel's Lament   (Paul Bailey, 1986)
The "lament" of the title of the British writer's sixth novel is the expression of grief of its central character, Gabriel Harvey, when he learns, in Minnesota, that his mother had committed suicide some thirty years earlier within a few weeks of leaving home.

454   Galahad at Blandings   (P. G. Wodehouse, 1965)
The names of the people and places in the stylishly comic novels by the British-born writer (a US citizen from 1955) have long been a source of delight and object of research for devotees both sides of the Atlantic. The Galahad of this title, nick-named "Gally," is the younger brother of one of the author's leading characters, Clarence Threepwood, 9th Earl of Emsworth, whose residence is at Blandings Castle, near Market Blandings, somewhere in rural Shropshire. Wodehouse had himself lived in the town of Emsworth in southern England, and British writer Richard Usborne, who has made a study of the topography of Blandings, reckons that Market Blandings represents Buildwas, ten miles from Shrewsbury, Shropshire. Threepwood was the name of Wodehouse's home at Emsworth. Owen Dudley Edwards, in *P. G. Wodehouse* (1977), suggests that the name Blandings itself comes from Beatrix Potter's *The Tale of Pigling Bland* (1913). The novel, the tenth in the Blandings Castle series, was first published in the USA as *The Brinkmanship of Galahad Threepwood*.

455   The Gallery   (John Horne Burns, 1947)
The American writer's best-known novel is an episodic story set in Italy and North Africa and based on his service in the US Army in World War II. The "portraits" that make up the story are unified by their setting, the Galleria Umberto Primo in Naples in 1944, and this is the "gallery" of the title, as an arcade through which the various characters pass or the place where they meet.

456   The Game   (Jack London, 1905)
The "game" is boxing, and the title is ironic. The American writer's novelette tells how a young fighter is begged by his fiancé to abandon boxing. He insists on one last fight, but an accidental slip on the canvas results in his death.

457   The Gang's All Here   (Robert E. Lee, 1959)
The play by the American playwright is based on the life of President Harding, and tells how a man of mediocre talent and ability is pushed into the prominence of public life by crafty politicians. The title reflects a chorus from W. S. Gilbert and Arthur Sullivan's operetta *The Pirates of Penzance* (1879): "Hail, hail, the gang's all here."

458   General Ludd   (John Metcalf, 1980)
The British-born Canadian author's third novel takes its title from the Luddites, the group of 19th-century English textile workers who destroyed machinery as a

protest against mechanization. The novel's central character, Jim Wells, is a modern Luddite, a poet who protests at debased forms of communication, whether audiovisual, sartorial, or verbal, and who sets out to "smash" them.

459   The Genteel Tradition at Bay   (George Santayana, 1931)
The American philosopher's essay is an attack on what he called a "New England disease" but which was more widely known as "the genteel tradition." This was the term applied in the late 19th century to a group of American writers who promoted a literary and moral standard that emphasized correctness and conventionality and that opposed any "realistic" description of the American scene.

460   The Gentle People   (Irwin Shaw, 1939)
The comedy by the American writer, subtitled *A Brooklyn Fable*, tells how two harmless middle-aged men on a fishing trip are harassed by a gangster. They lure him into their boat, row him out to sea, drown him, then continue with their trip. The title is thus ironic. The play is a "parable" since it was intended to suggest a way of dealing with Fascists, as a solution to an urgent problem of the day.

461   Gentlemen Prefer Blondes   (Anita Loos, 1925)
The title of the American writer's novel, the story of the blonde Lorelei Lee, refers to the generally recognized fact that western men find blondes more attractive than brunettes. The statement is spelled out in the first chapter: "Gentlemen always seem to remember blondes." Loos followed the novel with the less successful *But Gentlemen Marry Brunettes* (1926). Loos is generally assumed to have originated the title.

462   Geronimo Rex   (Barry Hannah, 1972)
The American writer's first novel tells how an aspiring writer boasts of his physical resemblance to the Apache chieftain Geronimo, whose independence he greatly admires. Hence the title, which puns on the Latin title of various European kings, such as *Georgius Rex* ("King George").

463   Gerontion   (T. S. Eliot, 1920)
The poem by the Anglo-American writer represents the meditation of "an old man in a dry month," and takes its title from Greek *gerontion*, "little old man."

464   The Getting of Wisdom   (Henry Handel Richardson [Ethel Florence Lindesay Richardson], 1910)
The Australian writer's work, generally regarded as her masterpiece, is a semiautobiographical account of the destruction of a schoolgirl's innocence in her struggle to achieve academic success and popularity. By pretending to be other than she is, she eventually "gets wisdom," and leaves school able to face the outside world and its many uncertainties. The title has a biblical ring, but nowhere occurs in the exact quoted form. Two verses in Proverbs are close, however: "Happy is the man that findeth wisdom, and the man that getteth understanding" (3:13), and "He that getteth wisdom loveth his own soul: he that keepeth understanding shall find good" (19:8).

465   The Ghost in the Machine   (Arthur Koestler, 1967)
The Hungarian-born British writer's study of the nature of mind takes its title from the expression introduced by the British philosopher Gilbert Ryle in his work *The Concept of Mind* (1949), in which he uses it to refer to the mind (the "ghost") as distinct from the body (the "machine").

466   Giants in the Earth   (O. E. Rölvaag, 1927)
The Norwegian-born American writer's best known novel, about Scandinavian pioneer life in the American Mid-West, tells the story of Peder Holm, whose struggle with the untamed frontier resembles a battle against trolls and giants. The title, here in its English translation, is biblical in origin: "There were giants in the earth in those days." (Genesis 6:4.) The work, subtitled *A Saga of the Prairie*, was first published in two parts in Norway with titles translating respectively as *In Those Days* (1924) and *The Kingdom Is Founded* (1925).

467   The Gift of Stones   (Jim Crace, 1988)
The British writer's first novel centers on a clan of flint-carvers at a time just before the start of the Bronze Age. The tribe are able to chip and refine bits of flint into knives and other tools, yet this ability, the "gift" of the title, sets them apart from other clans, who are thus obliged to barter with them for their artifacts.

468   Giles Goat-Boy   (John Barth, 1966)
The American writer's novel tells how the University (a metaphor for the world) is controlled by a computer, able to program itself and tyrannize people. However, it gets out of hand, and one of its developers seeks to reprogram it through a Grand Tutor, who will bring in a "New Syllabus" (a new philosophy). To do this, he selects George Giles, whom he had raised among goats as a goat, although he was actually found as a baby in the computer's tapelift. George enters the computer but paralyzes it instead of reprogramming it. He is therefore sent back to the goats of his boyhood as a scapegoat.

469   The Ginger Man   (J. P. Donleavy, 1955)
The Irish writer's first novel has as its antihero Sebastian Dangerfield, who is not only a (married) redhead but a man of action ("ginger"), squandering cash on liquor and having constant affairs with women. Hence the title.

470   The Girl of the Golden West   (David Belasco, 1905)
The play by the American playwright centers on "The Girl" who runs a saloon in a mining camp of the the the "Golden West" (so named for its golden corn). It was on this play that Puccini based his opera *La Fanciulla del West* (1910), the first grand opera on an American theme.

471   A Girl of the Limberlost   (Gene Stratton-Porter, 1909)
The story continues the American author's popular novel *Freckles* (1904), and is about a girl who hunts moths in Indiana swamplands in order to earn money for her education. According to a local story, the Limberlost Swamp, near which Porter

herself lived as a girl, is named for a hunter, "Limber Jim" McDowell, who was once lost there.

472   The Girl with the Green Eyes   (Clyde Fitch, 1902)

The play by the American playwright is a study of Jinny Austin, a pathologically jealous woman. Green is the color of jealousy.

473   Girls in Their Married Bliss   (Edna O'Brien, 1964)

The title of the third volume in the Irish-born writer's trilogy is ironic, since the story concerns the blighted marriages of two couples. The overall title of the three novels is *The Country Girls Trilogy*, taking this from the first in the series, *The Country Girls* (1960). This was also the author's first novel, written when in London after leaving her native Ireland in 1960.

474   The Girls of Slender Means   (Muriel Spark, 1963)

The British writer's novel is set in 1945, when "all the nice people in England were poor." The story centers on the members of the May Teck Club, which has been founded in a fashionable district of London "for the Pecuniary Convenience and Social Protection of Ladies of Slender Means below the age of Thirty Years, who are obliged to reside apart from their Families in order to follow an occupation in London." The euphemistic phrase "of slender means" simply means "poor," therefore, and the novel depicts the everyday lives of the young women (the "girls") as they discover sex, swap boyfriends, and share the one good-quality dress they have between them.

475   The Glass Menagerie   (Tennessee Williams, 1944)

The American writer's first successful play has a title that immediately refers to the collection of small glass animals owned by Laura, daughter of the central character, Tom Wingfield. At a broader level, it alludes to the "little people," the impoverished Wingfield family, whose world is visibly falling apart.

476   A Glass of Blessings   (Barbara Pym, 1958)

The British writer's novel centers on Wilmet Forsyth, a rich, high-born but foolish woman who imagines the exciting and passionate lives that the priests and parishioners in her local village must be having. She fancies herself in love with a handsome teacher, and assumes that he returns her love. As the story gradually unfolds, it becomes clear that all her assumptions are mistaken. The title comes from George Herbert's poem *The Pulley* (1633):

> When God at first made man,
> Having a glass of blessings standing by;
> Let us (said he) pour on him all we can:
> Let the world's riches, which dispersed lie,
> Contract into a span.

477   The Glittering Prizes   (Frederic Raphael, 1976)

The novel by the American-born British writer tells of the fortunes of a group of Cambridge contemporaries after their graduation. The chief of them is a novelist, who is tempted to make a foray into the mass media. The title quotes words from a speech by the Earl of Birkenhead to the students of Glasgow University in 1923: "The world continues to offer glittering prizes to those who have stout hearts and sharp swords."

478 The Glory (Vladimir Nabokov, 1971)

The Russian-born American writer's novel is a comic portrait of the wanderings of Martin, a sensitive young Russian émigré, and of his victory over his fear in futile but poetically significant acts. It originally appeared in Russian as *Podvig* (1931). Nabokov explains in his Foreword:

> The book's—certainly very attractive—working title (later discarded in favor of the pithier *Podvig*, 'gallant feat,' 'high deed') was *Romanticheskiy vek*, 'romantic times,' which I had chosen partly because I had had enough of hearing Western journalists call our era 'materialistic,' 'practical,' ultilitarian,' etc., but mainly because the purpose of my novel [...] lay in stressing the thrill and the glamour that my young expatriate finds in the most ordinary pleasure as well as in the seemingly meaningless adventures of a lonely life. [...] 'Fulfillment' would have been, perhaps, an even better title for the novel: Nabokov cannot be unaware that the obvious translation of *podvig* is 'exploit' [...]; but if you perceive in 'exploit' the verb 'utilize,' gone is the *podvig*, the inutile deed of renown. The author chose therefore the oblique 'glory,' which is a less literal but much richer rendering of the original title with all its natural associations [...]. It is the glory of high adventure and disinterested achievement; the glory of this earth and its patchy paradise; the glory of personal pluck; the glory of a radiant martyr.

479 Go Down, Moses (William Faulkner, 1942)

The title of the seven interrelated stories by the American writer, about complex race relations in the South, comes from a spiritual in which God bids Moses persuade Pharoah to release his people from slavery:

> Go down, Moses,
> Way down in Egypt land,
> Tell old Pharoah,
> Let my people go.

480 Go Tell It on the Mountain (James Baldwin, 1953)

The American writer's first novel, recounting a young black boy's coming to terms with the religious beliefs of his father, has a title that suggests a biblical text but that does not actually occur in the Bible. Its closest evocation is possibly the following: "O Zion, that bringest good tidings, get thee up into the high mountain; [...] say unto the cities of Judah, Behold your God!" (Isaiah 40:9).

481 The Godfather (Mario Puzo, 1969)

The American writer's novel concerns the underground struggle for power of the head of a New York crime family, Don Vito Gorleone, and he is the "godfather" of the title. The novel, or rather the 1972 movie based on it, widely popularized this slang sense of the word.

482   God's Little Acre   (Erskine Caldwell, 1933)

The American writer's novel deals with the shiftless and amoral mountain-dwellers of Georgia. The title relates to the plot of land that the central character, Ty Walden, has set aside so that its income goes to the church. However, he has to shift "God's little acre" constantly so as not to interfere with his gold-digging. *God's Acre* (from German *Gottesacker*) is itself a traditional euphemism for a churchyard.

483   The Gods Themselves   (Isaac Asimov, 1972)

The American writer's science fiction novel tells what happens when humans invent the Positron Pump, a device that sucks energy from a parallel universe and that threatens to destroy not only its inhabitants but humans as well. The title comes from Shakespeare's *King Lear*:

> Upon such sacrifices, my Cordelia,
> The gods themselves throw incense.   [V.iii.20]

484   Gog   (Andrew Sinclair, 1967)

The British writer's sixth novel takes its title and the name of its central character from the legendary giant of British folklore. (He and Magog were the only survivors of a race of giants destroyed by Brutus, the legendary founder of Britain.) Gog appears in the novel in the person of a huge naked man washed up on the Scottish coast in the summer of 1945, and the book is an account of his walk to London to claim his inheritance as a representative of the British. *Magog* (1972), Sinclair's next novel, was a sequel, and the trilogy was completed with *King Ludd* (1988), about the mythical king of Britain who is said to have given the name of London.

485   The Golden Bough   (Sir James Frazer, 1890–1915)

The Scottish anthropologist's famous comparative study of the religious beliefs of primitive man takes its title from the golden bough (Latin, *ramus aureus*, identified with the mistletoe) which, in classical mythology, Aeneas had to find and pluck for Proserpine before entering the Underworld. This in itself was an echo of an ancient ritual in which a runaway slave broke off a branch from a sacred tree before killing a priest and taking his place. Frazer set himself the task of establishing why the mistletoe, regarded normally as a mere parasite, should have acquired such mystical properties. Frazer was already familiar with the identically titled painting by J. M. W. Turner, depicting a tree overlooking Lake Nemi, Italy.

486   The Golden Bowl   (Henry James, 1904)

The American writer's novel centers on a golden bowl with an invisible flaw, symbolizing the various flawed relationships in the narrative. (The bowl is dramatically dashed to the floor by one of the characters.) The reference is to a biblical passage:

> Or ever the silver cord be loosed, or the golden bowl be broken, or the pitcher be broken at the fountain, or the wheel broken at the cistern.   [Ecclesiastes 12:6]

487   The Golden Boy   (Clifford Odets, 1937)

The American playwright's most successful play tells the story of a young Italian American who is expected to become a violinist but who thinks it will be easier to win fame and fortune as a "golden boy" in the boxing ring. The title is ironic, since he and his girl are killed in an automobile accident. The play actually popularized the term "golden boy" for a successful young man, not only by its title but in its text: "He walks down the street respected—the golden boy!" (III. i).

488   The Golden Gate   (Vikram Seth, 1986)
Described by Gore Vidal as "The Great Californian Novel," the Indian-born writer's ingenious work is written entirely in verse, including even the front matter (Acknowledgments, Dedication, and Contents), end matter (About the Author), and the title itself: "*The Golden Gate* by Vikram Seth" (pronounced "Sate"). It is a satire of life among groups of friends and lovers in California's "Silicon Valley," and the Golden Gate of the title is not only the actual strait and bridge of the name but also a symbol of the outwardly stable but inwardly volatile lives and loves of its characters.

489   The Golden Honeycomb   (Kamala Markandaya, 1977)
The Indian writer's historical novel has as its theme her country's struggle for independence. It centers on three generations of an imaginary princely family, "The Golden Honeycomb" of the title being the huge palace of its head, Bawajiraj III, Maharajah of Devapur. Much of the novel's action takes place in the palace, whose "honeycomb" can be said to symbolize both the growth of corruption in privileged Indian society and the gradual disintegration and decomposition of the British Empire.

490   The Golden Legend   (H. W. Longfellow, 1851)
The American poet explained the origin of his long dramatic poem and its title in an introduction:

> The old *Legenda Aurea* or Golden Legend, was originally written in Latin, in the thirteenth century, by Jacobus de Voragine, a Dominican friar, who afterwards became Archbishop of Genoa, and died in 1292. [...] I have called this poem the Golden Legend, because the story upon which it is founded seems to me to surpass all other legends in beauty and significance. [...] The story is told, and perhaps invented, by Hartmann von der Aue, a Minnesinger of the twelfth century.

491   Golk   (Richard Stern, 1960)
The American author's first novel has as its title the name of a television program that is a sort of "Candid Camera," catching people at embarrassing moments. It catches the novel's central character, Herbert Hondorp, and he enjoys the experience so much that he takes a job with the program.

492   Gone to Earth   (Mary Webb, 1917)
The British writer's novel tells the story of a wild, nature-loving young woman who dies trying to save her pet fox from the hunt. Hence the title, which is the hunting expression for a quarry that has sought refuge in its hole or burrow.

493   Gone with the Wind   (Margaret Mitchell, 1936)
The American author's only work, a historical bestseller about life in the South during and after the Civil War, takes its title from the poem *Non Sum Qualis Eram* (1896) by the English poet Ernest Dowson:

> I have forgot much, Cynara! gone with the wind,
> Flung roses, roses, riotously, with the throng.

The novel was originally called *Tomorrow Is Another Day*, the words with which it now closes. Mitchell herself changed this, as she did the heroine's name from Pansy (O'Hara) to Scarlett. The specific reference of the title is to the South *before* the Civil War, as is made clear by the on-screen prologue to the famous film (1939) of the novel:

> There was a land of Cavaliers and Cotton Fields called the Old South. Here in this patrician world the Age of Chivalry took its last bows. Here was the last ever seen of the Knights and their Ladies fair, of Master and Slave. Look for it only in books, for it is no more than a dream remembered, a Civilization gone with the wind.

494   The Good Companions   (J. B. Priestley, 1929)

The British writer's bestselling novel tells how Jess Oakroyd breaks away from the increasingly bleak world of mounting employment, tears up her National Insurance card, and joins a traveling concert party called "The Good Companions." Hence the title.

495   The Good Earth   (Pearl Buck, 1931)

The American writer's novel is a story of northern China, and recounts birth, marriage, and death in a Chinese peasant family. The title refers to the fertile land that brings the family their wealth, although all three sons turn away from the soil to lead other lives.

496   Good Night, Sweet Prince   (Gene Fowler, 1943)

The American writer's biography of John Barrymore, published the year after the actor's death, takes its title from Shakespeare's *Hamlet*, with the words that Horatio addresses to Hamlet after *his* death:

> Now cracks a noble heart. Good-night, sweet prince,
> And flights of angels sing thee to thy rest.   [V.ii.373]

497   The Good Soldier   (Ford Madox Ford, 1915)

The events of the British writer's novel, subtitled *A Tale of Passion*, are narrated by the American John Dowell, who discovers that for the past nine years his wife has been the mistress of his best friend, Captain Ashburnham, the "good soldier" of the title. When Ford's publisher, John Lane, was reluctant to use the author's original title, *The Saddest Story*, Ford wrote back irritably:

> Why not call the book "A Roaring Joke"? Or call it anything you like, or perhaps it would be better to call it "A Good Soldier"—that might do.

498   A Good Time Was Had by All   (Stevie Smith, 1937)

The title of a collection of poems by the English poet comes from the traditional words used to conclude a report in a parish magazine of a church picnic or social evening.

499   Goodbye to All That   (Robert Graves, 1929)

The British writer's autobiographical novel describes his experiences in World War I, as well as postwar life in Wales, Oxford, and Egypt. It ends with a farewell to "god-awful" England, its characters and historical time. The title echoes Hemingway's Farewell to Arms (published the same year.)

500   Goops and How to Be Them   (Gelett Burgess, 1900)

"Goops" are balloon-headed creatures used by the American writer to teach manners to children. The book itself combines pictures and text and has the subtitle: *Manual of manners for polite infants, inculcating many juvenile virtues, both by precept and example. Goop* later came to mean much the same as *goof,* i.e., stupid person, and Burgess presumably based the word on this.

501   The Grapes of Wrath   (John Steinbeck, 1939)

The American writer's classic novel is an account of a family's battle with starvation and financial ruin as its members move west from a land of drought to seek fruit-picking work in California. The symbolic title (the anger of the people ferments as they search for work and food) is a phrase adopted from Julia Ward Howe's *Battle Hymn of the Republic* (1862):

> Mine eyes have seen the glory of the coming of the Lord:
> He is trampling out the vintage where the grapes of wrath are stored.

"Grapes of wrath" here refers to the wrath of God, and is a phrase of biblical inspiration, such as: "I have trodden the winepress alone; and of the people there was none with me: for I will tread them in mine anger" (Isaiah 63:3), or: "He treadeth the winepress of the fierceness and wrath of Almighty God" (Revelation 19:15). Steinbeck sent the title to his publisher, Pascal Covici, on September 16, 1938, with the comment: "I like the soft with the hard and the marching content and the American revolutionary content."

502   The Grass Harp   (Truman Capote, 1951)

The American writer's novel tells the story of a young orphan, Collin Fenwick, who goes to stay with his two elderly aunts. One of the aunts is driven by the other to take refuge in a treehouse, together with Collin and the black cook, and they are joined there by two "outcasts" from the town. The "five fools in a tree" are thus in a "raft in a sea of leaves," like Huckleberry Finn's raft, and it is this to which the title refers.

503   Gravity's Rainbow   (Thomas Pynchon, 1973)

The American writer's novel opens in London towards the end of World War II, when V-2 rockets are raining down, and is concerned overall with the "dream of annihilation" that has long obsessed western civilization. The title thus alludes both to the arc of the rocket and to the decline of civilization itself, as it apparently plummets to its own inevitable destruction.

504   The Great Brain   (John D. Fitzgerald, 1967)

The American writer's first story for children is set in Adenville, Utah, at the turn of the century. The "great brain" of the title is the narrator's brother, Tom, who is quick to exploit any situation and turn it to his own advantage.

505   The Great Divide   (William Vaughn Moody, 1906)
The play by the American writer is concerned with the "great divide" between East
and West, as represented respectively by the heroine and the man she marries. The
play's original title was *The Sabine Woman*. Its present title was adopted in 1909.

506   Great Expectations   (Charles Dickens, 1860–1)
The "great expectations" of the title are those of the central character, the poor orphan Philip Pirrip ("Pip"), who aspires to become a gentleman, to come by good
money, and to marry into society. He does receive money and promises of further
wealth from a mysterious benefactor, who turns out to be an escaped convict. His
"great expectations" fade, however, when he goes to London and is left penniless.
He finally passes through the various stages of his "great expectations" and emerges
chastened and wiser from his experiences.

507   The Great Fake Book   (Vance Bourjaily, 1987)
The American writer's novel is the story of a young man's search for his father. It
takes its title (and inspiration) from the fictional "Songs for Professional Musicians," which is explained to the central character as follows: "Now if you know you
chords, you kin fake 'bout any song you'd ever want to play from just this one book
here." The novel is thus the "working book of magic spells" that both men take their
fake book to be.

508   The Great Fortune   (Olivia Manning, 1960)
The British author's novel is the first part of *The Balkan Trilogy*, itself the first half
of a sequence of six novels portraying the marriage of a young English couple, Guy
and Harriet Pringle, set against the backdrop of World War II in Europe and
Africa. The entire sequence, based on the author's own experiences, is completed by
The Levant Trilogy and is itself entitled *Fortunes of War*. This first volume is set in
Romania and takes its title from the concept that that country is like a person who
has inherited a great fortune but who has lost it through folly. The title also ties in
with the overall title of the series.

509   The Great God Brown   (Eugene O'Neill, 1926)
The experimental play by the American playwright, in which the actors wear masks
as in the Greek theater, depicts the complicated relationships that exist between the
artist, Dion Anthony, his wife Margaret, and their friend, a successful businessman,
William A. Brown. This last is thus the "great god" of the title. As described in the
play itself, he is a "visionless demigod of our new materialistic myth." He is finally
shot, and dies in the arms of a prostitute, who affirms the existence of (the real)
God. For a similar title by the same writer, *cf.* **The Emperor Jones**.

510   The Great Meadow   (Elizabeth Madox Roberts, 1930)
The "great meadow" is Kentucky, and the American writer's novel tells how that
state was settled by emigrants from Virginia, how they fought the Indians, and what
the hardships were that these pioneers endured.

511   The Great Pursuit   (Tom Sharpe, 1977)

The British author's sixth novel returns to the theme of his third, **Porterhouse Blue**, and is a satire on university life, especially at professorial level. The title puns on those of the two best-known works by the Cambridge literary critic F. R. Leavis, *The Great Tradition* (1948) and *The Common Pursuit* (1952). Sharpe's novel is a burlesque on Leavis's disdain for "popular" literature.

512   The Great White Hope   (Howard Sackler, 1968)

The American writer's best-known play is based on the life of Jack Johnson (1878–1946), the first black American to become world heavyweight boxing champion. White Americans hated Johnson for his arrogance and his many white mistresses. He had also particularly offended white supremacists by knocking out James J. Jeffries, who had come out of retirement to try and regain the title "for the white race." Hence the ironic title.

513   The Green Hat   (Michael Arlen [Dikram Kouyoumdjian], 1924)

The Bulgarian-born British writer's bestseller shocked in its day. Its central character, Iris Storm, is a "shameless, shameful lady" and a personification of the "bright young things" of the 1920s. The green hat that she wears is symbolic of her waywardness. When her secret is revealed at the end of the story, that her husband committed suicide on learning that he had syphilis, she roars off in her car and is killed when it hits a tree. On the grass beside the road, thrown from the car, lies her green hat.

514   The Green Knight   (Iris Murdoch, 1993)

The British writer's novel has a cast of disparate characters, almost all of whom possess some kind of mystical significance. One of them kills a mugger in self-defense, but he comes back to life to form part of their company and break the spell that binds them. They dispute who he could be:

> "I think he's Mr. Pickwick," said Louise. "Oh no! Never!" said Sefton. "I think he's more like Prospero." "I think he's like the Green Knight," said Aleph.

The book is full of literary and religious references, and here it is to the character in the 14th-century poem *Sir Gawain and the Green Knight*. The precise import of the name in the novel is enigmatic, and could be lost on some readers. In an interview with David Blow for *Waterstone's 1993 Christmas Catalogue*, Murdoch explained:

> I'd been thinking about Sir Gawain over a long period and, because the story in the poem is so wonderful, I wanted to take it over in some sort of way.

515   The Green Man   (Kingsley Amis, 1969)

The British writer's tenth novel, a mixture of social satire, comic tale, and ghost story, takes its title ostensibly from the haunted coaching inn at Fareham, Hertfordshire, where it is set. However, there is another "green man" in the form of a supernatural monster, a creature of branches and twigs that is conjured by the inn's special ghost, the evil Underhill.

516   Green Mansions   (W. H. Hudson, 1904)
The British writer's novel, part adventure story, part tragic love story, is set in the Venezuelan jungle, the "green mansions" of the title. Hudson was himself born in Argentina of American parentage, but became a British subject in 1900.

517   Green Pastures   (Marc Connelly, 1930)
The American writer's play is a comedy based on Roark Bradford's retelling of black American stories that were interpretations of biblical lore. Its title is thus biblical, and comes from the well-known line: "He maketh me to lie down in green pastures" (Psalm 23:2).

518   The Greening of America   (Charles Reich, 1971)
The title of the American writer's book refers to the rural regions of America, with "greening" not in the environmental sense but alluding to a sudden growth and maturity as a conscious counterculture to urban life. Reich concludes:

> The extraordinary thing about this new consciousness is that it has emerged out of the wasteland of the Corporate State. For one who thought the world was irretrievably encased in metal and plastic and sterile stone, it seems a remarkable greening of America.

The title was turned to punning advantage by Max Apple for his story *The Oranging of America* (1976), a blend of reality and fantasy.

519   Greenmantle   (John Buchan, 1916)
The Scottish writer's novel, more ambitious than **The Thirty-Nine Steps**, takes its heroes through occupied Europe to the Turkish frontline city of Erzerum. One of the "baddies" they encounter is the alluring Hilda von Einem, who aims to consolidate Turkish support for the Germans by using the seer Zimrud ("Emerald"), who wears a green cloak, to fulfill a prophecy of deliveration. "Greenmantle" is his codename, taken from an old Turkish miracle play called *Kasredin*. The seer dies, and one of the "goodies," Sandy Arbuthnot, is persuaded by von Einem to don his green cloak. The story ends with a siege, in which von Einem is killed, and with the Russians breaking through the Turkish defenses to liberate the city. Arbuthnot, still in his green cloak, has thus fulfilled the prophecy.

520   Grendel   (John Gardner, 1971)
The American writer's novel is a retelling of the Anglo-Saxon classic *Beowulf* from the point of view of Grendel, the monster that Beowulf fights and kills. Hence the title.

521   The Group   (Mary McCarthy, 1963)
The American writer's novel centers on the love lives of a group of girls following their graduation from Vassar in 1933. Hence the title.

522   Gullible's Travels   (Ring Lardner, 1917)
The American writer's collection of satirical tales about the newly rich has a title based (fairly obviously) on Defoe's *Gulliver's Travels*.

523   Guys and Dolls   (Damon Runyon, 1932)
The American writer's first book is a collection of short stories about the unlikely romantic relationships that can develop between men ("guys") and women ("dolls"). The title was popularized by the successful 1950 Frank Loesser musical based on the stories.

524   Hackenfeller's Ape   (Brigid Brophy, 1953)
The British writer's first novel was conceived as "a narrative poem on the [...] theme of the liberation of animals." It concerns the efforts of a zoologist to prevent scientists sending the ape of the title, named Percy, into space. Hackenfeller's Ape, the hypothetical *Anthropopithecus hirsutus africanus*, is the size of a gorilla, but has the characteristics of a chimpanzee, so that its close resemblance to humans makes it a ready subject for experimentation.

525   "The Hairy Ape"   (Eugene O'Neill, 1922)
The American playwright's expressionist play takes its title from the nickname (hence the quotes) of its main character, Yank, the brutal and stupid leader of the stokers on a transatlantic liner. (The nickname was his shipmates' version of "filthy beast," the epithet given him by an aristocratic young woman in a chance encounter.) In New York on Easter Sunday, he goes to the zoo to see the real ape there, as the only creature with whom he can feel kinship, but it kills him when he sets it free.

526   Ham on Rye   (Charles Bukowski, 1982)
The American writer's fourth novel is autobiographical, and recounts the story of Henry Chinaski (Charles Bukowski) as a child and adolescent. The title refers to the popular snack, here contrasting the "ham" or falseness of the adult world in its contact with the "rye" or harshness of youth.

527   The Hamlet of A. MacLeish   (Archibald MacLeish, 1928)
The dramatic monologue by the American poet is the story of (Shakespeare's) Hamlet used as a symbol for the way "the knowledge of ill is among us," and the way in which we try to deal with it.

528   The Hand of Ethelberta   (Thomas Hardy, 1875–6)
The novel centers on a young widow, Ethelberta Peterwin, and the three suitors who court her, hoping to win her hand (of the title) in marriage. Despite her family's protestations, she finally marries the elderly but affluent Lord Mountclere, while an earlier and more suitable suitor, Christopher Julian, secures the hand of her sister, Picotee.

529   The Hand-Reared Boy   (Brian Aldiss, 1970)
The novel by the British writer, famous for his science fiction, is the first of series of volumes of fictional autobiography, recounting the sexual and spiritual growth of the central character, Horatio Stubbs. The book covers Stubbs's boyhood, and the punning title refers to his masturbatory fantasies and first sexual encounters.

530   A Handful of Dust   (Evelyn Waugh, 1934)
The British writer's novel, a black comedy, is a satire on English upper-class society, with its central character depicted as a man whose old-fashioned values cannot sustain him in the changing modern world. Despite the humor, Waugh's portrayal has been seen as a serious comment on the empty morality and shifting values of 1930s England. The title comes from T. S. Eliot's poem *The Waste Land* (1922):

> And I will show you something different from either
> Your shadow at morning striding behind you
> Or your shadow at evening rising to meet you;
> I will show you fear in a handful of dust.

531   The Handmaid's Tale   (Margaret Atwood, 1985)
The Canadian author's anti-feminist sixth novel is set in the Republic of Gilead, a bleak, futuristic North America, where society is ruled by a repressive oligarchy of religious fundamentalists who have "gone back to basics" with a vengeance. The "handmaid" of the title is the heroine, Offred, who is one of the few fertile women left, and who is farmed out to an elite family as a surrogate mother. The title itself echoes that of one of the narratives in Chaucer's *Canterbury Tales*, but also alludes more specifically to the "handmaid" in the Old Testament story of Leah and Rachel and their marriage to Jacob: "And she gave him Bilhah her handmaid to wife: and Jacob went in unto her" (Genesis 30:4).

532   Hanging by Her Teeth   (Bonnie Greer, 1993)
The American writer's novel tells of a black American woman's search for her absent father, and herself, in Europe, and of the characters and events she encounters in the course of her odyssey. The title refers to Degas's painting *Lala au Cirque Fernando, Paris*, a portrait of a black acrobat hanging by her teeth.

533   Happenstance   (Carol Shields, 1980)
The American writer's fifth novel is divided into two parts: "The Husband's Story" and "The Wife's Story." It is the record of five days, the first separation in a long and happy marriage. The title alludes to the chance occurrences that brought this about.

534   The Harder They Fall   (Budd Schulberg, 1947)
The novel by the American writer is a study of the sport of boxing as a corrupt industry. Its title refers to the proverbial saying: "The harder they come, the harder they fall."

535   Hatter's Castle   (A. J. Cronin, 1931)
The British writer's best-selling first novel deals with the career of James Brodie, a tyrannical and over-ambitious family head who by trade is a hatter.

536   Hawksmoor   (Peter Ackroyd, 1985)
The British writer's third novel is set in London partly in the 18th century and partly in the 20th. The title is the name of the 20th-century detective, Nicholas

Hawksmoor, who investigates a series of murders of hobos and boys that have occurred near churches. The churches were designed in the 18th century by Nicholas Dyer, a pupil of the (real) architect Christopher Wren. Dyer had designed his churches to an occult plan and consecrated them with human sacrifices. Hawksmoor cannot solve the crimes, and is driven to a breakdown. The title also alludes, however, to the *real* church architect and pupil of Wren, Nicholas Hawksmoor (1661–1736). In consequence, Ackroyd attracted some criticism for perverting Hawksmoor's memory by associating him with the fictional satanist Dyer.

537   He Knew He Was Right   (Anthony Trollope, 1868–9)
The title of the British writer's novel is ironic. The story itself is that of the gradual mental and moral decline of a suspicious husband, who finally dies.

538   Hearing Secret Harmonies   (Anthony Powell, 1975)
The twelfth and last volume in the British writer's sequence **A Dance to the Music of Time** has a title which seems to suggest that the "music of time" has, after all, a hidden concord that some may perceive during the "dance."

539   The Heart Is a Lonely Hunter   (Carson McCullers, 1940)
The American writer's novel tells of a deaf and mute boy, John Singer, growing up in a small Southern town, and of the tragedy that befalls the four people who admire him. Singer himself subsequently commits suicide. The title is taken from a line in the poem *The Lonely Hunter* (1896) by the Scottish writer Fiona MacLeod (William Sharp): "My heart is a lonely hunter that hunts on a lonely hill."

540   The Heart of Midlothian   (Walter Scott, 1818)
The novel takes its title from the old Edinburgh Tolbooth, or prison, known as the "Heart of Midlothian," where much of the action is set. The prison itself was so nicknamed for its central position in Midlothian, the district that was formerly synonymous with the old county of Edinburgh. The prison was demolished in 1817.

541   The Heart of the Matter   (Graham Greene, 1948)
The title of the novel by the British Catholic convert alludes generally to its underlying theme: sin. More directly, it refers to the anguish in the heart of its central character, Major Scobie, whose gradual downfall is caused by the conflict between his Catholicism and his love for two women.

542   Heartbreak House   (G. B. Shaw, 1919)
The Irish writer's play, an indictment of the cultured leisured classes of Western society, describes the impact made by a young woman on the eccentric inhabitants of the "house without foundations" named in the title. The title itself evokes those of Thomas Love Peacock's prose satires *Headlong Hall* (1816), *Nightmare Abbey* (1818), and *Crotchet Castle* (1831).

543   Heaven's My Destination   (Thornton Wilder, 1934)
The American writer's comic novel about an evangelically religious salesman takes its title from the poem printed at the beginning of the book (with the names of the main character and his home town in italics):

George Brush is my name;
America's my nation;
Ludington's my dwelling place,
And Heaven's my destination.

Wilder added an explanatory note: "Doggerel verse which children of the Middle West were accustomed to write in their school-books."

544   The Hedgehog and the Fox   (Isaiah Berlin, 1953)

The British philosopher's work is a study of Tolstoy as a writer in whom the intellectual's desire for a universal principle of life would not yield to the novelist's awareness of diversity. The title alludes to the saying, originally formulated by the 7th-century BC Greek poet Archilocus, that, "The fox knows many things, but the hedgehog knows one *big* thing." As Berlin himself puts it in the book:

There exists a great chasm between those on one side, who relate everything to a single central vision [...] and, on the other side, those who pursue many ends, often unrelated and even contradictory [...]. The first kind of intellectual and artistic personality belongs to the hedgehogs, the second to the foxes.

545   The Heidenmauer   (J. Fenimore Cooper, 1832)

The American novelist's romance is set in 16th-century Bavaria in the town of Dürkheim at a time when society is emerging from Catholic dominance. The narrative tells of the love and marriage of a forester, Berchtold Hintermayer, and Meta Frey, daughter of prominent local citizen. The title alludes to a ruined fortress near the town that is the home of the man who at one time planned to marry Meta's mother.

546   Her Story   (Dan Jacobson, 1987)

The South African-born British writer's seventh novel is set in both the past and the future, and is presented as a story by a female author written in the year 2040 and discovered in 2296. It is thus a sort of *history* (or historical romance) that is *her story*. Hence the punning title.

547   Here Comes Everybody   (Anthony Burgess, 1965)

The British writer's book has a subtitle that explains its purpose: *An Introduction to James Joyce for the Ordinary Reader.* The title is a quote from Joyce's *Finnegans Wake* (1939): "There goes Everyman, Here Comes Everybody, the H.C.E. of our culture-lag." (The initials "H.C.E." occur throughout the novel, and are those of the central character, H. C. Earwicker.) Burgess's book was published in the United States (also in 1965) under the title *Re Joyce*.

548   Herself Surprised   (Joyce Cary, 1941)

The British writer's novel is the first of a trilogy based on his theory that "we are alone in our worlds." All three were published in 1958 under the title *First Trilogy*, which the author introduced by explaining that he aimed "to show three people, living each in his own world by his own ideas, and relating his life and struggles, his triumphs and miseries in that world." The three characters are two men in love with the same woman, and she is Sara, the central figure of the first novel, who is "her-self surprised" at her intuitive response to the world. *Cf.* To Be a Pilgrim, The Horse's Mouth.

549   The Hidden Persuaders   (Vance Packard, 1957)
The book by the American writer is a popular exposé of advertising practices, with the advertisers themselves the "hidden persuaders" of the title. (A short section in the book on subliminal advertising caused a furore at the time of publication.)

550   Hideous Kinky   (Esther Freud, 1992)
The British author's first novel tells the tale of life on the road in Morocco in the 1960s with an eccentric hippie mother from the point of view of her young daugh-ter. The title represents the favorite catchwords of the little girl and her older sister, Bea. But it also symbolizes the weird and wonderful life they lead:

> Hideous was Bea's and my favourite word. "Hideous" and "Kinky." They were the only words we could remember Maretta ever having said. "Hideous kinky. Hideous kinky," I chanted to myself. "It is ... if you want to get into Morocco," Mum answered.   [Chapter 1]

551   High Tor   (Maxwell Anderson, 1937)
The play in prose and verse by the American writer takes its title from its setting, the mountain of High Tor overlooking the Hudson, where the protagonist goes in order to escape civilization.

552   him   (E. E. Cummings, 1927)
The American writer's surrealist poem-and-play is intended to convey the struggle its author had in reconciling the conflicting claims of marriage, parenthood, and art. "Him" is actually the name of the protagonist, while the heroine is "Me."

553   The Hippopotamus   (Stephen Fry, 1993)
The British writer's third novel centers on the lazy writer Ted Wallace, who is tempted out of his slothful existence only by the lure of £250,000 to investigate some strange occurrences at a country house. He is thus the "hippopotamus" of the title.

554   His Little Women   (Judith Rossner, 1990)
The American writer's eighth novel is a feminist revisionist's reworking of Louisa May Alcott's *Little Women* (1868), contrasting the Victorian ideals of family, moth-erhood, and sisterhood with the broken family of the late 20th century. The coun-terpart for the four girls' mother, Marmee, is three different women, who have all been married to the same man, Sam Pearlstein, the counterpart for Mr. March. The three are thus "his little women."

555   The History Man   (Malcolm Bradbury, 1975)
The British writer's novel is a satirical "history" of life in a provincial English uni-versity, centering on Howard Kirk, a history lecturer. It is also a campus novel to

end all campus novels, which the author may have realized would date in time and so come to be regarded as a historical novel. Bradbury based the book on his own experiences as an academic, and in an "Author's Note" teasingly explains that it is "a total invention with delusory approximations to historical reality, just as is history itself."

556   A History of the World in 10½ Chapters   (Julian Barnes, 1989)
The British writer's fifth book is half novel, half collection of short stories. It describes a number of close escapes for the human race, such as the Flood, the sinking of the *Titanic*, a terrorist massacre, and two separate visits to Mt. Ararat. It begins with Noah's Ark and ends with heaven, pausing two thirds of the way through with the "half chapter," a direct meditation by the author on the nature of love. This is clearly intended to have a bearing on the other chapters, although the author's thesis, that love affects the course of history, is certainly not borne out by the events in those chapters. The title mirrors those of more orthodox "histories of the world," with the fractional number both disrupting the round figure of 10 and intimating the unorthodoxy of this particular history.

557   Hitty, Her First Hundred Years   (Rachel Field, 1927)
The American writer's fifth novel for children centers on the wooden doll Hitty, made for a girl in New England in the early 19th century. The story recounts her many adventures and misadventures since that time.

558   The Hobbit   (J. R. R. Tolkien, 1937)
The famous fantasy story for children by the British writer opens with the words: "In a hole in the ground there lived a hobbit." Hobbits are "small people, smaller than dwarves." This one was called Bilbo Baggins. The word "hobbit" had come to Tolkien unbidden, and he was puzzled about its origin. He later suspected it could have been suggested by Sinclair Lewis's *Babbitt*, whose hero's character is similar to that of Bilbo.

559   The Hollow Men   (T. S. Eliot, 1925)
The poem by the Anglo-American writer concerns itself with the emptiness of human life and "death's other Kingdom." Its first section has the lines:

> We are the hollow men
> We are the stuffed men
> Leaning together
> Headpiece filled with straw. Alas!

The title may have been influenced by Conrad's story *Heart of Darkness* (1902), in which Kurtz, one of the central characters, is demented by years of solitude, evil, and "hollow at the core." Eliot used the words in which a native boy announces his end, "Mistah Kurtz—he dead," as the epigraph for *The Hollow Men*.

560   Home and Beauty   (W. Somerset Maugham, 1919)
The play by the British writer concerns a World War I "grass widow" who remarries, whereupon her original husband turns up. Its title comes from the line "England,

home and beauty" in the song by the British composer Samuel James Arnold, *The Death of Nelson* (1811). The American title of Maugham's play was *Too Many Husbands*.

561   Home from the Hill   (William Humphrey, 1958)

The American writer's first novel tells the story of a family whose men are hunters, living and dying by their own bloody code. The title quotes from R. L. Stevenson's poem *Underwoods* (*Requiem*) (1887):

> Home is the sailor, home from sea,
> And the hunter home from the hill.

562   Honey in the Horn   (Harold L. Davis, 1935)

The American writer's tale of life among the pioneers of early Oregon takes as its title a phrase from the classic American rural song "Turkey in the Straw":

> Sugar in the gourd and honey in the horn,
> I never was so happy since the hour I was born.

563   Hopeful Monsters   (Nicholas Mosley, 1990)

The British writer's complex novel has intellectual and political revolution in Europe as its theme. It follows the stories of two characters, Eleanor Anders and Max Ackerman, who act as alternate narrators. They first meet in 1928 at a performance of *Faust* in the Black Forest. Their lives converge, diverge, and ultimately interweave, when they realize that they are the "hopeful monsters" of the title: "things born perhaps slightly before their time; when it's not known if the environment is quite ready for them."

564   Horseman, Pass By   (Larry McMurtry, 1961)

The American writer's first novel is the story of three generations of cowboys, as told from the point of view of a 17-year-old boy. As he looks on, the Old West of cowboys and traditional values collides with the New West, where nothing matters except making money. When the novel was reissued in 1963, it was retitled *Hud*, for the amoral stepson of the boy's grandfather, who aims to sell the cattle and take over the ranch. The first title quotes from W. B. Yeats's poem *Under Ben Bulben* (1919):

> Cast a cold eye
> On life, on death.
> Horseman, pass by!

565   The Horse's Mouth   (Joyce Cary, 1944)

The British writer's novel is the third of a trilogy (*see* **Herself Surprised**). The central character is the artist Gulley Jimson, whom Cary based on an amalgam of William Blake and Stanley Spencer. The title relates to the familiar phrase *from the horse's mouth*, meaning a direct source of information. Cary explains that he chose it because it refers to "the voice that commands Gulley to be an artist, and makes him struggle to realise his imagination in spite of all discouragement."

566   Hôtel du Lac   (Anita Brookner, 1984)
The title of the British writer's fourth novel is the name of the hotel by Lake Geneva, Switzerland, that is the place of retreat of a young woman in disgrace with her family for having a mind of her own about marriage. In the hotel she makes some unexpected new acquaintances, who tell her their own sad stories.

567   The Hotel New Hampshire   (John Irving, 1981)
The novel by the American writer follows the life of a large and eccentric New Hampshire family who experience sex and violence while inhabiting three different dwellings with the same name as the title.

568   The Hound of Earth   (Vance Bourjaily, 1955)
The American author's second novel concerns the responsibility of Americans for nuclear power. It describes the last days of an atomic scientist, who has fled his work and family because his ties with them remind him of the people he has been instrumental in killing. He takes up a bare existence only to be hunted down by his "hound of earth," a persistent humanitarian impulse that obliges him to perform small acts of kindness to everyone he meets.

569   House Divided   (Ben Ames Williams, 1947)
The American author's historical novel is a lengthy romance following the fortunes of a wealthy Virginia family during the Civil War. The title quotes from Abraham Lincoln's speech of June 16, 1858 at the Republican State Convention, Springfield, Illinois: "A house divided against itself itself cannot stand," itself adapted from the biblical sentence: "If a house be divided against itself, that house cannot stand" (Mark 3:25).

570   A House for Mr. Biswas   (V. S. Naipaul, 1961)
The Trinidadian writer's best-known novel is set in Trinidad's East Indian community and tells of the quest of the central character, Mohun Biswas, to own a home of his own. His fortunes are closely linked to the various houses in which he meantime lives. He eventually acquires his house, a ramshackle property in Port of Spain, but dies soon afterwards.

571   House Made of Dawn   (N. Scott Momaday, 1968)
The American writer's first novel is the story of Abel, a Native American caught between the traditional world of Indian heritage and that of the white man. After a varied and often stressful life in Los Angeles, he returns to his reservation where, although damaged by the white man, he eventually recovers his innate serenity and realizes that his true home is in a place of harmony with the natural world, a "house made of dawn."

572   The House of Mirth   (Edith Wharton, 1905)
The American writer's novel, a satire on the cruel and empty world of New York high society, takes its ironic title from the Bible: "The heart of fools is in the house of mirth" (Ecclesiastes 7:4).

573 How Much? (Burt Blechman, 1961)
The American author's first novel has a title that encapsulates the question asked by its protagonists, the Halpern family, as they face bankruptcy, war, and constant failure: "How much, dear God, how much does it cost to be happy?"

574 Howl (Allen Ginsberg, 1956)
The poem by the American poet, with its lengthy lines and surreally random content, gained instant fame (and notoriety) as the manifesto of the Beat movement. It is effectively both a shout of protest and an anthem of liberation. The poem was designed to be declaimed ("howled") with maximum straining of the nerves and vocal cords. (Like other Beat poets, Ginsberg often read or recited his poems aloud in public.)

575 Humboldt's Gift (Saul Bellow, 1975)
The American writer's long and complex seventh novel concerns the relationship between Charlie Citrine, a successful dramatist, and his friend (later his enemy), the poet and madman Von Humboldt Fleisher. Humboldt dies, but leaves two "gifts" to Charlie: a manuscript, that solves his financial problems, and a letter of reconciliation.

576 Humping My Bluey (Graham McInnes, 1966)
The British-born writer was taken to Australia as a child but as a young man emigrated to Canada. The book is the second part of his autobiography, describing life in Melbourne in the 1930s and ending with his departure for Canada in search of his father. The title means "hitting the trail," or literally "carrying my belongings." (A *bluey* is an Australian bushman's bundle, traditionally wrapped in a blue blanket.)

577 Hurry On Down (John Wain, 1953)
The British writer's picaresque first novel tells how its central character and "anti-hero," Charles Lumley, revolts against his grammar school and university upbringing, and the "respectable" life they have brought him, and instead goes rapidly "down" in society, taking a series of menial jobs. The title comes from Nellie Lutcher's popular song of 1947:

> Hurry on down to my place, baby,
> Nobody home but me.

578 I Am a Camera (John Van Druten, 1951)
The British-born American writer's play was based on Christopher Isherwood's *Goodbye to Berlin* (1939), describing decadence and social corruption in Germany during Hitler's rise to power. Its title comes from words in the original: "I am a camera with its shutter open, quite passive, recording, not thinking." Van Druten's play in turn formed the basis for the Broadway musical *Cabaret* (1966).

579 I Cannot Get You Close Enough (Ellen Gilchrist, 1990)
The American writer's volume contains three novellas titled *Winter*, *De Havilland Hand*, and *Summer in Maine*. Each of these features Anna Hand, the central character

in Gilchrist's novel *The Anna Papers* (1988). The title of the present collection comes from Anna's final words in *Summer in Maine*, which were addressed to her lover: "I cannot get you close enough. [...] We never can get from anyone else the things we need to fill the endless terrible need." The words imply not only her recognition that her love affair has failed, and that her efforts to reunite her family have come to nothing, but that human beings are unable to fully relate to one another.

580   I Ching Kanada   (Dave Godfrey, 1976)
The Canadian writer's collection of prose-poem meditations is based on the hexagrams of the *I Ching*, the ancient Chinese book of divination. Hence the title, which can also be punningly understood as "I Sing Canada."

581   I, Claudius   (Robert Graves, 1934)
The British writer's famous historical novel is a first person account of the colorful life of the Roman emperor Claudius (10 B.C.–A.D. 54). The title quotes from the opening words:

> I Tiberius Claudius Drusus Nero Germanicus This-that-and-the-other (for I shall not trouble you yet with all my titles), who was once, and not so long ago either, known to my friends and relatives and associates as "Claudius the Idiot," or "That Claudius," or "Claudius the Stammerer," or "Clau-Clau-Claudius," or at best as "Poor Uncle Claudius," am now about to write this strange history of my life.

582   I Know Why the Caged Bird Sings   (Maya Angelou, 1969)
The American writer's autobiography of her years up to the age of 16, ending with the birth of her child and including her rape at age eight, takes its title from a line in Paul Laurence Dunbar's poem *Sympathy* (1899):

> It is not a carol of joy or glee,
> But a prayer that he sends from his heart's deep core [...]
> I know why the caged bird sings!

583   I Leap Over the Wall   (Monica Baldwin, 1949)
The British writer's book describes her return to the world after 28 years in a convent. She traced the title to a Baldwin family Latin motto, *Per Deum Meum Transilio Murum*, "With the help of my God I leap over the wall," which relates to the escape of an earlier Baldwin. As she explains in the book:

> Nearly 400 years ago, my ancestor Thomas Baldwin of Diddlesbury leaped to freedom from behind the walls of the Tower of London [...]. His name with an inscription and the date "July 1585" can still be seen where he carved it on the wall of his cell in the Beauchamp Tower.

The motto itself echoes a biblical line: "By my God have I leaped over a wall" (2 Samuel 22:30).

584   I Sing the Body Electric   (Walt Whitman, 1867)
The American poet's famous composition was untitled in the original 1855 edition of **Leaves of Grass**. The poem is a hymn to human anatomy and sexuality and to the form of men, women, and children.

585   I Want It Now   (Kingsley Amis, 1968)
The title of the British writer's ninth novel, a love story, seems to imply that its two protagonists, Simona Baldock and Ronnie Appleyard, desire money or sex (or both). However, although these aspects continually feature, the focus on money leads to considerations of class and social values, and that on sex to considerations of human relationships and public morality.

586   An Ice-Cream War   (William Boyd, 1982)
The British writer's novel recounts the conflict that flared up during World War I between the British and German colonies in East Africa. The title refers to the region's torrid heat. As one character remarks: "It is far too hot for sustained fighting [...] we will all melt like ice-cream in the sun!"

587   The Iceman Cometh   (Eugene O'Neill, 1946)
The play by the American playwright concerns the "pipe dreams" of a group of alcoholics in a saloon, who are waiting for one of their number, the salesman Hickey. The title directly refers to a joke about the iceman and his wife that Hickey traditionally makes. Hickey himself is symbolically regarded as the "Iceman of Death," so that the title really means "Death cometh." The words have a biblical resonance, and echo a phrase from the parable of the ten virgins: "Behold, the bridegroom cometh" (Matthew 25:6). There are, too, a number of parallels between the play and the parable. However, the character of Hickey is quite different, and the allusion may actually be to lines from Macaulay's poem *Lays of Ancient Rome* (1842):

> To every man upon this earth
> Death cometh soon or late.

588   The Ides of March   (Thornton Wilder, 1948)
The American writer's novel is a fictionalized account of the life of Julius Caesar, who was murdered on the ides (15th) of March. The phrase that gave the title was made familiar by Shakespeare in his historical play *Julius Caesar* ("Beware the ides of March"), though Plutarch recorded Caesar himself as having said: "The ides of March have come."

589   Idiot's Delight   (Robert E. Sherwood, 1936)
The play by the American writer is concerned with the imminent World War II, and the futility of the efforts of "the little people" to stop it. One of the characters has words alluding to the title: "Poor, dear God. Playing Idiot's Delight. The game that never means anything, and never ends." Idiot's delight itself is a type of solitaire card game.

590   If Not Now, When?   (Primo Levi, 1985)
The Italian writer's novel with the Jewish experience of World War II as its theme has a title that in the original Italian was *Se non ora, quando?* (1982). This was a quotation from the 1st-century Talmudic sage Hillel, and in full runs: "If I am not for myself, who is for me? And when I am for myself, what am I? And if not now, when?" (*Talmud: The Wisdom of the Fathers*, translated by Jacob Neusner).

591   Ile   (Eugene O'Neill, 1919)
The one-act play by the American dramatist is the story of a sea captain searching for whale oil, or "ile," at the cost of his wife's sanity and the risk of a mutiny.

592   I'll Take Manhattan   (Judith Krantz, 1985)
The American novelist's steamy bestseller has a title based on the Rodgers and Hart song "Manhattan" (1925). The song itself actually has "We'll have Manhattan."

593   Illywhacker   (Peter Carey, 1985)
The Australian author's second novel is the "autobiography" of a 139-year-old confidence trickster. The title is an Australian colloquial term, of unknown origin, for such a person.

594   Image of a Drawn Sword   (Jocelyn Brooke, 1950)
The British writer's haunting novel depicts the gradual transformation of a young bank clerk in the army under the influence of military authority. The title relates to the image that he has tattooed on his forearm as a symbol of his acceptance of his new way of life.

595   In a Glass Darkly   (J. S. Le Fanu, 1872)
The collection of five short stories by the Irish writer purports to be cases from the papers of "Dr. Martin Hesselius, the German Physician," this being the first of a line of psychic investigators in English literature. The title is adapted from a biblical phrase: "For now we see through a glass, darkly" (1 Corinthians 13:12).

596   In a Shallow Grave   (James Purdy, 1975)
The American writer's novel has as its theme the redemption of suffering through love, a theme that is developed through the experiences of a 26-year-old Vietnam veteran, Garnet Montrose. The "shallow grave" of the title is the pile of corpses under which Montrose had lain for several days before being rescued and returned to his native Virginia. This comes to represent the shallow psychological grave of his past, from which he must now also be rescued.

597   In Abraham's Bosom   (Paul Green, 1926)
The American writer's play tells of the attempts of the mulatto Abraham McCranie to help black Americans by setting up a school for them. His white father helps him, but after the father's death his white half-brother refuses to give further help and Abraham kills him, only to be shot by a mob as he shouts a prophecy of freedom for his race. The title, though obviously referring to the central character, is ultimately biblical in origin: "The beggar died, and was carried by the angels into Abraham's bosom" (Luke 16:10). Sleeping or lying "in Abraham's bosom" is thus a metaphor for being dead.

598   In Between the Sheets   (Ian McEwan, 1978)
The British author's second volume of short stories, with their themes of lust, violence, and despair, takes its title from the poem *Comeclose and Sleepnow* (1967) by Roger McGough:

Let me die a youngman's death
Not a clean & in-between-
The-sheets, holy-water death,
Not a famous-last-words
Peaceful out-of-breath death.

599   In Cold Blood   (Truman Capote, 1966)
The American writer's "nonfiction novel," as he called it, is the account of the murder in 1959 of a Kansas farming family. They were killed deliberately, "in cold blood," and the murderers were subsequently (in 1965) captured, tried, and executed equally deliberately "in cold blood."

600   In Dubious Battle   (John Steinbeck, 1936)
The American writer's novel deals with a fruit strike in a Californian valley and the attempts of radical leaders to organize the striking pickers. The strike fails, and one of the two leaders is killed. The title is from Milton's *Paradise Lost* (1667), referring to the contest between Satan and his angels and the hosts of heaven "in dubious battle."

601   In the American Grain   (William Carlos Williams, 1925)
The volume of essays by the American writer portrays well-known individuals in history who typified the "American grain" of character in being homely rather than heroic.

602   In the Belly of the Beast   (Jack Henry Abbot, 1981)
The American convict's book is a description of life in prison (the "beast") of the title. The subtitle, *Letters from Prison*, spells out the allusion.

603   In the Night Kitchen   (Maurice Sendak, 1970)
The children's picture book by the American writer and illustrator tells how a small boy, woken by a noise in the night, falls through the dark into a "Night Kitchen" where three fat bakers mix him into their batter. The story was partly inspired by an advertisement for a New York bakery that Sendak had seen as a child: "We Bake While You Sleep!"

604   In This Our Life   (Ellen Glasgow, 1941)
The American writer's novel is about a neurotic girl who disrupts the family life of her relatives and is killed when fleeing the police. The novel gives no clue regarding the relevance of the title, which itself at first glance seems to come from some Shakespeare passage, such as the following from *As You Like It*:

And this our life, exempt from public haunt,
Finds tongues in trees, books in the running brooks,
Sermons in stones, and good in everything.   [II.i.15]

However, it appears to be simply a general phrase, and as such occurs in various works dating from the 17th century, such as Thomas Heywood's poem *The Hierarchy of the Blessed Angels* (1635), Carlyle's *Sartor Resartus* (1831), and George Meredith's poem *Modern Love* (1862):

> Ah, what a dusty answer gets the soul
> When hot for certainties in this our life!

With regard to this last, *cf*. **Dusty Answer.**

605 In Youth Is Pleasure (Denton Welch, 1945)

The British writer's only novel is a study of the inner life of an adolescent boy, a life dominated by the erotic and the macabre. The title is taken from the poem "Lusty Juventus" by the 16th-century poet Robert Wever:

> In a harbour grene aslepe whereas I lay,
> The byrdes sang swete in the middes of the day,
> I dreamíd fast of mirth and play:
> In youth is pleasure in youth is pleasure.

606 Including Finnigin (Strickland Gillilan, 1910)

The collection of comic poems by the American writer takes its title from its main poem, which was (obviously) included. This was about an Irish railroad foreman called Finnigin (or Finnegan) who had been told to "keep it short" when reporting accidents. The telegram he sent on one occasion was used by Gillilan as a refrain for a poem entitled *Finnigin to Flannigan*, as in its sixth stanza:

> Bilin' down's repoort, wuz Finnigin!
> An' he writed this here: "Musther Flannigan—
> Off agin, on agin,
> Gone agin.—FINNIGIN."

607 The Incredible Journey (Sheila Burnford, 1961)

The Scottish-born Canadian writer's story for children tells how two dogs and a cat make an "incredible journey" through the wilds of Canada back to their home. (Such a journey is theoretically possible, but highly unlikely, and "incredible" is a more telling word than perhaps the author intended.)

608 The Indian in the Cupboard (Lynne Reid Banks, 1980)

The British writer's seventh novel for children tells the story of a small boy, Omri, and the plastic toys in his cupboard. One of these is the Indian, Little Bull, who turns out to have a mind of his own.'

609 The Indian Princess (J. N. Barker, 1808)

Subtitled *La Belle Sauvage*, the play was the first Indian play by an American and the first to use the story of Pocahontas, the "Indian Princess" of the title. The work was accompanied by songs and was called "an operatic melodrame."

610 Infants of the Spring (Anthony Powell, 1976)

The first volume of the British writer's autobiography, overall entitled *To Keep the Ball Rolling*, appears to derive its title from one or other of two Shakespeare plays (probably the first):

Berowne is like an envious sneaping frost
That bites the first-born infants of the spring.   [*Love's Labour's Lost*
I.i.100]

The canker galls the infants of the spring
Too oft before their buttons be disclos'd.   [*Hamlet*, I.iii.39]

611   Inherit the Wind   (Jerome Lawrence and Robert E. Lee, 1955)
The play by the American playwrights is a thinly disguised account of the so called
"Monkey Trial" of 1925 in Dayton, Tennessee, when a young scientist, John T.
Scopes, was found guilty of teaching the doctrine of evolution. The debate between
Clarence Darrow, for the defense, and William Jennings Bryan, for the prosecution,
rocked the country for several months. The title is biblical in origin: "He that troubleth his own house shall inherit the wind" (Proverbs 11:29).

612   Innocence Is Drowned   (Walter Allen, 1938)
The British writer's first novel deals with the attempts of a working-class family to
come to terms with the cruel realities of life in the months preceding World War
II. The title comes from the well-known lines from Yeats's poem *The Second Coming* (1921):

Things fall apart; the centre cannot hold;
Mere anarchy is loosed upon the world,
The blood-dimmed tide is loosed, and everywhere
The ceremony of innocence is drowned.

For another title from these lines, *cf.* **Things Fall Apart**.

613   The Innocent   (Ian McEwan, 1990)
The British writer's fourth novel is an unusual love story set in Berlin during the
Cold War. The central character is a Post Office technician, Leonard Marnham,
who enters the world of intrigue and deception as a political, emotional, and sexual
"innocent."

614   Intruder in the Dust   (William Faulkner, 1948)
The American writer's novel concerns an ageing black American who is wrongly
accused of the murder of a white man. His innocence is proved by 16-year-old
Chick Mallison, who violates a grave in his search for evidence. He is thus the "intruder in the dust" of the title.

615   Invisible Man   (Ralph Ellison, 1952)
The novel by the black American writer has a title that relates to its nameless black
narrator, who is chosen by Communists to play a political role but who finds that
they are merely using him as a symbolic black American. He is thus an "invisible
man" to them, as he is to everyone else.

616   Invitation to a Beheading   (Vladimir Nabokov, 1958)
The Russian-born American writer's mock anti-utopian novel was originally published in Russian in 1938. Its central character is Cincinnatus C., in prison awaiting

execution for his crime of "gnostical turpitude," since his soul has not been receptive to other people. Nabokov based the title on that of Baudelaire's poem *L'Invitation au voyage* in *Les Fleurs du Mal* (1857), which is invoked at various points in the novel.

617   The Ipcress File   (Len Deighton, 1962)

The British author's first famous spy novel tells how an operation to trace a missing biochemist brings the (nameless) narrator up against a conspiracy to brainwash the entire country. The acronym of the title stands for "*I*nduction of *P*sychoneuroses by *C*onditional *R*eflex with St*ress*."

618   Iron John   (Robert Bly, 1990)

The title of the American writer's influential but idiosyncratic *Book About Men*, as it is subtitled, is the name of a fearsome creature lurking under a lake. The author explains: "Every modern male has, lying at the bottom of his psyche, a large primitive being covered with hair." The creature is the central character in what is essentially a rambling folk tale, itself a complex metaphor about the importance to men of myth and ritual.

619   The Iron Heel   (Jack London, 1908)

The American writer's novel, purportedly written in 1932, tells of events said to take place between 1912 and 1918, when the great capitalist monopolies of the United States band together in a fascist-style organization, the "Iron Heel," which gains control of the country. The name of the organization prefigures the Iron Guard, the fascist grouping formed in Romania in 1927.

620   is 5   (E. E. Cummings, 1926)

The American writer's fourth book of poems has an eccentric title typical of him. It implies "two times two is five," as an unexpected and miraculous equation rather than the expected and sensible "is four."

621   It Can't Happen Here   (Sinclair Lewis, 1935)

"It" is the fascist dictatorship which the American novelist imagines has been established in the United States. However, Lewis intended the title ironically, since the novel was a direct response to Hitler's dictatorship in Germany, which *had* happened. Lewis wanted to warn his fellow Americans against steps that could well be taken by reactionary demagogues then in positions of influence in the States.

622   It Doesn't Take a Hero   (Norman Schwarzkopf, 1992)

The American army commander's account of the 1991 Gulf War, in which he led the coalition forces, takes its title from a comment that he made after the war: "It doesn't take a hero to order men into battle. It takes a hero to be one of those men who goes into battle."

623   Ivanhoe   (Walter Scott, 1819)

The title refers to the novel's medieval central character, Wilfred of Ivanhoe, who incurs the displeasure of his father, Cedric, because of his love for his father's ward,

Rowena. Scott took the name from the village of *Ivinghoe*, Buckinghamshire. He recalled an old rhyme but changed the spelling of the name. (His spelling was not necessarily a mistake, and the name actually appears as *Ivanhoe* in a document dated 1665. Scott could not have seen this, however, since it was published only in 1905.) The rhyme is as follows:

> Tring Wing and Ivinghoe
> For striking of a blow
> Hampden did forego
> And glad he could escape so.

624   Jake's Thing   (Kingsley Amis, 1978)

The central character of the British writer's fifteenth novel is Jake Richardson, a 59-year-old Oxford don, whose general grudge against the world (his "thing") is reflected at a personal level in his impotence, which means an inability to control his anatomical "thing," formerly active and reliable.

625   Jasmine   (Bharati Mukherjee, 1989)

The Indian-born Canadian writer's third novel is the story of an Indian peasant woman whose progress through life takes her from the Punjab to Florida, then to New York and Iowa, and finally, as the novel closes, to California. With each new move she takes a new name, symbolizing the gradual realization of her ambition to be an American. First she is Jyoti, then Jasmine, then Jase, then Jane. The title selects the second of these as representing the first stage of her ongoing journey and her search for her identity.

626   Java Head   (Joseph Hergesheimer, 1919)

The title of the American writer's novel is the name of the home of its central character, shipowner and retired captain Jeremy Ammidon, which he has so called to symbolize "the safe and happy end of an arduous voyage."

627   J.B.   (Archibald MacLeish, 1958)

The initials of the successful businessman who is the central character of the American poet's verse drama are intended to suggest the name of Job, the Old Testament patriarch who is tested by God. The work was suggested by his story and is constantly contrasted with it.

628   Jerry of the Islands   (Jack London, 1917)

The American writer's novel is named for the Irish setter pup that is its central character. The islands are the Solomon Islands, from which Jerry's master, Van Horn, obtains black labor. When Van Horn is killed, Jerry is taken by the local chief and trained as a watchdog.

629   Jew Süss   (Lion Feuchtwanger, 1925)

The German writer's long historical novel about a German Jewish community is set in the 18th century and has a Jew named Süss as its central character. The original German title, *Jud Süss*, is translated literally in British editions of the book, but in American editions the novel is usually known as *Power*.

630   The Jewel in the Crown   (Paul Scott, 1966)

The first of the British writer's novels in the four that make up *The Raj Quartet*, portraying political and personal conflict in India in the days leading up to Independence, derives from the phrase "jewels in the crown" at one time used for the colonies of the British Empire. It is understandable that *the* jewel should be India, partly because of that country's importance, and partly because the famous Kohinoor diamond, from India, has been part of the British crown jewels since 1849. In the book itself, "The Jewel in Her Crown" (*sic*) is the title of a "semi-historical, semi-allegorical" picture showing Queen Victoria surrounded by representative figures of her Indian Empire, and depicting an Indian prince "bearing a velvet cushion on which he offered a large and sparkling gem."

631   John Bull's Other Island   (G. B. Shaw, 1904)

The Irish writer's play deals with the conflict over Home Rule between England and Ireland, with the civil engineer Tom Broadbent representing England ("John Bull") gaining ascendancy over his Irish counterpart, Larry Doyle. "John Bull's other island" is thus Ireland.

632   Johnny Got His Gun   (Dalton Trumbo, 1939)

The American writer's famous antiwar novel was published in the United States on September 3, 1939, the very day that England and France declared war on Germany. The story concerns 20-year-old recruit Joe Banham, hospitalized with horrific injuries (he is deaf and blind and has no arms, legs, or mouth). His aim is to discharge himself and earn his keep as a living testimony to the effects of war. He is refused this request, however, because what he asks is "against regulations." The title of the book is based on the popular song by Monroe H. Rosenfeld, *Johnny Get Your Gun* (1886).

633   Journal of a Disappointed Man   (W. N. P. Barbellion [Bruce Cumings], 1919)

The British author describes his feelings of deep disappointment and frustration on learning that, as a scientist, he has little time to live. The book was published in the year of the writer's death at age 30 from disseminated sclerosis.

634   Journey's End   (R. C. Sherriff, 1928)

The British writer's play is one of the best known about World War I, which proved to be the "journey's end" for many men fighting in the trenches. The title is ostensibly a quotation from Dryden's *Palamon and Arcite* (1700):

> Like pilgrims to th'appointed place we tend;
> The world's an inn, and death the journey's end.   [Book 3]

However, in his autobiography *No Leading Lady* (1968), Sherriff writes:

> One night I was reading a book in bed. I got to a chapter that closed with the words: "It was late in the evening when we came at last to our Journey's End." The last two words sprang out as the ones I was looking for. Next night I typed them on a front page for the play, and the thing was done.

635 Juice   (Stephen Becker, 1958)
The American writer's novel has justice as its theme. When the central character, Joseph Harrison, kills a pedestrian in an auto accident, his friends and boss try to use the law and power of money and status (the "juice" of the title) to whitewash the occurrence. Harrison himself, however, demands a proper judgment so he can redeem his error.

636 July's People   (Nadine Gordimer, 1981)
The South African writer's novel centers on the struggle for land between whites and blacks. The white protagonists escape revolution by running away with, and becoming captives of, their lifelong black servant, July. Hence the title.

637 The Jungle   (Upton Sinclair, 1906)
The American writer's novel that famously exposed the Chicago meat-packing industry took its title from the metaphorical sense of "jungle" to refer to a place of brutality and exploitation, where the "law of the jungle" prevails. *Cf.* **The Asphalt Jungle, The Blackboard Jungle**.

638 Junkie   (William Lee (William S. Burroughs), 1953)
The American writer's novel is a fictionalized account of his experiences as a "junkie," or drug addict.

639 Juno and the Paycock   (Sean O'Casey, 1924)
The tragicomedy by the Irish writer has for its two protagonists the vain idler Jack Boyle, who spends his time "sthruttin' about from mornin' till night like a paycock" (peacock) in and out of Dublin pubs, and who solves his problems by having another drink, and his heroic wife Juno, who battles with him, with poverty, and with the Irish "Troubles" of the day.

640 Jurassic Park   (Michael Crichton, 1991)
The American writer's blockbuster novel tells how a billionaire develops a theme park on an island near Costa Rica in which he succeeds in recreating dinosaurs. These prehistoric creatures lived in the Jurassic period of the Mesozoic Era. Hence the name of the park (and title of the book). Steven Spielberg's movie based on the book was a major box office success of 1993.

641 Just So Stories   (Rudyard Kipling, 1902)
The British writer's stories for children give the fantastically imagined "origins" of the main physical characteristics of certain animals, e.g., "How the Camel got his Hump," the implication being that such distinctive features were gained "just so," that is, simply as described.

642 Kaddish   (Allen Ginsberg, 1961)
The American poet wrote the long poem of this name on the death of his mother, Naomi Ginsberg. Its title is the Jewish name, meaning "holy one," for a portion of the daily ritual of the synagogue, comprising thanksgiving and praise and concluding

with a prayer for universal peace. The portion is traditionally recited by orphan mourners.

643   Kalki   (Gore Vidal, 1978)

The American writer's novel tells how the American James Kelly settles in the Himalayas after the Vietnam war, changes his name to Kalki, and announces that he is the tenth avatar of the Hindu god Vishna. His coming to earth, he claims, means the end of human existence as we know it.

644   The Kandy-Kolored Tangerine-Flake Streamline Baby   (Tom Wolfe, 1965)

The American author's first book is a collection of essays satirizing pop heroes of the 1960s. It is cast in the form of a "pop monologue" promoting the latest car models. The automobile, as distinct from the motorcycle or amplifier, which symbolize counterculture, is regarded by Wolfe as a "symbol of traditional American awareness." The title, with its pop-style psychedelic wording, thus relates to the automobile.

645   Keep the Aspidistra Flying   (George Orwell, 1936)

The British writer's novel tells the story of a young bookseller's assistant, whose aspirations and humiliations are similar to the author's own. The title puns on the phrase "keep the flag flying" (in the sense of keeping up the fight), but for "flag" substitutes the name of the house plant that in the interwar years in Britain was traditionally regarded as "a symbol of dull middle-class respectability" (*Oxford English Dictionary*).

646   A Kestrel for a Knave   (Barry Hines, 1968)

The British writer's second novel, about a young boy misfit who learns about life through training his kestrel hawk, derives its title from *The Boke of St. Albans* (1486):

> An Eagle for an Emperor, a Gyrfalcon for a King; a Peregrine for a Prince, a Saker for a Knight, a Merlin for a Lady; a Goshawk for a Yeoman, a Sparrowhawk for a Priest, a Musket for a Holy water Clerk, a Kestrel for a Knave.

In 1974 the book was reissued as *Kes*, the boy's pet name for his hawk.

647   A Kid for Two Farthings   (Wolf Mankowitz, 1954)

The British author's second novel reflects his own Cockney childhood. It centers on a small boy (a kid), Joe, who buys a young goat (a kid) in a London East End market believing it to be a unicorn. The title directly relates to a Passover song that alludes to the custom of sacrificing a kid at this festival. "Two farthings" is a token small amount, as in the biblical text: "Are not five sparrows sold for two farthings?" (Luke 12:6).

648   Killing a Mouse on Sunday   (Emeric Pressburger, 1961)

The Hungarian-born American screenwriter's novel centers on a survivor from the Spanish Civil War who emerges from retirement twenty years later to murder a brutal police chief. The title comes from Richard Braithwaite's poem *Barnaby's Journal* (1638), describing Banbury, "the most Puritan of Puritan towns":

> To Banbury came I O profane one!
> Where I saw a Puritane one
> Hanging of his cat on Monday
> For killing of a mouse on Sunday.

When the novel became a movie its title was changed to *Behold a Pale Horse* (1964), from Revelation 6:8. In his book *Million-Dollar Movie* (1992), Pressburger's collaborator, Michael Powell, tells how he was concerned about the title, and said as much. Pressburger explained that he had chosen it because it was "a cat and mouse story."

649   Kind Hearts and Coronets   (Roy Horniman, 1907)

The novel by the British writer tells of the individuals whom the hero murders in order to gain succession to a dukedom, although betraying himself at his moment of triumph. The title was adopted from Tennyson's poem *Lady Clara Vere de Vere* (1842):

> Kind hearts are more than coronets,
> And simple faith more than Norman blood.

650   A Kind of Loving   (Stan Barstow, 1960)

The British writer's novel, set in an industrial town in the north of England, tells how an office worker is forced to marry his pregnant girlfriend. The novel concentrates on the realities of life, in which "love" is not the fine and uplifting thing people dream of experiencing, but a routine progression of infatuation, sex, pregnancy, and a marriage to a person one no longer loves, or with whom one had merely "a kind of loving" in the first place.

651   The Kindly Ones   (Anthony Powell, 1962)

The British author's sixth novel in the 12-volume series entitled **A Dance to the Music of Time** has a title that translates the euphemistic Greek name of the Furies, *Eumenides.* These were the goddesses, as the narrator's governess taught him in his childhood, who "inflicted the vengeance of the gods by bringing in their train war, pestilence, dissension on earth; torturing, too, by the strings of conscience." The novel opens in 1914, the year when World War I began, with the nine-year-old narrator living with his parents near the military base of Aldershot and observing the rising personal and national tension. It concludes a quarter-century later, with the outbreak of World War II, and the Furies about to wreak the second vengeance of the gods.

652   The Kindness of Strangers   (Donald Spotto, 1990)

The American writer's biography of Tennessee Williams takes its title from Blanche Dubois' last words in Williams' play *A Streetcar Named Desire* (1947), when she is about to be taken off to an institution: "I have always depended on the kindness of strangers." The words have proved popular with other writers, as have variants on them, such as **The Comfort of Strangers** and the Canadian movie *The Company of Strangers* (1990).

653   Kinflicks   (Lisa Alther, 1976)

The central character of the American writer's first novel, Ginny Hull Babcock, visits her dying mother in hospital and recalls all the "kinflicks," or home movies, that were her mother's record of "family firsts" (the first tooth, the first smile, and so on). The word itself probably came about as a pun on *skinflick*, a slang term for a porno movie (which involves a "flick," or film, of "skin," or nudity). *Skinflick* (1979) is the title of a novel about a homosexual private eye by the American writer Joseph Hansen.

654   King Coal   (Upton Sinclair, 1917)

The novel by the American writer is based on "sworn testimony, taken under government supervision," during an investigation of the Colorado coalmining industry after the strike of 1914–15. The title puns on the nursery rhyme about "Old King Cole."

655   King Rat   (James Clavell, 1962)

The British-born American author's first novel is based on the three years he spent in a Japanese prisoner-of-war camp in World War II. Rats, cholera, lice, and filth abound in the camp, but they are challenged by "the King," an adaptable American corporal, determined to survive at any cost. The title refers to him and to his dominant role among the inmates, whose own animal existence is like that of the rats themselves.

656   The Kingdom by the Sea   (Paul Theroux, 1983)

The book is an account of the American writer's travels by train and on foot around the coast of Britain, the "kingdom by the sea" of the title. The title is intended ironically, since the author constantly encountered expressions of cheap patriotism, and found much that was dull and depressing. It is itself a quote from Edgar Allan Poe's poem *Annabel Lee* (1849):

> *I* was a child and *she* was a child,
> In this kingdom by the sea.

657   Kiss Kiss, Bang Bang   (Pauline Kael, 1968)

The American movie critic explained the title of her book on her work in a "Note on the Title":

> The words "Kiss Kiss Bang Bang," which I saw on an Italian movie poster, are perhaps the briefest statement imaginable of the basic appeal of movies.

658   Kiss Me, Kate   (Bella Spewack and Samuel Spewack, 1948)

The play-within-a-play by the East European-born American playwrights, husband and wife, is based on Shakespeare's *The Taming of the Shrew*, and its title is a quote from that play. The words are those of Petruchio to Katharina (the "shrew" of the play's title): "Kiss me, Kate, we will be married o' Sunday" (II.i.318).

659   Kleinzeit   (Russell Hoban, 1974)

The American writer's second novel takes its title from the name of its central character, who believes that it means "hero" in German, but who is told by another character that it actually means "smalltime."

660   Krapp's Last Tape   (Samuel Beckett, 1958)

The short play by the Irish-born French playwright consists of a monologue by its sole character, Krapp, who listens to a tape recording he made thirty years earlier and finds that it has lost all meaning now that he is an old man.

661   Laddie   (Gene Stratton-Porter, 1913)

The autobiographical account of the American author's childhood has a title character based on her brother Leander ("Laddie"), drowned at age 18.

662   Lady into Fox   (David Garnett, 1922)

The title of the British writer's "first serious book" is to be taken literally, since it relates to the novel's central event: the sudden and unexplained transformation of Mrs. Tebrick's young wife Silvia into a fox, and the gradual alteration of her human nature into that of a feral beast, a "cunning little vixen." The author described his tale as a *"reductio ad absurdum* of the problem of fidelity in love."

663   Lady Lazarus   (Sylvia Plath, 1962)

The poem describes the American poet's history of suicide attempts. (She referred to herself as "a woman with the great and terrible gift of being reborn.") Hence the title, with its allusion to the biblical Lazarus, who was brought back to life by Jesus.

664   The Lady's Not for Burning   (Christopher Fry, 1949)

The play by the British playwright, set in an Irish town in 1400, is a comedy about the love between a young witch, falsely accused of murder, and a discharged soldier from the Flanders wars, who confesses to the murder. The witch is sentenced to be burned the next day. However, the "murdered" man turns up and the witch and soldier leave the town together. The title quotes a line from the play itself.

665   Lalla Rookh   (Thomas Moore, 1817)

The Irish poet's series of oriental tales in verse takes its title from the name of its central character, *Lalla Rookh,* daughter of the Mogul emperor Aurungzebe. In a note to the work, Moore explains that her name means "tulip-cheek." The reference would be to a person with a delicate complexion and rosy cheeks.

666   Lamb   (Bernard MacLaverty, 1980)

The Northern Irish writer's first novel has as its theme the nature of love and the sacrifices it can involve. It is the story of a troubled priest and a wayward boy on the run from the church and the state, in a series of shared experiences that gradually climax to end in tragedy. The characters' names are meaningful, and the title is that of the priest, Michael Lamb, who as the novel opens has doubts about hs vocation as Brother Sebastian. The 12-year-old boy is Owen Kane, who as his name implies is involved in a "kill or cure" solution to the problems of both himself and his mentor.

667   Lanark   (Alasdair Gray, 1982)

The Scottish writer's novel is divided into four books and ranges from descriptions of his native Glasgow to fantastical adventures in the city of Unthank, the whole representing a vast dystopia. Lanark (in reality the name of a Scottish town and county) is its central character, newly arrived in Unthank. In a previous incarnation, in Glasgow, he was Duncan Thaw. Gray delights in the nuances that names can have, and Scottish names in particular. At one point in the novel two of the characters discuss Lanark and his name:

> "Lanark has been around for a long long time," said Wilkins. "I think he deserves a three-syllable name, don't you?"
> "Oh, he certainly deserves it," said the other man. "There's nothing wrong with a two-syllable name. I'm called Uxbridge, but Lanark has earned something more melodious. Like Blairardie."
> "Rutherglen, Garscaden," said Wilkins.
> "Gargunnock, Carmunnock, Auchenshuggle," said the other man.
> "Auchenshuggle has four syllables," said Wilkins.

668   The Land Is Bright   (George S. Kaufman and Edna Ferber, 1941)

The popular play by the American writers takes its title from Arthur Hugh Clough's poem *Say Not the Struggle Nought Availeth* (1862):

> In front the sun climbs slow, how slowly,
> But westward, look, the land is bright.

669   The Land of Little Rain   (Mary Austin, 1903)

The 14 sketches by the American writer, based on personal observation, are an account of the California region "between the high Sierras south from Yosemite east and south [...] beyond Death Valley and on illimitably into the Mojave desert."

670   A Laodicean   (Thomas Hardy, 1881)

The novel tells the story of Paula Power, a young woman who wavers in her faith and her love, and she is the "Laodicean" of the title. The origin of this name for a vacillating person is biblical, alluding to the church of the Laodiceans, which was "lukewarm, and neither cold nor hot" (Revelation 3:16).

671   Lark Rise to Candleford   (Flora Thompson, 1945)

The British writer's autobiographical trilogy was originally published in separate volumes as *Lark Rise* (1939), *Over to Candleford* (1941), and *Candleford Green* (1943). The series chronicles rural life in Oxfordshire in the late 19th century, with "Lark Rise" representing Juniper Hill, the village near Brackley where the author was born, and "Candleford" being Fringford, near Bicester, where she worked as a post office assistant in her teens. *Lark Rise* opens:

> The hamlet stood on a gentle rise in the flat, wheat-growing north-east corner of Oxfordshire. We will call it Lark Rise because of the great number of skylarks

which made the surrounding fields their springboard and nested on the bare earth between the rows of green corn.

"Lark Rise" is now the name of a field near the cottage where Thompson was born. Eagle and Carnell (see Select Bibliography, p. 232) note that it is "still the haunt of larks today."

672   The Last Enemy   (Richard Hillary, 1942)
The British writer's account of his wartime experiences in the Royal Air Force was published in the year before his death, aged 23. The book tells how the young officer returns to combat after being severely wounded, only to meet the "last enemy": "The last enemy that shall be destroyed is death" (1 Corinthians 15:26). Hillary died when his plane crashed in the south of Scotland.

673   Last Exit to Brooklyn   (Hubert Selby, Jr., 1964)
The title of the American author's first novel, a collection of six stories of human isolation and despair, is that of an expressway sign symbolically overlooking a cemetery of solid concrete. The tales themselves were drawn from the author's experiences "hanging out" in Brooklyn's nastiest bars.

674   The Last Frontier   (Howard Fast, 1941)
The American writer's historical novel, set in 1878, tells how a tribe of Northern Cheyenne are virtual prisoners in their reservation, where they are sick and hungry. Led by Dull Knife and Little Wolf, they attempt to flee to their northern homeland. Dull Knife's group is captured, starved, and massacred, but Little Wolf's contingent is allowed to remain in Powder River country. The Indians' struggle for freedom agsnist the might of the United States, which seeks to enslave or annihilate them, is the "last frontier" they have to cross.

675   The Last Hurrah   (Edwin O'Connor, 1956)
The American writer's novel is about an ageing Boston-Irish politician fighting his last campaign. Hnce the title, which the novelist appears to have created himself. The phrase has entered the language to describe a politician's farewell.

676   The Last Leaf   (O. Henry, 1907)
The American writer's short story concerns a girl dying of pneumonia in a Greenwich Village apartment. She resolves to go when the last leaf of five remaining has dropped off a vine outside her window. One leaf does not fall, and she recovers. The title was earlier that of a poem of 1831 by Oliver Wendell Holmes.

677   The Last Leaf   (Oliver Wendell Holmes, 1831)
According to the American writer, the poem was "suggested by the appearance in one of our streets of a venerable relic of the Revolution, said to be one of the party who threw the tea overboard in Boston Harbor." The actual subject is Thomas Melville, Herman Melville's grandfather. The title puns on the last leaf of a tree to fall in winter, as a relic of time gone by, and the last leaf of tea thrown into Boston Harbor.

678   The Last Picture Show   (Larry McMurtry, 1966)
The American writer's novel, set in the town of Thalia (modeled on Archer City, Texas) in 1951, is a study of the way high-school boys center their lives on the gratification of their sexual needs. This involves the films showing at the local movie house, which closes at the end of the novel when the protagonist leaves for Korea.

679   The Last Tycoon   (F. Scott Fitzgerald, 1941)
The title of the American author's novel refers to the great motion-picture producer Pat Grady. His death is arranged by his former partner, Monroe Stahr, who takes up with Brady's daughter, Cecilia, when the woman he loves marries someone else. In the novel's closing pages Stahr is himself killed in a plane crash. The title was suggested to Fitzgerald by the U.S. critic Edmund Wilson. Fitzgerald's two working titles were *Stahr: A Romance* and *The Love of the Last Tycoon: A Western*. Shortly before his death, Fitzgerald told gossip columnist Sheilah Graham, with whom he had a long affair, that he wanted to get the reaction of Maxwell Perkins, his editor, to *The Love of the Last Tycoon*. He accordingly included this title on a page of possible titles, crossing the others out with a note: "This is the familiar Fitzgerald formula but the boy grows tired."

680   Laughing Boy   (Oliver La Farge, 1929)
The American writer's novel has a title that is the name of one of the novel's two main characters, a young Navajo silversmith and horse trader. The other chief character is Slim Girl, whom he loves but who alienates him by meeting a white lover.

681   Laughter in the Dark   (Vladimir Nabokov, 1938)
The novel by the Russian-born American writer tells of a doomed sexual quest, in which the protagonist, Albinus, falls prey to a greedy and sadistic young woman. The "dark" of the title apparently refers to the increasingly depressed response of the reader to the plot and to the central character. At the same time both story and character evoke a bitter laughter. In his critical study, *Nikolai Gogol* (1944), Nabokov notes how "one likes to recall that the difference between the comic side of things, and their cosmic side, depends upon one sibilant," and a similar juxtaposition seemingly applies here. A noted Nabokov critic comments:

> The title goes two ways: it records the laughter of the cosmic joker who has made a pawn of Albinus, blinding and tormenting him, but it also summarizes Nabokov's response to life, his course for survival. [Vladimir Nabokov, *The Annotated Lolita*, edited, with preface, introduction, and notes, by Alfred Appel, Jr., 1993.]

The novel was originally published in Russian as *Kamera Obskura* (1932), and (as *Camera Obscura*) this was the title of the English translation, published in London in 1936. The present title is that of the revised edition, published in New York in 1938.

682   Lavengro   (George Borrow, 1851)
The English writer's novel or narrative, subtitled *The Scholar, The Gypsy, The Priest*, purports to tell the story of the writer's own wandering life. It has a title that is the

Romany word for "philologist." This was the nickname given Borrow himself in his youth by Ambrose Smith, who appears in the book as the Gypsy Jasper Petulengro: "We'll no longer call you Sap-engro [Snake Master] brother," said he, "but rather Lav-engro, which in the language of the Gorgios meaneth Word Master" (Chapter 17).

683   Lazarus Laughed   (Eugene O'Neill, 1927)
The poetic drama by the American playwright is based on the biblical Lazarus, who after being raised from the dead by Jesus, begins to laugh "in the laughter of God," so signifying a message of universal love and the denial of death. Cf. **Lady Lazarus**.

684   Leaven of Malice   (Robertson Davies, 1954)
The Canadian writer's novel is the second in the so-called *Salterton Trilogy*. It pokes fun at Canadian provincialism and has a plot centering on the repercussions that ensue from the false announcement of an engagement. The title quotes from a biblical passage:

> Therefore let us keep the feast, not with old leaven, neither with the leaven of malice and wickedness; but with the unleavened bread of sincerity and truth.   [1 Corinthians 5:8]

The novel was later dramatized under the title *Love and Libel* (1960).

685   Leaves of Grass   (Walt Whitman, 1855)
The first edition of the American poet's collection contained 12 poems, with the many subsequent editions adding new compositions but retaining the title. The poems themselves are about fertility and mortality, or life and death, set against the background of the world of nature. Grass is the constantly recurring image of the collection's longest poem, *Song of Myself* (e.g., "I believe a leaf of grass is no less than the journey-work of the stars"), and the "leaves of grass" of the title are those that grow everywhere from the bodies and mouths of the dead where they sleep, symbolizing "life out of death."

686   A Legacy   (Sybille Bedford, 1956)
The best-known novel by the German-born British author draws on family memories and is an account of German aristocratic life before World War I. The legacy of the title are the memories themselves, which have come down to the narrator, Francesca, although she is uncertain which memories are those of her father and his first wife's family and which are her own.

687   Legs   (William Kennedy, 1975)
The American writer's second novel is a fictionalized biography of Jack "Legs" Diamond, the prohibition gangster and entertainer, whose story is narrated and interpreted by the lawyer Marcus Gorman.

688   The Leopard's Spots   (Thomas Dixon, Jr., 1902)
The American writer's novel aimed to show what fearful results would ensue if the black American were "lifted above his station." The title is of biblical origin: "Can

the Ethiopian change his skin, or the leopard his spots?" (Jeremiah 13:23). (The second half of this question was intended to suggest the first half in the reader's mind.)

689 A Lesson Before Dying (Ernest Gaines, 1993)

The novel by the black American writer tells the story of a killing and its consequences in a rural Louisiana parish in the 1950s. The title alludes to lines from Beilby Porteus's poem *Death* (1759):

> Teach him how to live,
> And, oh! still harder lesson! how to die.

690 Let the People Sing (J. B. Priestley, 1939)

The British author's novel, about people fighting to save a village hall from being commandeered for commercial interests, takes its title from a song that characters in the story compose and sing:

> Let the people sing,
> And freedom bring
> An end to a sad old story.
> Where the people sing,
> Their voices ring
> In the dawn of the people's glory.

The phrase appears to have originated with Priestley himself although it evokes similar lines in two hymns: "Let all on earth their voices raise," and "Let all the world in every corner sing." The title was widely taken up for new songs and radio programs, and virtually became a slogan of World War II.

691 Let Us Now Praise Famous Men (James Agee, 1941)

The American writer's book, with integral photographs by Walker Evans, is an account of three poor white families in the rural South during the Depression. The title is biblical in origin: "Let us now praise famous men, and our fathers that begat us" (Ecclesiastes 44:1). It is not ironic, because Agee's intentions were celebratory, not condemnatory. The men and women of the families deserve our praise, not our pity.

692 LETTERS (John Barth, 1978)

The American writer's novel consists of 88 letters exchanged between himself (as the "Author"), five characters from his earlier works, and one new one, Lady Amherst, and opens with an inventive attempt to explicate the implications of its own title. The (upper case) letters which spell out the title on the title page are made up of smaller (lower case) letters which in turn spell out the book's subtitle, "an old time epistolary novel by seven fictitious drolls and dreamers, each of which imagines himself actual." Each letter (epistle) in the book is "lettered" rather than numbered, and these letters form a complicated acrostic which leads once again to the subtitle. Moreover, each of the book's seven sections is prefaced with a calendar on which the identifying letter of each epistle is superimposed on the date on which it was sent, and the pattern of identifying letters forms the shape of the letter that heads that particular section. The whole work is thus literally "well-lettered."

693   Life Studies   (Robert Lowell, 1959)
The collection of poetry and prose by the American writer is divided into four parts and takes its title from the fourth. This opens with recollections of Lowell's family and childhood and closes with poems about his adult experiences in marriage, in prison as a conscientious objector, and in hospital as a mental patient.

694   The Light and the Dark   (C. P. Snow, 1947)
The British author's second novel in the sequence of 11 entitled **Strangers and Brothers** is set in Cambridge and explores the character of its manic-depressive central figure, Roy Calvert, an academic whose speciality is the study of Manichean beliefs. The doctrines of this heretical sect embrace one of the central themes of Snow's sequence, the dualism between soul and body, and these are respectively the "light" and "dark" of the title.

695   Light Can Be Both Wave and Particle   (Ellen Gilchrist, 1989)
The American writer's fourth collection of short stories takes its title from the papers of Anna Hand, the central character of her second novel, *The Anna Papers* (1988). These reveal that Anna had chosen the title to be that of her "one last book." The title itself implies that every person is an individual particle in the universe but that each of us can in some way identify with the "waves" of nature and human history.

696   Light in August   (William Faulkner, 1932)
The complicated plot of the American writer's novel centers on the mulatto Joe Christmas, whose mixed blood generates most of the narrative's development and argument. Faulkner's general premise is that events happening here and now have universal significance. As they occur, time seems to stand still, so that all is revealed in a clear light, like that of days at the end of August, when the fine, fresh air has a sense of sadness about it.

697   Light Thickens   (Ngaio Marsh, 1982)
The last of the thirty-odd detective novels by the New Zealand writer centers on a murder in the middle of a production of Shakespeare's *Macbeth*. The title thus appropriately quotes from that play:

> Light thickens, and the crow
> Makes wing to the rooky wood;
> Good things of day begin to droop and drowse,
> Whiles night's black agents to their preys do rouse.   [III.ii.50]

698   Listening to Billie   (Alice Adams, 1978)
The American writer's third novel is the (selective) life history of a woman, Eliza Hamilton Quarles, who after the early death of her husband has a series of more or less successful love affairs. She is aided in her passage through the various relationships by a vivid recollection of a night club performance by Billie Holiday, the "Billie" of the title.

699   The Little Foxes   (Lillian Hellman, 1939)
The play by the Americn playwright is a study of the rampant capitalism that the author believed had seriously damaged and diluted the traditional values of the Southern states. The new Southerners were rapacious and ruthless, like "the little foxes, that spoil the vines" (Song of Solomon 2:15). See also **Another Part of the Forest.**

700   The Little French Girl   (Anne Douglas Sedgwick, 1924)
The novel by the American-born British writer recounts the romantic entanglements of Alix Vervier, a French girl sent to England by her worldly mother to marry a rich Englishman.

701   Little Gidding   (T. S. Eliot, 1942)
The poem, the third of the Anglo-American writer's *Four Quartets* (1943), takes its title from the village of Little Gidding, Cambridgeshire, England, which Eliot visited in 1937 on the occasion of the tercentenary of Nicholas Ferrar (1592-1637), the cleric who founded a religious community there in 1625. The poem links the English Civil War, when the monastery was dispersed, with the devastation and destruction of World War II.

702   The Little Shepherd of Kingdom Come   (John Fox, Jr., 1903)
The American writer's bestselling novel centers on Chad Buford, a young shepherd, who comes to the Cumberland Mountain settlement of Kingdom Come, and tells of his romantic involvements there at the outbreak of the Civil War. The novel was dramatized in 1916.

703   Loitering with Intent   (Muriel Spark, 1981)
The British writer's novel is set in the late 1940s and narrated by Fleur Talbot, a young woman writing her first novel who lives "on the edge of the literary world." She is the "loiterer" of the title, and has a job with the Autobiographical Association, where she is engaged in editing and embellishing the illiterate and boring memoirs of its snobbish chairman. She notices that the people he describes undergo experiences similar to those of the characters in her own novel, and discovers that he has acquired a copy of it and is plagiarizing parts of it. Her "intent" is thus to steal the memoirs from his office and hold them in ransom for the return of her manuscript. The legal expression "loitering with intent" is used to describe idling in the street for an unlawful purpose.

704   London Fields   (Martin Amis, 1989)
The British writer's complex sixth novel, set in inner city London in 1999, takes its title from the name of a district in the East End (though its central character, Keith Talent, lives in west London.) The author prefaces the book with a "Note," which is worth quoting in full:

> A word about the title. Several alternatives suggested themselves. For a while I toyed with *Time's Arrow*. Then I thought *Millennium* would be wonderfully bold (a common belief: *everything* is called *Millennium* just now). I even flirted, late at

night, with *The Death of Love*. In the end the most serious contender was *The Murderee*, which seemed both sinister and deeply catchy. And I wavered and compromised with things like *London Fields, or The Murderee: Final Version...* But as you see I kept ironic faith with my narrator, who would have been pleased, no doubt, to remind me that there are two kinds of title—two grades, two orders. The first kind of title decides on a name for something that is already there. The second kind of title is present all along: it lives and breathes, or it tries, on every page. My suggestions (and they cost me sleep) are all the first kind of title. *London Fields* is the second kind of title. So let's call it *London Fields*. This book is called *London Fields*. *London Fields...*

705   The Lonely Londoners   (Samuel Selvon, 1956)
The novel by the Trinidad-born British writer tells how Caribbean immigrants were lured to London and the "Mother Country" after World War II by the labor shortage. The central character is Moses Alouetta, a good-natured Trinidadian, who acts as a reluctant father figure to his fellows, the innocent or feckless "lonely Londoners" of the title.

706   Lonesome Dove   (Larry McMurtry, 1985)
Many of the American writer's novels are about his native Texas, and this one is no exception. It is set in the late 1870s, and centers on the small livestock business run by two former captains in the Texas Rangers in Lonesome Dove, the town named in the title, just above the Mexican border. It is uncertain to what extent McMurtry intended the name to symbolize the fate or condition of any of the huge cast of characters that people his work.

707   A Long and Happy Life   (Reynolds Price, 1962)
The American writer's novel, set in North Carolina, centers on Rosacoke Mustian, who naively assumes that marriage to Wesley Beavers (by whom she gets pregnant) will bring her the romantic state of the title.

708   Long Day's Journey into Night   (Eugene O'Neill, 1941)
The semiautobiographical play by the American dramatist is a harrowing domestic tragedy, ending with the characters contemplating their own destruction. The title echoes various phrases and metaphors, but appears to be O'Neill's own creation. Lines in Christina Rossetti's poem *Up-Hill* (1862) are close, however:

> Will the day's journey take the whole long day?
> From morn to night, my friend.

709   The Long Valley   (John Steinbeck, 1928)
The title of the American writer's collection of 13 stories refers to their setting: the towns and farms of the Salinas Valley in California.

710   The Longest Journey   (E. M. Forster, 1907)
The British writer's novel concerns the life and experiences of Rickie Elliot, a Cambridge university student, who finally loses his life in an attempt to save his half-brother, Stephen Wonham. The title comes from Shelley's *Epipsychidion* (1821):

> Who travel to their home among the dead
> By the broad highway of the world, and so
> With one chained friend, perhaps a jealous foe,
> The dreariest and the longest journey go.

711   Look Back in Anger   (John Osborne, 1956)

When the original handwritten manuscript of the British writer's play was put up for auction in 1992 it was clear that its author had had difficulty selecting an appropriate title. His original choice appears to have been *Bargain from Strength*. He obviously felt this was unpromising, however, so tried two others: *Close the Cage Behind You* and *My Blood Is a Mile High*. These were closer, but still not quite right. He finally considered *Man in a Rage*, *Angry Man*, and *Farewell to Anger*, before crossing all these out and settling on the title that became a catch-phrase in its own right. The title also gave the term "angry young men" for the group of anti-establishment writers of his day.

712   Look Homeward, Angel   (Thomas Wolfe, 1929)

The American writer's novel, a thinly disguised autobiography, tells the story of a sensitive youth coming of age in North Carolina, and later in the North, and finally breaking with his family to set out on a pilgrimage in search of "the lost lane-end into heaven, a stone, a leaf, an unfound door." The title is from Milton's poem *Lycidas* (1638): "Look homeward, Angel, now, and melt with ruth" (l. 164).

713   Look, Stranger!   (W. H. Auden, 1936)

The British poet's collection of poems took its original title from that of the first poem in the book, which begins:

> Look, stranger, at this island now
> The leaping light for your delight discovers.

The words "at this island" appear as "on this island" in another edition. Hence the American title of the collection which was *On This Island*. The British title was given the collection by Auden's publishers, and the poet himself had simply wished to call it *Poems 1936*. He disliked the publishers' title, saying it sounded "like the work of a vegetarian lady novelist," and it was subsequently dropped.

714   Lookout Cartridge   (Joseph McElroy, 1974)

The American writer's fourth novel centers on the efforts of one Cartwright to track down the thief of several rolls of film from a secretly shot movie that may or may not have captured scenes of a political crime. The title puns on *cartridge* as a roll of film and as the name of the central character, whose thoughts are similarly "captured."

715   Lord Jim   (Joseph Conrad, 1900)

The central character of the Polish-born British writer's novel is the ship's officer Jim, nicknamed *Tuan Jim* ("Lord Jim") by the natives of Patusan, the remote trading post where he becomes an agent.

716   Lord of the Flies   (William Golding, 1955)
The British writer's allegorical first novel, telling of the gradual moral degeneration of a party of schoolboys marooned on a desert island after a plane crash, takes its title from the name of the biblical "prince of the devils," Beelzebub, whose name, literally translated from the Hebrew, is generally rendered in English as "lord of the flies." In the story itself, the name "Lord of the Flies" is specifically applied to the fly-infested pig's head that the boys have impaled on a stick. (In the course of the narrative, one of the boys, nicknamed Piggy, is teased by the others, tortured, and eventually killed.)

717   The Lord of the Rings   (J. R. R. Tolkien, 1954–5)
The British writer's long and ambitious work, a sequel to **The Hobbit** (1937), has as its central character Sauron the Great, the self-styled Ruler of Middle-earth and Lord of Mordor, whose strength and authority depend on the possession of the Rings of Power, especially the One Ring or "Ruling Ring" which he had long lost and which he now seeks to recover. There were altogether 19 rings: the Three Rings of the Elves, the Seven Dwarf-rings, and the Nine Rings of Mortal Men "doomed to die." The rings themselves were worn on the finger.

718   Lord Weary's Castle   (Robert Lowell, 1946)
The American poet's collection of poems takes its title from a folk ballad about Lord Weary, who refused to pay his stonemason, Lambkin, for building his castle and whose wife and child were consequently murdered by Lambkin in revenge.

719   A Lost Lady   (Willa Cather, 1923)
The "lost lady" of the American writer's title is the novel's central character, Marian Forrester, the young wife of a Western pioneer and railroad builder, whose weakness for drink and cheap men leads her astray and who eventually disappears after her husband's death. "Lost" thus has both a literal and a figurative sense.

720   Love and Friendship   (Alison Lurie, 1962)
The American writer's first novel is a campus comedy about two people trapped in an affair. The title is perhaps borrowed from A. B. Lindsley's comedy *Love and Friendship, or, Yankee Notions* (1809). However, the English writer Jane Austen had earlier used the title for her juvenile parody of a sentimental novel, published in 1790, and that was probably the actual inspiration. Not only is Lurie's heroine called Emmy, but the novel's restricted canvas and wit are features typical of Austen's fiction.

721   Love in a Cold Climate   (Nancy Mitford, 1949)
The British writer's novel, with the instability of love as its theme, has a title that appears to allude to a letter of 1787 from the English poet Robert Southey to his brother (about Mary Wollstonecraft's letters from Sweden and Norway):

> She has made me in love with a cold climate, and frost and snow, with a northern moonlight.

722   The Love Song of J. Alfred Prufrock   (T. S. Eliot, 1915)

The striking title of the Anglo-American writer's poem, with its unexpected juxta-position of "Love Song" and a formal personal name, has resulted in speculation about the name itself. Does the antihero in some way seek "proof" in a "frock," for example? Does the initial "J." represent the name of Eliot's friend Jean Verdenal? No definitive answer has yet been proposed. The title is anyway ironic, since the middle-aged Prufrock is too timid to take the step that would free him from the empty rituals of his genteel world.

723   The Loved One   (Evelyn Waugh, 1948)

The British writer's novel is a macabre comedy about Californian funeral practices, and is set in the fictional Whispering Glades Memorial Park (loosely based on the Forest Lawn cemetery, Los Angeles). Its title represents a morticians' euphemism for a corpse.

724   The Luck of Roaring Camp   (Bret Harte, 1868)

The American writer's story is set in the California gold-mining settlement of Roaring Camp. A child is born there to the prostitute Cherokee Sal. When his mother dies, the boy, christened Thomas Luck, is adopted by the miners, whose hard-bitten nature is softened by the young child. The following year, the settle-ment is engulfed when the river rises, and one of the miners, attempting to save "The Luck," is drowned with the child in his arms. The title thus not only names the setting and the central character, but leaves open the nature of the luck ("The Luck") that he both wins and loses.

725   Lucky Jim   (Kingsley Amis, 1954)

The hero (rather, antihero) of the British author's first novel is Jim Dixon, a history lecturer in a provincial English university. The story tells of his misadventures, mis-takes, and downright disasters, so that the title is ironic. It comes from an Ameri-can song by Frederick Bowers and Charles Horwitz which tells how a man waited for his childhood friend to die so that he could marry the girl they both wanted. Unhappily married, however, he wishes he were also dead: "Oh, lucky Jim, how I envy him."

726   Lummox   (Fannie Hurst, 1923)

The novel by the British writer tells the story of Bertha, a semi-articulate Scandi-navian girl who sinks lower and lower but "has a great soul." The title is a colloquial term for an ungainly or stupid person, as Bertha is.

727   Lustra   (Ezra Pound, 1916)

The American poet's collection of poems takes its title from the plural of the Latin word *lustrum*, the term for a purificatory sacrifice performed by the Roman censors every five years on completion of the census.

728   Machine Dreams   (Jayne Anne Phillips, 1984)

The American writer's first novel is a family chronicle, and develops through a suc-cession of narrators whose stories at first seem unrelated. It gradually becomes apparent, however, that they are all linked by experiences connected in some way with machines. The novel ends with a description of the holocaust of Vietnam, in which both non-human machines and human dreams are shattered.

729   The Madness of a Seduced Woman   (Susan Fromberg Schaeffer, 1983)

The American writer's fifth novel is based on an actual murder trial in Vermont in the early 20th century. In this, Agnes Dempster was tried for the murder of her rival and pronounced insane, mainly on psychiatric evidence that her insanity resulted from "the madness of a seduced woman." Schaeffer does not share this verdict, and her novel examines the evidence in detail from the point of view of Agnes's lawyers, friends, and father.

730   A Maggot   (John Fowles, 1985)

The British writer's sixth novel is set in the 18th century and is a fantastic reworking of a real-life murder investigation. The title uses "maggot" in the then current sense of the word to mean "whim," "quirk," although the word itself appears in more than one sense in the novel.

731   The Magnificent Ambersons   (Booth Tarkington, 1918)

The novel by the American writer forms part of a trilogy, itself titled *Growth* (1927), with the other two volumes being respectively *The Turmoil* (1915) and *The Midlander* (1923). The middle volume tells the story of a snobbish aristocratic family, represented by old Major Ambersor., his daughter Isabel, and her arrogant son George, who is the novel's central character. He ultimately meets his "comeuppance," and the adjective of the title is ironic.

732   Main Street   (Sinclair Lewis, 1920)

The American writer's novel tells of the futile efforts of Carol Kennicott, a doctor's wife, to bring culture to the Midwest town of Gopher Prairie, where she lives on Main Street, its chief thoroughfare. According to the novel, this particular Main Street "is the continuation of main streets everywhere." Lewis based Gopher Prairie on his home town of Sauk Centre, Minnesota, which had a Main Street of the type he describes.

733   The Maltese Falcon   (Dashiell Hammett, 1930)

The American writer's novel is one of the first in the "hard-boiled" genre of detective fiction. It has a complex plot, but involves an attempt to recover a valuable statuette of a falcon which one of the characters is suspected of possessing, and which eventually passes to the novel's central character, private eye Sam Spade.

734   A Man for All Seasons   (Robert Bolt, 1961)

The stage play by the British dramatist on the life and execution of Sir Thomas More (1478–1535) began as a radio play (1954). The title comes from a description of More by his contemporary, Robert Whittington, in his book *Vulgaria* (1521), in which it was a passage for schoolboys to put into Latin:

More is a man of angel's wit and singular learning; I know not his fellow. For where is the man of that gentleness, lowliness and affability? And as time requireth, a man of marvellous mirth and pastimes, and sometimes as sad a gravity, as who say: a man for all seasons.

It translates a comment on More by Erasmus, who in the prefatory letter to his *In Praise of Folly* (1509) says that he played "*omnium horarum hominem*" ("a man of all hours").

735   The Man Who Came to Dinner   (Moss Hart and George S. Kaufman, 1939)

The play by the two American playwrights is a friendly burlesque on the writer Alexander Woollcott, represented by the central character, Sheridan Whiteside, and he is the "man who came to dinner." As such, he is the guest of a Midwestern family who stays on after breaking his leg to become a meddling nuisance in his hosts' home.

736   The Man Who Cried I Am   (John A. Williams, 1967)

The black American writer's fourth novel tells how its central character, Max Reddick, a black man successful in the white world, strives to confirm and assert his identity. This does not come from the white world but from himself. As he says: "All you ever want to do is remind me that I am black. But, goddam it, I also am."

737   The Man Who Dies   (D. H. Lawrence, 1931)

The British writer's novel was originally called *The Escaped Cock*, apparently for a little toy rooster coming out of an egg that Lawrence had seen in a shop window. When part of the story was published in an American magazine, however, he agreed to the change of title. It refers to "The Man," who rises from his tomb and lives for a while with peasants near Jerusalem (where they own the rooster) before going to Lebanon. There death is taken out of him by a priestess and he is designated as Osiris.

738   The Man Who Loved Children   (Christina Stead, 1940)

The Australian writer's novel is set in America but draws on the author's own childhood circumstances when her widowed father remarried and she became "the eldest of a large family." The book is a portrait of a family in crisis, and the title refers to the central character, unhappily married Sam Pollit, father of a brood of six children, with a seventh on the way. He deludes himself that he loves everyone and everything, and cannot understand why his marriage has gone wrong: "Mother Earth [...] I love you, I love men and women, I love little children and all innocent things. [...] I feel I am love itself—how could I pick a woman who would hate me so much."

739   The Man Who Mistook His Wife for a Hat   (Oliver Sacks, 1985)

The book, by a noted British psychiatrist, presents 24 case studies of neurological dysfunction, including that of the musician of the title who cannot comprehend the totality of the objects he sees. The work inspired a number of artistic re-creations, including a play by Harold Pinter, a movie with Robert De Niro, and an opera by Michael Nyman.

740   The Man Who Was Thursday   (G. K. Chesterton, 1908)
The novel by the British writer is a fantasy about a group of revolutionaries, secretly sworn to destroy the world. There are seven members of the Central Anarchist Council, who call themselves by the names of the days of the week for reasons of security: the research dynamiter Button is "Monday," Gogol is "Tuesday," the Marquis de St Eustache is "Wednesday," the poet Gabriel Syme is "Thursday," Professor de Worms is "Friday," and Dr Bull is "Saturday." The name of "Sunday," as the President of the Council, is not revealed. When it emerges that "Thursday" is not a poet at all but a Scotland Yard detective, doubt is cast on the identity of the others. "Wednesday," for example, turns out to be Inspector Ratcliffe.

741   The Man with the Blue Guitar   (Wallace Stevens, 1937)
The title poem of the American poet's volume of verse is so named from a painting by Picasso, and is a meditation on the relationship between art and nature. When charged with distorting reality, the man with the guitar replies: "Things as they are/Are changed upon the blue guitar." That is, words have their own reality rather than that of the external objects they appear to represent. See also **The Blue Guitar**.

742   The Man with the Golden Arm   (Nelson Algren, 1949)
The American writer's novel centers on a Polish immigrant dealer in a Chicago poker parlor. His name is Francis Majcinek, but he is known as Frankie Machine and is nicknamed "The Man with the Golden Arm," because of both his rapid reflexes when dealing and his drug addiction.

743   Manhattan Transfer   (John Dos Passos, 1925)
The American writer's novel, an imaginative sociological study of life in the swarming metropolis that is New York City, takes its title from the station maintained in the 1920s by the Pennsylvania Railroad in New Jersey meadows between Newark and Jersey City, where passengers changed trains between New York City and points south and west. The title thus represents the variegated life of New York City itself.

744   Manual Labor   (Frederick Busch, 1974)
The American writer's second novel concerns the struggle of a couple, Anne and Phil Sorenson, to overcome the death of their unborn child. They do so by rebuilding an old house, the manual labor thus following the vain labor of a childless mother.

745   A Many-Splendoured Thing   (Han Suyin, 1952)
The novel tells of the love of a Eurasian woman doctor in Hong Kong during the Korean War for a war correspondent. The British author (real name Rosalie Comber) took her title from the poem *The Kingdom of God* (1913) by the English mystic poet Francis Thompson:

The angels keep their ancient places;—
Turn but a stone, and start a wing!
'Tis ye, 'tis your estrangèd faces,
That miss the many-splendoured thing.

The American film of the novel bore the extended title *Love Is a Many-Splendored Thing* (1955), and its popular theme song, of the same name, gave the words a romantic association that Thompson never originally intended.

746   Maple   (Robert Frost, 1923)
The American poet's narrative poem in blank verse takes its title from its subject, a New England girl named Maple. Others take the name to be "Mabel," but it actually refers to her kinship with the trees.

747   Mapp and Lucia   (E. F. Benson, 1935)
The British writer's absorbing novel is one of a series about a pair of cunning middle-aged ladies, who are distrustful of everyone and everything and who are scheming rivals. They first meet in this book, and the title names them. The first is Miss Elizabeth Mapp. The second is Emmeline Lucas, "universally known to her friends as Lucia." They had each appeared individually in earlier books.

748   The Marble Faun   (William Faulkner, 1924)
The American writer's book of pastoral verse takes its title from the identically named Italian romance of 1860 by Nathaniel Hawthorne. This was itself named for (the copy of) Praxiteles' statue of a resting satyr in the Capitoline Museum, Rome.

749   The Marble Faun   (Nathaniel Hawthorne, 1860)
The American writer's novel concerns a sculptor, a young New England woman, who with her friend, Miriam, is an art student in Rome. She becomes acquainted there with a handsome Italian count, who physically and in character resembles the Marble Faun of the Greek classical sculptor Praxiteles. The story of passion and murder develops from this point.

750   Marching On   (James Boyd, 1927)
The historical novel by the American writer is set in the time of the Civil War and tells the story of a young man who attempts to win a bride above his social station. The title quotes from the last line of the first stanza of Julia Ward Howe's *Battle Hymn of the Republic* (1862): "His truth is marching on."

751   Marco Millions   (Eugene O'Neill, 1927)
The play by the American playwright concerns the historic explorer Marco Polo, who in his desire to make "millions" is persistently blind to the fact that Kublai Khan's granddaughter, Kukachin, is in love with him.

752   The Mask of Anarchy   (P. B. Shelley, 1832)
The poet's work is a poem of political protest written as a response to the so-called "Peterloo Massacre" in Manchester in 1819, in which a radical meeting was broken

up by a cavalry charge, resulting in about 500 injuries and 11 deaths. The "mask" of the title is a pageant (masquerade) of British political leaders, whom Shelley blames for the "triumph of Anarchy" in the country. Much of his anger was directed specifically at the foreign secretary, Lord Castlereagh:

> I met Murder on the way—
> He had a mask like Castlereagh.

753   The Master of the Inn   (Robert Herrick, 1908)
The novelette by the American writer concerns the home ("inn") for mentally and physically sick men that a doctor (the "master") runs in the New England countryside. The story ends with the destruction of both "master" and "inn" in a fire.

754   Maybe   (Burt Blechman, 1967)
The American writer's fifth novel tells the story of Myra Russell, who compulsively wastes money and time. Hence the title, which encapsulates her problem: "Maybe the biggest problem in life is how to spend it."

755   Maybe the Moon   (Armistead Maupin, 1992)
The narrator of the American writer's novel is a dwarf film actress, Cadence Roth, who seeks fame after starring as a lovable elf in a popular movie in which she remained unseen because she played the part inside a rubber suit. When a tall pianist enters her life she "shoots the moon" with a crazy scheme to achieve her objective. The title hints at her aspiration, and is quoted as a possible name for a new movie in a letter from its screenwriter:

> P.S. How does *Maybe the Moon* sound as a title? [...] I think it strikes just the right note of striving for the impossible.

The moon itself appears or is mentioned several times in the novel, at one point in the exact words of the title:

> "He has a kid, honey. It's his whole life. He's not gonna ask me to come and live with him." "Maybe he will." "Yeah, and maybe the moon is cheese."

756   The Medium Is the Massage   (Marshall McLuhan, 1967)
The work by the Canadian cultural critic propounds his theory that humans are passively manipulated by the media, or as he put it, "all media work us over completely." The title puns on McLuhan's famous maxim, "The medium is the message," which he used as the title of the first chapter of his earlier book, *Understanding Media* (1964).

757   Memento Mori   (Muriel Spark, 1959)
The British author's third novel is a black comedy, in which the humor hides a more serious strand, as a meditation on the inevitability of death, an awareness of which is necessary to bring relish to life.The main characters are thus in their seventies and eighties, and one by one receive an anonymous telephone call with an identical message: "Remember you must die." These words are the English translation of the Latin title, which itself is used for an object, such as a skull, that reminds people of the inevitability of death.

758   The Memorial   (Christopher Isherwood, 1932)
The British writer's novel explores the mutual hostility that existed between the pre- and postwar generations. It is a memorial both to those, like the author's father (the book's dedicatee), who lost their lives in World War I, and to Isherwood's own generation, affected by a conflict in which they were too young to take part. The title indirectly refers to these two memorials, but directly alludes to the war memorial which is due to be unveiled as the novel's second section opens.

759   Men in White   (Sidney Kingsley, 1933)
The play by the American playwright and actor deals with with a crisis in the life of a surgeon (a "man in white") when faced with a conflict between personal and professional loyalties. The original title of the play was *Crisis*.

760   The Men's Club   (Leonard Michaels, 1981)
The American writer's first novel is the story of a group of men who get together to form a kind of consciousness-raising "club," with each telling the story of his life. However, what the reader gets is simply fragments of stories, albeit moments of intense self-awareness. The overall theme of the novel is the power that women have to fascinate men. The "men's club" thus fails in its attempt to ban the presence of women.

761   The Mezzanine   (Nicholson Baker, 1988)
The American writer's novel is a detailed account of an office-worker's lunch hour on a mezzanine floor. At the same time, the title indicates the intermediate layers of contemporary life that the book describes.

762   The Middle of the Journey   (Lionel Trilling, 1947)
The novel by the Americn writer concerns the emotional and intellectual state of the middle-aged man, John Laskell, when his daughter is accidentally killed by the drunken husband of the woman with whom he is having an affair and who is nursing him back to health after a near-fatal illness. After considering opposing philosophical viewpoints on the cause of the tragedy, Laskell finally reaches his "middle-of-the-road" conclusion that human beings are neither fully controlled by external forces nor fully possessed of a free will.

763   The Middle Parts of Fortune   (Frederic Manning, 1929)
The Australian writer's novel is based on his experiences as an army private in World War I. Its reputation derived from the 1920 bowdlerized edition issued under the title *Her Privates We*, "by Private 19022." The author's identity was not acknowledged until 1943, eight years after his death, and the unexpurgated version, under the present title, was not published until 1977. Each of the novel's chapters has a Shakespearean epigraph, and both titles (with the substitution of one word from an earlier line) come from the bawdy exchange between Hamlet and the nonentities Rosencrantz and Guildenstern, with whom Manning allies the infantrymen, on the subject of Fortune as a "strumpet."

Hamlet: Then you live about her waist or in the middle of her favours?
Guildenstern: Faith, her privates we.
Hamlet: In the secret parts of Fortune? O, most true; she is a strumpet. [II.ii.4]

764 Middle Passage (Charles Johnson, 1990)
The black American writer's third novel is a pastiche of 19th-century American
sea-faring fiction. It tells the story of Rutherford Calhoun, a newly-freed slave, who
works his passage on board a slave clipper bound for Africa. The voyage for him is
a "middle passage," a time when the past and the future have little or no significance, and he uses it to confront his own identity and, by implication, black identity in America generally.

765 A Midnight Clear (William Wharton [pseudonym], 1982)
The American writer's antiwar third novel concerns a group of teenaged GIs trying to survive Christmas 1941 in a snowbound no-man's-land. Its title is based on
the opening line of Edmund Hamilton Sears' poem *The Angel's Song* (1850), familiar as a Christmas carol:

> It came upon the midnight clear,
> That glorious song of old.

766 The Midnight Folk (John Masefield, 1927)
The British writer's fantasy novel for children centers on an orphan who at night
meets animals and toys from his younger life. These are the "midnight folk" with
whom he has adventures while searching for a treasure.

767 Midnight's Children (Salman Rushdie, 1981)
The Bombay-born British writer's novel presents a part true, part fantasy picture of
India, as told through the personal history of the narrator, Saleem Sinai, one of
1001 children born with magic powers on the stroke of midnight, August 15, 1947,
the precise time and date when India gained independence from Britain (and the
year when Rushdie himself was born). Hence the title.

768 The Midwich Cuckoos (John Wyndham, 1957)
The British science fiction writer's novel tells how strange, yellow-eyed children are
mysteriously born to mothers in the village of Midwich. They are "cuckoos" in the
sense that they are alien, like the chicks that hatch from eggs laid by cuckoos in the
nests of other birds.

769 Mine Eyes Have Seen (Alice Dunbar Nelson, 1918)
The black American writer's one-act play questions the responsibility of black men
to serve in the military in the face of racial oppression in America. The title quotes
the well-known first line of Julia Ward Howe's *Battle Hymn of the Republic* (1862):
"Mine eyes have seen the glory of the coming of the Lord."

770 The Mint (T. E. Lawrence, 1955)
The account of the British author's experience of life in the ranks of the Royal Air
Force has a title that refers metaphorically to the young men's impressionable time,
when they are "minted" or molded by service life.

771   Miss Lonelyhearts   (Nathanael West, 1933)
The title of the American writer's novel is a nickname for its central character, a man who writes advice to the lovelorn in a New York newspaper. As the narrative itself explains: "*Miss Lonelyhearts* tells the story of a reporter [...] detailed to write an agony column and answer daily the letters desperate with human misery addressed to his paper." The nickname appears to have been invented by West for a journalist of this kind (at first originally female), and it came to be adopted generally for someone able to advise those with personal problems, whether in a newspaper or magazine or more generally.

772   M'liss   (Bret Harte, 1860)
The American writer's novelette tells of the adventures of a willful young girl in mining country. Her name is a short form of her full name, Melissa Smith.

773   Moby-Dick   (Herman Melville, 1851)
The American author's famous realistic acount of a whaling voyage, symbolizing the conflict between man and his fate, takes its title from the whale who is the central character. His name may have been based on that of *Mocha Dick*, a fierce white whale that had caused deaths and damage some 12 years earlier. Melville may have read an account of this whale by J.N. Reynolds in *The Knickerbocker Magazine* (1839). It is not clear how Melville hit on his own name for the whale.

774   The Monikins   (J. Fenimore Cooper, 1835)
The "Monikins" of the American writer's allegorical satire are four monkeys who travel Europe and meet an English knight, Sir John Goldencalf, and an American sea-captain, Noah Poke. All the names are in similar vein, and those of the monkeys themselves, who come from the Arctic regions, are Dr. Reasono, Lord Chatterino, Lady Chatterissa, and Mistress Vigilance Lynx.

775   The Moon and Sixpence   (W. Somerset Maugham, 1919)
The British writer's novel, based on the life of Gauguin, tells the story of a London stockbroker who in middle age suddenly decides to desert his wife, family, and business to become a painter. The title came from a review of Maugham's earlier book **Of Human Bondage** in the *Times Literary Supplement*, which said that like many young men he was "so busy yearning for the moon that he never saw the sixpence at his feet." (The sixpence was a silver coin, just as the moon is silver.)

776   Moon-Calf   (Floyd Dell, 1920)
The title of the American writer's semiautobiographical novel describes its central character, Felix Fay, who moons through life "in the day-dreams which books unfold before him." As a nickname for an absentminded person, *mooncalf* literally means "moon child."

777   Moon Tiger   (Penelope Lively, 1987)
The British writer's seventh novel tells the story of a popular historian, Claudia Hampson, who thinks of writing a history of the world as she lies dying in hospital

but instead tells her own life story. In this, she recalls her lover, a tank officer killed in World War II while she was in Cairo. The title is the name of the brand of mosquito repellent that burned in their bedroom in Luxor.

778 More Joy in Heaven (Morley Callaghan, 1937)

The Canadian author's novel is a fictionalized account of the career of the bank robber Red Ryan, the account itself being presented as a parable of a reformed criminal in a violent world. The title is based on a biblical verse: "Joy shall be in heaven over one sinner that repenteth, more than over ninety and nine just persons" (Luke 15:7).

779 More Pricks Than Kicks (Samuel Beckett, 1934)

The series of short stories by the Irish-born French writer centers on Belacqua Shuah, solipsist and Peeping Tom, an outsider in Dublin. His life chiefly consists of different sexual encounters with women, until his death in the operating theater and subsequent burial erase memory of him from the minds of all who knew him. The title puns on the biblical text: "It is hard for thee to kick against the pricks" (Acts 9:5). The implication is that Shuah's life was more about mechanical sex ("pricks") than genuine thrills or pleasures ("kicks").

780 Morning Glory (Somerset de Chair, 1988)

The first volume of the autobiography of the eminent British politician, historical biographer, and war hero, takes its title from the slang expression for sexual intercourse in the early morning, before rising from bed. His publishers subtitled it *Memoirs from the Edge of History*, an appellation not entirely to the subject's liking, as he made plain in an interview in the London *Times* (November 29, 1994) on the occasion of its republication:

> The author [...] is horrified by their choice. "Rather pompous don't you think," he says. "I wanted them to call it *The Indiscretions of a Self-Confessed Heterosexual*. But the publishers said 'Oh no! We couldn't *possibly*'." Well actually, they could. For these rambling memoirs [...] still linger in the memory as the remarkably frank confessions of a man who has been married four times and admits: "I love women—all women."

781 A Mortal Antipathy (Oliver Wendell Holmes, 1885)

The American writer's novel concerns a young man, the son of a wealthy American family, whose growth to manhood is normal in all respects save one, his "mortal antipathy" to beautiful young women. This is the result of an incident in his childhood, when he was dropped into a thornbush by a young female cousin. Needless to say, he is cured of the distressing malady, and marries happily.

782 Morte d'Urban (J. F. Powers, 1962)

The American writer's first novel is a satire charting the gradual corruption and final downfall of a proselytizing priest, Father Urban, attached to the (fictional) Clementine Order. The title is adapted from Thomas Malory's cycle of Arthurian legends, *Le Morte Darthur* ("The Death of Arthur") (1485).

783   Mourning Becomes Electra   (Eugene O'Neill, 1931)

The work by the American dramatist is a trilogy of plays based on Aeschylus' *Oresteia*, which tells the story of Orestes and Electra, brother and sister, who kill their mother Clytemnestra to avenge their father, Agamemnon, whom Clytemnestra and her lover Aegisthus had murdered. In O'Neill's plays, Electra is represented by Lavinia, daughter of Ezra Mannon, a general returning from the Civil War, representing Agamemnon. The memorable title was explained by O'Neill himself as follows:

> By the title *Mourning Becomes Electra* I sought to convey that mourning befits Electra; it becomes Electra to mourn; it is her fate; black is becoming to her and it is the color that becomes her destiny.   [Quoted in Arthur Gelb and Barbara Gelb, *O'Neill*, 1965]

784   The Mousetrap   (Agatha Christie, 1952)

The famous long-running play was adapted from the British author's earlier short story *Three Blind Mice* (1948), itself named from the familiar nursery rhyme. *The Mousetrap* is a title borrowed from Shakespeare, and is the name given by Hamlet to the "play within a play" that he arranges "to catch the conscience of the king" by representing the crimes of Claudius, his uncle:

> *King*   What do you call the play?
> *Hamlet*   The Mouse-trap. [...] This play is the image of a murder done in
>   Vienna: Gonzago is the duke's name; his wife, Baptista.   [III.ii.249]

785   A Moveable Feast   (Ernest Hemingway, 1964)

The posthumously published memoir of the American writer tells of the author's experiences in Paris. In the church calendar, a "moveable feast" is one such as Easter, that does not fall on a fixed date. As Hemingway writes in the book itself:

> If you are lucky enough to have lived in Paris as a young man, then wherever you go for the rest of your life, it stays with you, for Paris is a moveable feast.

786   Moving On   (Larry McMurtry, 1970)

The American writer's fourth novel has as its main characters Pete and Patsy Carpenter, who wish to "move on" from their affluent Texan backgrounds to gain some kind of individual achievement. Pete hopes to photograph cowboy skills for a book on rodeo. He fails, however, and instead becomes a collector of old books. He has moved, but he has not moved on. Each person's past is not significant in the present.

787   Moving Parts   (Steve Katz, 1977)

The American writer's fifth novel is not really a novel at all, but a collection of stories, diary entries, photographs, and the like. A photograph of Katz bearded is followed by one of a barbershop and then by one of Katz clean-shaven. Katz's face is thus just one of the "moving parts" that makes up the whole work.

788   The Moving Toyshop   (Edmund Crispin [Bruce Montgomery], 1946)

The British thriller writer's novel opens with the apparent disappearance of a toyshop in Oxford. Hence the title, which comes from Pope's comment on women in his poem *The Rape of the Lock* (1714):

> With varying vanities from ev'ry part,
> They shift the moving toyshop of the heart.

789   Mr. Britling Sees It Through   (H. G. Wells, 1916)

The British writer's novel is largely autobiographical, and has a contemporary set-ting, in World War I, which the central character, the art critic and writer, Hugh Britling, "sees through," as he does the personal tragedy of the loss of his son, killed in the war. The present tense of the title reflects Wells's belief that the war would be over by 1916, when he expected that he himself would have "seen it through."

790   Mr. Fortune's Maggot   (Sylvia Townsend Warner, 1927)

The British writer's novel evolved from a dream that she had in 1925, in which she saw a middle-aged missionary who "stood alone on an ocean beach, wringing his hands in despair." The missionary became Mr. Timothy Fortune, the novel's central figure, and his "maggot" (a whimsical or perverse fancy) is to convert the popula-tion of Fauna, a small Polynesian island. (*Cf.* **A Maggot**.)

791   Mr. Love and Justice   (Colin MacInnes, 1960)

The novel is the third in the trilogy by the English author that began with **City of Spades**. Like its predecessor, **Absolute Beginners**, it is set in the criminal under-world, and is an allegory about a pimp, Frankie Love, and a police officer, Edward Justice. Their meaningful names are those of the title.

792   Mr. Norris Changes Trains   (Christopher Isherwood, 1935)

The British writer's novel, set in a corrupt Berlin between the wars, tells how Arthur Norris, the seedy "gent" who is its central character, sells secrets to the Nazis while pretending to be a Communist. He is thus duplicitous, and "changes trains" accordingly. Isherwood had originally planned to incorporate this novel, with its variant title *The Last of Mr. Norris*, and **Goodbye to Berlin** in a single work to be called *The Lost*.

793   Mr. Weston's Good Wine   (T. F. Powys, 1927)

The novel by the British writer, ultimately an allegory of love and death, opens when two strangers travel in a Ford delivery truck to an English village. The elderly driver announces himself as Mr. Weston, a wine merchant, distributing his special brand of wine, called "Mr. Weston's Good Wine." The title comes from Jane Austen's *Emma* (1816):

> She believed he had been drinking too much of Mr. Weston's good wine, and felt
> sure he would want to be talking nonsense.   [Chapter 15]

794   Mulligan Stew   (Gilbert Sorrentino, 1979)

The American author's fifth and best-known novel is a literary potpourri in which he displays all the aspects of novel-writing, from the actual act of composition to the writer's notebooks and letters and the thoughts of his characters. Hence the title, from the "mulligan stew" that is made from odds and ends of food.

795 Murder in the Cathedral (T. S. Eliot, 1935)
The religious play by the Anglo-American writer has as its subject the "murder in the cathedral" of Archbishop Thomas Becket at Canterbury in 1170, following his opposition to Henry II's attempts to control the clergy. The first performance of the play was actually in Canterbury cathedral.

796 Murmuring Judges (David Hare, 1991)
The English dramatist's play about the British criminal justice system takes its title from an old legal expression meaning to speak ill of the judiciary. To "murmur" a judge is to complain about his actions. In Scottish law, this is still an offense.

797 Murther and Walking Spirits (Robertson Davies, 1991)
The narrator of the Canadian author's novel is murdered on page one. The story is thus related from the perspective of a dead man. Hence the title, which quotes from Samuel Butler (1612–1680):

> When Murther and Walking Spirits meet, there is no other Narrative can come near it.

798 The Mutiny on the Bounty (James Norman Hall and Charles Bernard Nordhoff, 1932)
The narrative by the two American writers tells the true tale of the mutiny in 1787 by the crew of the British warship *Bounty* against their cruel captain, William Bligh.

799 The Mutual Friend (Frederick Busch, 1978)
The American author's third novel, as its title implies, is about Charles Dickens, but merely that part of his life from 1867 to 1870. His "mutual friend" is his companion, George Dolby, who takes over the narrative from Dickens and explains that it is difficult to guarantee the accuracy of the accounts.

800 My Ántonia (Willa Cather, 1918)
The American writer's novel, a realistic portrayal of the Midwest, takes its title from the name of its central character, the immigrant Czech girl Ántonia Shimerda, who longs to escape from the farm to the town. (Her name is accented on the first syllable.)

801 My Heart and My Flesh (Elizabeth Madox Roberts, 1927)
The American writer's novel tells of the three love affairs of Theodosia Bell, a young Kentucky woman. Her first lover is burned to death and her second deserts her. She finally finds peace with a simple cattle rancher. The title comes from the Bible: "My heart and my flesh crieth out for the living God" (Psalm 84:2).

802 My Life Story (Marlene Dietrich, 1979)
The famous U.S. movie actress and singer's autobiography might have had a less prosaic title if she had accepted the (somewhat tongue-in-cheek) advice of the English

theatre critic Kenneth Tynan (*see* **Oh! Calcutta!**) who in a private letter to her dated June 28, 1977 wrote as follows:

> Titles: none of the ones you suggest seems quite right to me. Flashback as you say, is serviceable, but slightly predictable. Ghosts I Have Laid smacks just a *leetle* of bad taste. Here are one or two others that come to mind—none of them, I fear, anything like the ideal:
>   Survivor (sounds boastful)
>   Autograph (which means an original manuscript as well as a signature)
>   The Face I Face (from that song)
>   Mirror Writing
>   Travelling Light
>   All You Need to Know (sounds churlish: comes from the Keats quotation: "Beauty is truth, truth beauty: that is all/You know on earth, and all you need to know." But it still sounds churlish. How about I Enjoy Being a Churl?)
>   Open Secrets
>   Before I Forget
>   But I'll go on thinking and the moment anything more promising turns up I'll rush it to you. [Kathleen Tynan, ed., *Kenneth Tynan: Letters*, 1994]

803   My Name Is Aram   (William Saroyan, 1940)
The American writer's autobiographical collection of stories recounts the exuberant experiences of a group of Armenian children in California, with the title referring to their protagonist, nine-year-old Aram Garoglanyan. Saroyan himself was born into a family of Armenian immigrants to America. *Aram* is a typically Armenian name (as for the composer Aram Khachaturyan.)

804   My Turn to Make the Tea   (Monica Dickens, 1951)
The British writer's popular account of life in the office of a local weekly newspaper has an intentionally ironic title. Dickens (the great-granddaughter of Charles Dickens) was the only woman in the office, and it was *always* her turn to make the tea.

805   Myra Breckinridge   (Gore Vidal, 1968)
The American writer's satire of Californian life tells the story of the "disturbingly beautiful" Myra Breckinridge of the title, who goes to Hollywood in a mission to "re-create the sexes and thus save the human race from extinction." The reader learns in a casual aside that her husband, film critic Myron, has recently drowned. It emerges, however, that not only was she never married to Myron in the first place but that she actually *is* Myron, or was until she underwent a sex-change operation. In the story's final episode, Myra/Myron marries Mary-Ann Pringle, girlfriend of the original Myron's lecherous uncle, Buck Loner. The whole novel is thus an extravaganza of role reversal and sexual inversion, as the title, the central character's name, was perhaps intended to suggest, from the way in which it interacts with and is mirrored by the names of other characters.

806   The Mysterious Stranger   (Mark Twain, 1916)
The American writer's story appears in two versions. The first, published posthumously in 1916, was edited from various manuscripts by Twain's biographer A. B.

Paine. The story is set in the medieval Austrian village of Eseldorf, where a mysterious stranger, discovered to be the Devil, visits young Theodor Fischer and two of his friends. It subsequently emerged that Paine had not only deleted about a quarter of Twain's text, but had created a major new character, altered the names of others, and conflated three drafts to create his own story. The second version, published in 1969, is also set in Eseldorf, but the mysterious stranger is now an amiable young printer's devil, called only No. 44.

807   The Mystic Masseur   (V. S. Naipaul, 1957)
The Trinidadian writer's first novel is a satire on the power that popular superstition and bogus education can bring. It centers on an incompetent masseur, Pundit Ganesh Ramsummair, who gains popular prestige as a mystic and writer and who rises to become G. Ramsay Muir, Esq., M. B. E.

808   Naked Lunch   (William S. Burroughs, 1959)
The American author of the novel, a montage of human disintegration and degradation, was given its title by his friend Jack Kerouac, who helped type the manuscript. As Burroughs himself explains in the Introduction: "The title means exactly what the words say: NAKED Lunch—a frozen moment when everyone sees what is on the end of every fork."

The critic Eric Mottram elucidated it further as: "The moment a man realizes his cannibalism, his predatory condition, and his necessary parasitism and addictive nature."

809   The Name of the Rose   (Umberto Eco, 1981)
The Italian writer's first novel, in the original titled *Il Nomme della Rosa*, is basically a historical crime novel telling how a 14th-century monk, William of Baskerville, solves seven murders in the monastery he happens to be visiting. In his later book, *Reflections on The Name of the Rose* (1985), Eco explains that the title derives from the Latin hexameter with which the novel ends: "*Stat rosa pristina nomine, nomina nuda tenemus*" ("The past rose stands in name, we hold the mere names"). This comes from a satirical poem, *De contemptu mundi*, by the 12th-century monk Bernard of Cluny, and roughly speaking means that although things pass, their names remain. Eco also comments in the later book: "A title must muddle the reader's ideas, not regiment them."

810   The Narrows   (Ann Petry, 1954)
The American author's third novel, a story of love and betrayal, takes its title from its setting, the black neighborhood in Monmouth, Connecticut.

811   Natalie Natalia   (Nicholas Mosley, 1971)
The British author's eighth novel tells the story of a politician, Anthony Greville. The title represents the two names of the woman who is Greville's mistress. She is a contradictory character, on the one hand rapacious Natalie, on the other sweet and gentle Natalia.

812 National Velvet (Enid Bagnold, 1930)
The popular children's story by the British writer tells how a 14-year-old girl, Velvet Brown, acquires a horse in a raffle and eventually wins the Grand National on it. Hence the title. An American film of the book was released in 1945 with Elizabeth Taylor in the title role.

813 Nice Guys Finish Last (Leo Durocher, 1975)
In his autobiography, the American baseball coach recalled his remarks to reporters about the New York Giants in July 1946: "All nice guys. They'll finish last. Nice guys." This gave him the title of his book. However, Frank Graham of the New York *Journal-American* recorded his words rather differently: "Why, they're the nicest guys in the world! And where are they? In seventh place!" (This itself gave the title of Ralph Keyes's 1992 book on misquotations, *Nice Guys Finish Seventh*.)

814 Nice Work (David Lodge, 1988)
The British writer's eighth novel concerns a prim feminist lecturer and a chauvinist factory boss who in turn "shadow" each other for a year to broaden their experience. The title works on several levels, depending on the various senses of "nice" (agreeable, precise, delicate) while equally suggesting the well-known lines from George and Ira Gershwin's musical *Damsel in Distress* (1937):

> Nice work if you can get it,
> And you can get it if you try.

815 Nigger Heaven (Carl Van Vechten, 1926)
The (white) American writer's novel, set in Harlem in the jazz era, comprises a number of melodramatic episodes that conclude with a murder. The title is an old slang expression for the top gallery in a theater. The narrator explains:

> That's what Harlem is. We sit in our places in the gallery of this New York theater and watch the white world sitting down below us in the good seats.

816 The Night Has a Thousand Eyes (Cornell Woolrich, 1945)
The American writer's story of a vaudeville entertainer who can predict the future takes its title from *Among the Flowers* (1878) by the English poet Francis William Bourdillon:

> The night has a thousand eyes,
> And the day but one;
> Yet the light of the bright world dies,
> With the dying sun.

817 'Night Mother (Marsha Norman, 1983)
The play by the American playwright has just two characters, mother and daughter. At the beginning of the play, the daughter announces she is going to kill herself, and the rest of the action moves relentlessly to this outcome. The title quotes her final words while punning on night as "mother of the day."

818 The Night of the Iguana (Tennessee Williams, 1962)

The American dramatist's play is the story of T. Lawrence Shannon, a defrocked Episcopalian minister turned sleazy tour guide, whose crackup in a cheap Mexico hotel grants him a new acceptance of life and a kinder vision of God. The "night" of the title is the time when this occurs, and when an iguana is symbolically released from captivity.

819 The Nine Tailors (Dorothy L. Sayers, 1934)

The title of the British novelist's thriller alludes to "Tailor Paul," the name of one of the church bells of Fenchurch St. Paul, which play a part in the plot. The saying "Nine Tailors Make a Man" is quoted on the novel's last page. "Nine tailors" is a corruption of "nine tellers," meaning nine strokes on a bell, which traditionally announced the death of a man.

820 Nineteen Eighty-Four (George Orwell, 1949)

The British writer's famous novel of life in a totalitarian state was set in a random future year at the time of its composition. Orwell settled on this particular year by simply reversing the last two figures of the year when he actually wrote the book, 1948, intending it as a contemporary warning, not as an actual prophecy. The title he had originally planned for the book was *The Last Man in Europe*.

821 98.6 (Ronald Sukenik, 1975)

The American writer's third novel is a comic indictment of the 1960s generation for failing to produce a satisfactory model for society. The central section of the novel details the attempts of countercultural revolutionaries to set up a commune, and it is this to which the title refers, representing the body temperature being monitored when a woman from the commune miscarries the child supposed to be this world's future.

822 No Country for Young Men (Julia O'Faoláin, 1980)

The Irish writer's novel is set in Dublin in 1979 and centers on the effect of the Irish Civil War of 1922 on the present and previous generations of two interrelated families. Its title is adopted from the opening lines of Yeats's poem *Sailing to Byzantium* (1928):

> That is no country for old men. The young
> In one another's arms birds in the trees—
> Those dying generations—at their song.

823 No Drums—No Trumpets (Alec Le Vernoy, 1983)

The English translation of the French writer's World War II memoirs has a title based on the expression "without trumpets or drums," as applied to any inconspicuous or covert undertaking. The Scottish writer J.M. Barrie is said to have given the following advice to a young writer who did not know what to call his novel:

> "Are there any trumpets in it?"
> "No."
> "Are there any drums in it?"

"No."
"Then why not call it *Without Drums or Trumpets?*"

824 No! In Thunder (Leslie A. Fiedler, 1960)

The title piece of the American author's collection of "essays on myth and literature" argues that great modern writers have responded to ideals, institutions, and
even people with uncompromising negation. The title itself quotes words from
Herman Melville's letter to Nathaniel Hawthorne (April 16, 1851): "The grand
truth about Nathaniel Hawthorne. He says NO! in thunder; but the Devil himself
cannot make him say *yes.*"

825 No Fond Return of Love (Barbara Pym, 1961)

The British author's novel, one of many about the domestic lives of genteel, "unex-
ploited" women, was to have originally been called *A Thankless Task.* However, Pym
decided she wanted a title with "love" in it, so worked through *The Oxford Book of
English Verse* until she found one. It was in the first line of *Prayer for Indifference,* by
the 18th-century poet Fanny Greville, and served her purpose well, although with
a minor alteration:

> I ask no kind return of love,
> No tempting charm to please;
> Far from the heart those gifts remove
> That sigh for peace and ease.

826 No Other Life (Brian Moore, 1993)

The Northern Ireland-born Canadian writer's novel is set in a Caribbean island re-
sembling Haiti. It tells the story of a poor orphan from the hills who is trained by
priests for a career in the church but who stands for election as president of the island after the death of a dictator and who becomes part of the island's mythology.
The darkest part of the novel concerns the visit of the priest and politician to his
dying mother, who tells him, "There is no other life," that is, no life after death.
Hence the title, which on another level, however, could be taken to imply that there
is no hope for reform or revolution in earthly life.

827 None but the Lonely Heart (Richard Llewellyn, 1943)

The Welsh writer's sentimental story of a Cockney with a dying mother has a title
that appears to be the author's original creation, perhaps inspired by "None but the
weary heart," the popular title of a song by Tchaikovsky, and Carson McCullers'
The Heart Is a Lonely Hunter (or a blend of both).

828 North and South (Elizabeth Gaskell, 1854–5)

The English writer's novel is a study of the contrast between the values and customs of rural southern England and those of industrial northern England. Hence
the title, with its implied disparity, which is gradually resolved when the central
character, Margaret Hale, moves from a genteel and leisurely life in the southern
countryside to the working-class environment of a northern city and comes to
know and respect the millworkers there.

829   Nostromo   (Joseph Conrad, 1904)
The Polish-born British writer's novel, generally agreed to be the author's best, takes its title from the nickname of its central character, the Italian dockworkers' foreman Gian Battista Fidanza, known as *Nostromo*, from Italian *nostr'uomo*, "our man."

830   Notes of a Native Son   (James Baldwin, 1955)
The title of the black American writer's collection of essays ostensibly comes from its title essay, which is a study of Baldwin's relationship with his father. At another level, however, it refers to Richard Wright's bestselling novel *Native Son* (1940), which Baldwin criticizes in two of the essays: "Everybody's Protest Novel" and "Many Thousands Gone." Wright was Baldwin's mentor when the two writers were in France.

831   Nothing but the Night   (James Yaffe, 1957)
The American author's third novel is based on the Nathan Leopold–Richard Loeb murder case of 1924, with the case history seen through the eyes of one of the young men, not as a criminal but as a lonely child. The title comes from A. E. Housman's poem *A Shropshire Lad* (1896):

> In all the endless road you tread
> There's nothing but the night.

832   Nothing Like Leather   (V. S. Pritchett, 1935)
The British writer's third novel tells the story of Matthew Burkle, who hates sex and instead channels his energy into making money. The novel is set against the background of the leather trade. Hence the title.

833   Nothing Like the Sun   (Anthony Burgess, 1964)
The British writer's twelfth novel, subtitled *A Story of Shakespeare's Love-Life*, comes, predictably, from Shakespeare himself, and quotes a line from his *Sonnet CXXX*: "My mistress' eyes are nothing like the sun."

834   Novel on Yellow Paper   (Stevie Smith, 1936)
The British writer's unusual first novel, based mainly on autobiographical material, was written at the suggestion of her boss at the London publishing house where she worked as a personal secretary. She typed the novel in the firm's time on the firm's "very yellow" copying paper.

835   Now Barabbas Was a Rotter   (Ursula Bloom, 1977)
The British writer's biography of the English romantic novelist Marie Corelli (1855–1924) has a title that not only puns on the familiar biblical line, "Now Barabbas was a robber" (John 18:40), but alludes specifically to *Barabbas* (1893), Corelli's first successful novel.

836   Now in November   (Josephine Johnson, 1935)
The American writer's first novel centers on the lives of small farmers in Missouri. Every season for them is filled with foreboding, and the story culminates in a

ruinous fire. The title is a quotation from D. H. Lawrence's poem *November by the Sea* (1929): "Now in November nearer comes the sun down the abandoned heaven."

837   Now Voyager   (Olive Prouty, 1941)
The American writer's romantic tale, about a frustrated spinster who embarks on a doomed love affair, takes its title from a favorite phrase of Walt Whitman in *Leaves of Grass* (1881 edition). One example in "The Untold Want" is: "Now voyager sail thou forth to seek and find."

Nunquam *see* **Tunc**

838   O, How the Wheel Becomes It!   (Anthony Powell, 1983)
The British author's eccentric novel, quite unrelated to his sequence **A Dance to the Music of Time**, takes its title from one of poor Ophelia's deranged remarks in her madness in Shakespeare's *Hamlet*:

> You must sing a-down a-down,
> And you call him a-down-a.
> O how the wheel becomes it! It is the false steward that stole his
> master's daughter.   [IV.v.169]

("Wheel" here is either the refrain of the song that Ophelia sings or else the spinning wheel to which it was traditionally sung.)

839   O Pioneers!   (Willa Cather, 1913)
The American writer took the title of her novel from Walt Whitman's poem "Pioneers! O Pioneers" (1865), addressed to the pioneers of America, in which the words occur as a refrain in every stanza.

840   The O-Zone   (Paul Theroux, 1986)
The American writer's thirteenth novel complements his tenth, *The Mosquito Coast* (1981), in which a crazed inventor and his family flee an imagined nuclear holocaust to set up an ideal community in the jungles of Honduras. It describes an expedition by pampered New Yorkers into the proscribed U.S. interior, the Ozarks, or "O-Zone," contaminated by radioactive waste.

841   The Octopus   (Frank Norris, 1901)
The American writer's novel depicts the struggle for power between California wheat ranchers and "the Railroad." The latter is the "octopus" of the title, gradually encircling and strangling the ranchers.

842   The Odessa File   (Frederick Forsyth, 1972)
The British writer's second novel, a thriller, tells how Miller, a journalist covering the hunt for war criminals, uncovers a Nazi plot to smuggle arms to Arab terrorists in Israel. The first word of the title is the acronym of the (real) Nazi organization that Miller aims to penetrate, German *Organisation der SS-Angehörigen*, "Organization of SS members."

843   Odtaa   (John Masefield, 1926)
The British writer's novel of adventure (or misadventure) has a title that is an acronym for "*o*ne *d*amned *t*hing *a*fter *a*nother," an abbreviation of his own whimsical invention.

844   Of Human Bondage   (W. Somerset Maugham, 1915)
The partly autobiographical novel by the British writer, telling of the struggle for independence and professional recognition by a club-footed orphan, Philip Carey, takes its title from one of the books in Spinoza's *Ethics* (1677).

845   Of Love and Hunger   (J. Maclaren-Ross, 1947)
The story of the British author's first and best novel is set in 1939 against the growing threat of war and draws on the writer's experiences as a vacuum-cleaner salesman in south-coast resort Bognor Regis. The title comes from W.H. Auden and Louis MacNeice's *Letters from Iceland* (1937), a book to which the novel's narrator, Richard Fanshawe, is introduced by his lover, Sukie:

> Adventurers though, must take things as they find them,
>   And look for pickings where the pickings are.
> The drives of love and hunger are behind them,
>   They can't afford to be particular.

846   Of Mice and Men   (John Steinbeck, 1937)
The American writer's novel, which the author dramatized in its year of publication, concerns two itinerant farm laborers, George Milton and his strong but simple-minded friend, Lennie Small. Although both men dream of a farm of their own, George finally shoots Lennie after the latter has accidentally killed the wife of their bully boss, Curley. The title is a quote from Robert Burns' poem *To a Mouse* (1785):

> The best laid schemes o'mice and men
> Gang aft a-gley [often go wrong].

847   Of Thee I Sing   (George S. Kaufman, 1931)
The American playwright's comedy, with music by George Gershwin, is a satire on United States politics and centers on the presidential candidate John P. Wintergreen, whose party leaders decide that he must have a romance with "the most beautiful girl in America." Instead, he marries a campaign worker. The title alludes to the two women, and is the third line of Samuel F. Smith's patriotic hymn *America* (1831).

848   Of Time and the River   (Thomas Wolfe, 1935)
The American writer's semiautobiographical novel was originally titled *The October Fair*. Wolfe was persuaded by his editor to prune the vast manuscript down and divide it into two works, the first titled as now, the second **The Web and the Rock**. Critic Carl Van Doren has expressed the view that Wolfe's four novels are really only one: "A tumultuous series of scenes [...] haunted by the perpetual image of time as an infinite river in which men lead their short and trifling lives."

849   Oh! Calcutta!   (Kenneth Tynan, 1968)

The British writer and theatre critic's sexually explicit stage revue, premiered in the year that censorship in the London theater was abolished, has a bizarre title that Tynan explained in a private letter of June 28, 1966 to the impresario William Donaldson, the second section of which ran as follows:

> 2. Title. I made a long list of possibilities, including such outside chances as THE CONSENTING ADULTS SHOW, LET ME COUNT THE WAYS, HOW COME, etc. etc; but I've since found a beauty. I showed you a painting by the ancient French surrealist Clovis Trouille of a reclining girl displaying her bottom, with the caption: "Oh Calcutta!" While in Paris, I discovered that this is a pun— "Quel cul t'as!," meaning "What an arse you have!" I therefore suggest calling the show Oh Calcutta!, subtitled "An International Erotic Revue," and using the Trouille painting as a poster. Those who get the joke will get it, and those who don't will be intrigued. Anyway, it's unforgettable. [Kathleen Tynan, ed., *Kenneth Tynan: Letters*, 1994]

850   Oil for the Lamps of China   (Alice Tisdale Hobart, 1933)

The American writer's novel is an exposé of American oil companies and the way they sent clever young men to the Far East, only to drop them when they were expended. The title quotes an old expression used when winning anything or receiving a windfall. It is thus akin to "corn in Egypt," or "little fishes are sweet."

851   The Old Maid   (Edith Wharton, 1924)

The American writer's novelette tells the story of Tina, illegitimate daughter of Charlotte Lovell. Tina is brought up by Charlotte's cousin, Delia, without being told who her mother is. As she grows up, Tina gives all her affection to Delia and comes to regard "Aunt Chatty" as a typical middle-aged spinster or old maid. Hence the title.

852   The Old Man and the Sea   (Ernest Hemingway, 1952)

The "old man" of the American writer's title is the Cuban fisherman who is the novel's central character and who in his fight with a large fish represents the human race in its inevitable losing battle for existence. The title echoes the "Old Man of the Sea" who was a burden to Sinbad the Sailor in the *Arabian Nights* stories.

853   Old Mortality   (Walter Scott, 1816)

The title of the novel is the nickname of a historical person, one Robert Patterson, who wandered about Scotland in the late 18th century cleaning and repairing the graves of the Cameronians, or strict Covenanters, a Presbyterian sect. The novel itself is supposed to be based on the stories told by this supporter of their cause.

854   Old Possum's Book of Practical Cats   (T. S. Eliot, 1939)

"Old Possum" was the Anglo-American writer's nickname, first given him by Ezra Pound, who (tongue in cheek) said that he chose it because possums like to play dead while they are still alive. The children's verses tell of various cats, which are "practical" in that they are smart and purposeful (like the Gumbie Cat who teaches the mice music, or Mungojerrie and Rumpelteazer, who are "highly efficient cat-burglars").

855   The Old Wives' Tale   (Arnold Bennett, 1908)

The British writer's novel tells the stories of two sisters, lively Sophie and steady Constance, from their youth to the time when they are "old maids," neither having achieved anything of value outside their own lives. Bennett adopted the identical title of George Peele's play of 1595.

856   The Oldest Confession   (Richard Condon, 1958)

The American author's first novel, centering on an art theft, has a title that puns on the phrase "the oldest profession" (for prostitution).

857   Olivia   (Olivia [Dorothy Bussy], 1949)

The British writer's autobiographical novel, told in the first person, portrays the rapture, pain, and terror experienced by the 16-year-old Olivia when she falls in love for the first time (with Mlle. Julie, one of the two principals of her school). The author published the book under the pseudonym of her central character, which itself she may have chosen for its evocation of the spoken words "I love you."

858   Ommateum   (A. R. Ammons, 1955)

The American poet's first small collection of verse takes its title from the scientific term for an insect's compound or faceted eye. The word itself represents a Latin form of Greek *omma*, genitive *ommatos*, "eye."

859   Omoo   (Herman Melville, 1847)

The American writer's book, subtitled *A Narrative of Adventures in the South Seas*, is a fictional account of the author's experiences in the Society Islands in 1842. According to Melville, his title is the Marquesan word for "wanderer." The novel was a sequel to *Typee*.

860   On a Darkling Plain   (Wallace Stegner, 1940)

The American writer's third novel tells how a young veteran of World War I decides to live an isolated existence in Western Canada when he feels the need to detach himself from a human world that has betrayed him. The title quotes from Matthew Arnold's poem *Dover Beach* (1867):

> And here we are on a darkling plain
> Swept with confused alarms of struggle and flight,
> Where ignorant armies clash by night.

861   On the Road   (Jack Kerouac, 1957)

The American writer's semiautobiographical novel, a famous statement of the Beat movement, tells of the four road trips across America made by the young writer, Sal Paradise, and his friends as they search for new and exciting experiences. The title echoes Jack London's *The Road* (1907), an account of his hoboing experiences.

862 The Once and Future King (T. H. White, 1958)
The British writer's novel, in four sections, is based on the story of King Arthur and his knights. Its title is taken from one of the prime sources of the English version of the stories, Sir Thomas Malory's *Le Morte Darthur* (1469):

> And many men say that there is written on his tomb this verse: *Hic iacet Arthurus, rex quondam, rexque futurus* ("Here lies Arthur, once a king and a future king"). [Book 21, Chapter 7]

The individual titles of the four parts, all but the fourth published separately, are: **The Sword in the Stone**, *The Witch in the Wood* (1939) (later retitled *The Queen of Air and Darkness*), *The Ill-Made Knight* (1940), and *The Candle in the Wind* (added when the present book was published). A fifth part, *The Book of Merlyn* (1977), was published posthumously.

863 Once Upon a Time (John Barth, 1994)
The American author's novel, subtitled *A Floating Opera*, is both fictional and factual, in that on the one hand it enacts the myth of the eternal return, involving a quest and a perilous journey, from mysterious birth and initiation to a return through death and transfiguration, while on the other it is the author's personal story, at the same time intimating, by way of the title, that the true story is also a fairy tale. Barth gives this "true fiction" a musical context by returning to his first published creation, alluded to in the subtitle, **The Floating Opera**. This new "opera" floats on a sea of memory and desire, tracing its ultimate quest, and is arranged in the form of an "overture" and three acts, with two "entr'actes" between the acts.

864 One Fine Day (Mollie Panter-Downes, 1947)
The British writer's novel has been described as "almost a hymn of praise" to "the ordinary Englishwoman who did not fight in the war but lived through it as acutely as any soldier." As the title suggests, the action takes place within 24 hours, "one fine day" in one of the first summers of peace following World War II. The phrase is familiar as a near-cliché for the start of a story. But perhaps the title was suggested more romantically by Butterfly's aria *Un bel dì* (more familiar to English speakers as "One fine day") in Puccini's opera *Madama Butterfly* (1904).

865 One Flew Over the Cuckoo's Nest (Ken Kesey, 1962)
The American writer's first novel is set in a psychiatric ward, with one of the inmates, Chief Bromden, of Indian descent, as narrator. The ward is dominated by the sadistic Big Nurse. An eccentric Irishman, McMurphy, has himself transferred there from a prison and strives to gain control from Big Nurse. For assaulting Big Nurse, however, he is given shock treatment and eventually lobotomized. The Chief then smothers McMurphy as an act of mercy and escapes to the outside world. The mental hospital itself is thus the "cuckoo's nest" of the title, punning on *cuckoo* in its sense of "crazy," "eccentric." The title itself comes from the traditional nursery rhyme "Hinty Minty":

> One flew east, one flew west,
> One flew over the cuckoo's nest.

866   One Hundred Years of Solitude   (Gabriel García Márquez, 1967)

The Colombian writer's famous novel, the most widely read and admired Latin American novel of its time, tells the story of the small town of Macondo, from its foundation by the genius and madman José Arcadio Buendía, through expansion, revolutions, modernization, and final decay. The title refers to the burden of solitude borne by the successive generations of the Buendía family over the lengthy period covered by the novel. It first appeared in an English translation in 1970. (The original Spanish title was *Cien años de soledad*.)

867   Only When I Larf   (Len Deighton, 1968)

The British author's sixth novel, a departure from his usual spy fiction, was a comedy thriller about three English gangsters. The title, with its Cockney spelling, is a shortening of the phrase familiar from many jokes and cartoons, "It hurts only when I laugh." The American edition of the novel had the conventional spelling: *Only When I Laugh* (1987).

868   Oranges Are Not the Only Fruit   (Jeanette Winterson, 1985)

The British author's first novel is an autobiographical account of the sexual and religious experiences of her youth. Its title purports to be a quotation from Nell Gwynn, the orange-seller turned actress who was the mistress of Charles II. Oranges feature both literally and figuratively throughout the novel, with the implication that although the fruit is popularly regarded as "good for you," there is a more exotic or "forbidden" fruit that may be had. The negative statement is at first evoked positively in the book:

> My mother came to see me quite a lot. [...] When she couldn't come herself she sent my father, usually with a letter and a couple of oranges. "The only fruit," she always said. Fruit salad, fruit pie, fruit for fools, fruited punch. Demon fruit, passion fruit, rotten fruit, fruit on Sunday. Oranges are the only fruit.

869   The Orphan Angel   (Elinor Wylie, 1926)

The title of the American writer's book refers to the subject of the novel, the poet Shelley, whom she imagines not to have drowned, but to have been picked up by a passing ship and carried to America. (The sense is metaphorical, since Shelley was not literally an orphan.) The book was published the following year in Britain with the title *Mortal Image*.

870   Other Men's Flowers   (Earl Wavell, 1944)

The anthology of literary excerpts compiled by the British army commander takes its title from a phrase in Book III of Montaigne's *Essais* (1588):

> And one might therefore say of me that in this book I have only made up a bunch of other people's flowers, and that of my own I have only provided the string that ties them together.

The word "flowers" in the title also alludes to the literal sense of *anthology*, which is "flower-gathering." (In ancient Greece, *Anthologiai* were collections of short Greek poems, arranged by a single editor into a "nosegay.")

871   The Other Side   (Mary Gordon, 1989)

The American author's fourth novel is an Irish family saga, and centers on a single day in 1985 when elderly Vincent MacNamara reurns to his dying wife, Ellen. The narrative recounts their lives, together with the lives of their descendants. They reject their native Ireland, since America is no longer "the other side" but home. Hence the title, which further hints at the way "the other side" of each family member's story comes into focus.

872   Other Voices, Other Rooms   (Truman Capote, 1948)

The novel by the American writer concerns the quest for identity of Joel Knox, its 13-year-old central character, as he grows up on a Louisiana plantation. The narrative concerns not only the house where he lives but, beyond, the Cloud Hotel, the mysterious retreat of a crazy black American, Little Sunshine. The title is extracted from the story itself:

> It was a terrible, strange-looking hotel. But Little Sunshine stayed on: it was his rightful home, he said, for if he went away, as he had once upon a time, other voices, other rooms, voices lost and clouded, strummed his dreams.   [Chapter 5]

873   Our Country's Good   (Timberlake Wertenbaker, 1988)

The play by the Anglo-French-American dramatist is about a staging by Australian convicts of Farquhar's comedy *The Recruiting Officer* (1706) in the 1780s. It takes its title from George Barrington's prologue for the opening of the Sydney Play House in 1796 (when the actors were mainly convicts). His words come in Wertenbaker's play itself and include the lines:

> True patriots we; for be it understood,
> We left our country for our country's good [...]
> And none will doubt but that our emigration
> Has proved most useful to the British nation.

The first play to be staged at the Play House was actually Edward Young's tragedy *The Revenge* (1721).

874   Our Father   (Marilyn French, 1993)

The American feminist writer's fifth novel tells the story of four different sisters who hate one another when at their wealthy father's deathbed. On discovering that he had raped them all as children, however, they begin to bond, and are finally the best of friends and plan to set up home together. The title is taken from the opening words of the Lord's Prayer, and is appropriate for a father who has died and is "in heaven."

875   Our Gang   (Philip Roth, 1971)

The American writer's satire on the excesses of the Richard Nixon administration takes its title from "Our Gang," the name adopted by a group of child film actors in slapstick comedies from the 1920s.

876   Our Mutual Friend   (Charles Dickens, 1864–5)

The title refers to the novel's hero, John Harmon, who feigns death and whose identity is one of the mysteries of the many-stranded plot. The phrase was already in use when Dickens wrote the book, and for him is an exception to his many titles named for central characters. Some have objected that the phrase (and therefore the title) is a solecism, since it is impossible to share a friendship between two people (which is mutual) with a third party. The term "our common friend" might thus be more accurate.

877   Our Town   (Thornton Wilder, 1938)
The play by the American writer recounts the intimate history over the period 1901–13 of the inhabitants of a typical American town, Grover's Corners, New Hampshire.

878   Outside Over There   (Maurice Sendak, 1981)
The children's picture book by the American writer and illustrator tells how a baby is stolen by goblins, who substitute a changeling made of ice. The baby's sister, Ida, makes a journey to "outside over there" to fetch her back, but has problems identifying her among the babylike goblins.

879   The Owl Service   (Alan Garner, 1967)
The British writer's fifth novel for children, set in Wales, tells the story of three teenagers whose lives are influenced by a story from the Mabinogion, in which a woman made of flowers is turned into an owl as a punishment for causing the death of her husband. The legend comes alive when owl-like patterns on an old dinner service (the "owl service" of the title) vanish from the plates and seem to be turning into real owls. At the same time, the three find themselves re-enacting the original tragedy.

880   The Ox-Bow Incident   (Walter Van Tilburg Clark, 1940)
The story by the American writer, set in Nevada in 1885, tells how three supposed cattle rustlers are tracked down by a river with an ox-bow (a horseshoe-shaped bend). They are hanged just as word arrives that they were innocent.

881   The Painted Bird   (Jerzy Kosinski, 1965)
The Polish-born American author's first novel recounts his childhood experiences as a Jew in Poland during World War II. It takes its title from the practice of painting a bird and releasing it back into the wild. When the bird tries to rejoin its flock, it is torn to pieces for being different. As a young boy, Kosinski experienced many horrors in Nazi-occupied Poland. Ultimately, however, he was not like the painted bird, for he survived the depredations of his flock and lived to tell the tale.

882   Paddy Clarke Ha Ha Ha   (Roddy Doyle, 1993)
The Irish writer's prizewinning evocation of a childhood in Ireland is set in 1968 in a fictional suburb of Dublin and seen entirely throught the eyes of 10-year-old Paddy Clarke. He witnesses his parents' marriage disintegrate, so that his father moves out, though he cannot understand why this should be, since "She was lovely. He was nice." The title quotes from the chant with which members of the gang to which he belongs taunt him after he has had a fight with one of them:

Paddy Clarke—
Has no da.
Ha ha ha!

883 Painted Veils (James Huneker, 1920)

The American writer's novel is set against a background of the art world of New York. The title alludes to the artistic veneer that conceals the uninhibited lifestyles and lax morals of the characters.

884 The Painter of Signs (R. K. Narayan, 1976)

The title of the Indian writer's novel refers to its central character, Raman, who paints the sort of sign one sees in front of houses, offices, shops, and factories. Raman falls in love with Daisy, a modern young woman who is quite unsuited to him and who lays down various conditions that he must observe before she will marry him. The narrative contrasts the art that Raman must employ in his sign-painting with his preoccupation with Daisy's physical form. He does not see the "signs" that the various ups and downs of the relationship symbolize, and that Narayan parallels with the myths and legends of India. In the end, modernity triumphs over tradition, and Raman is left unmarried.

885 A Pair of Blue Eyes (Thomas Hardy, 1873)

The attribute of the title is that of the novel's central character, Elfride Swancourt, a vicar's daughter, who elopes with one lover, is betrothed to another, and marries a third. She finally dies, her charms having proved a fatal lure and ultimately an ill omen.

886 Pale Fire (Vladimir Nabokov, 1962)

The Russian-born American writer's novel, a parody of literary scholarship, contains an unfinished 999-line poem by the fictional John Shade, together with an inept commentary and index by the dead poet's neighbor, Charles Kinbote (who turns out to be the last king of Zembla, deposed in a revolution). The title is that of the poem itself, quoted in a passage where the poet names earlier works:

> (But this transparent thingum does require
> Some moondrop title. Help me, Will! *Pale Fire*.)   [961–2]

Kinbote's comment on the final five words is as follows: "Paraphrased, this evidently means: Let me look in Shakespeare for something I might use for a title. And the find is 'pale fire'. But in which of the Bard's works did our poet cull it? My readers must make their own research. All I have with me is a tiny vest pocket edition of *Timon of Athens*—in Zemblan! It certainly contains nothing that could be regarded as an equivalent of 'pale fire' (if it had, my luck would have been a statistical monster)." It actually is from *Timon of Athens*:

> The sun's a thief, and with his great attraction
> Robs the vast sea; the moon's an arrant thief,
> And her pale fire she snatches from the sun.   [IV.iii.442]

Moondrop itself, translating Latin *virus lunare*, is a vaporous foam that was formerly believed to be shed by the moon, when influenced by incantations, on certain herbs and objects. Shakespeare refers to it explicitly in another play, *Macbeth*, which may have been part of Nabokov's leg-pull:

> Upon the corner of the moon
> There hangs a vaporous drop profound;
> I'll catch it ere it come to ground.   [III.v.24]

887   Pale Horse, Pale Rider   (Katherine Anne Porter, 1939)

The American writer's collection of short stories is named for its title story, which tells of a doomed romance that ends when the young man dies during the influenza epidemic of 1919. (Porter wrote it after her own near fatal bout of influenza.) The title is biblical: "And I looked, and behold a pale horse: and his name that sat on him was Death" (Revelation 6:8).

888   Panic   (Archibald MacLeish, 1935)

The American writer's verse play evokes the financial crash of the Great Depression and describes the way panic transforms crashes into inevitable catastrophes.

889   Parade's End   (Ford Madox Ford, 1928)

The three volumes of the British writer's novel, sometimes referred to as *The Tietjens Trilogy*, was first published in the United States in one volume under the title above. Like E.M. Forster, Ford was preoccupied with the idea of the connected society, and his title deliberately echoes that of Forster's *Howards End* (1910). In that novel, the title was the name of a country house. In Ford's, the "parade" is the passing panorama of society, and the transmutation of the old, caring world into the new, mechanistic one. The "end" of the parade came when the peace of the opening years of the 20th century gave way to World War I.

890   A Passage to India   (E. M. Forster, 1924)

The British writer's novel is concerned with the barriers to mutual understanding between individuals and races as demonstrated in the reactions of the Indian and British communities in a small township to an Englishwoman's accusation of sexual assault against an Indian, Dr. Aziz. The novelist took the title from Walt Whitman's poem *Passage to India* (1868), itself inspired by the opening of the Suez Canal, which Whitman felt meant union with India, where civilization was perhaps born:

> Passage to India!
> Lo, soul, seest thou not God's purpose from the first?
> The earth to be spanned, connected by network.

The "passage" of Forster's title is generally held to refer to the one he himself made in 1921 when his second visit to India inspired him to revise and rework the notes made on his first visit in 1910, and so to produce his this novel. At the same time, the visit undertaken by three of the novel's characters to the mysterious Marabar Caves in India can also be regarded as a "passage." The trip ends in failure and thus symbolizes a mutual lack of understanding between the English and the Indians.

891   The Passing of the Third Floor Back   (Jerome K. Jerome, 1907)

The British writer's story, later his best-known play, concerns a mysterious, Christlike stranger who stays in a London lodging-house and works miracles for the benefit of fellow lodgers. The title refers to the part of the lodging-house where he "passed," at the rear of the third floor (which in the United States would be the fourth floor).

892 The Passion (Jeanette Winterson, 1987)

The British writer's third novel has as its central characters Henri, a young French peasant who is chicken chef to Napoleon, and Villanelle, a Venetian girl born with webbed feet. As the title implies, it is a novel about passion: its power, its grandeur, and also its obsessiveness and its ability to delude.

893 Paterson (William Carlos Williams, 1946–58)

The American writer's long poem, divided into five books, with an incomplete Book Six published posthumously in 1963 as an appendix, tells of the present and past of the city of Paterson, New Jersey, near the poet's hometown of Rutherford. The title name is also that of a character in the poem, a doctor, who combines details of the poet's private life with the public history of the region.

894 A Patriot for Me (John Osborne, 1966)

The British writer's play, both a spy story and a study of decadence in the Austro-Hungarian Empire in the early 20th century, takes its title from a comment by Emperor Francis II of Austria when told that a particular officer of his empire was a sterling patriot: "But is he a patriot for me?"

895 The Patriot's Progress (Henry Williamson, 1930)

The British writer's novel, subtitled "Being the Vicissitudes of Pte. John Bullock," describes the experiences in World War I of a London clerk, an English patriot who stands for all English patriots in that war. He undergoes deprivation and loses a leg, and eventually comes home after the war to confront an armchair patriot during the Armistice celebrations. "We'll see that England doesn't forget you fellows," says the latter, to which Bullock replies, "We are England." The title intentionally alludes to Bunyan's *The Pilgrim's Progress* (1678, 1684), and Bullock, like Christian, sets off with a burden on his back, although in his case it is his 70-pound pack of equipment. Unlike Christian, however, he does not reach the Celestial City, but returns to the City of London and his job as a clerk.

896 The Pearl (John Steinbeck, 1947)

The American writer's novelette, based on a true incident, tells how the father of a child stung by a scorpion seeks a pearl to pay the doctor who treats him. He finds a large one, but his neighbors plot to steal it and tragedy follows. When Steinbeck was writing the story his working title for it was *The Pearl of La Paz*, as the setting for the action is in and around this city. The title could also be considered symbolically (and ironically) if translated literally from the Spanish to mean "The Pearl of Peace." When the novel was first published, however, in the magazine *Woman's Home Companion*, the title chosen was *The Pearl of the World*. Steinbeck subsequently shortened this, apparently unconcerned that the two brief words would not evoke the allegory that the longer title implied. Some critics have also suggested parallels between Steinbeck's story and the anonymous 14th-century poem *Pearl*, about the grief of a father who has lost his daughter.

897   Pearl of Orr's Island   (Harriet Beecher Stowe, 1862)
The American writer's novel is set on the island of the title, a fishing community on the Maine coast. The central character is the orphan Mara Lincoln, who is reared there by her grandparents. They consider her a "pearl of great price." Hence the first word of the title.

898   Penrod   (Booth Tarkington, 1914)
The title of the American writer's novel is the first name of its central character, the 12-year-old American boy Penrod Schofield, "The Worst Boy in Town." Cf. Seventeen, the same author's later novel about an older boy.

899   Pentimento   (Lillian Hellman, 1973)
The American playwright's impressionistic memoirs of people that she knew takes its title from the artistic term for the revealing of a painting beneath another painted over it at a later date. The word *pentimento* itself is Italian for "repentance."

900   The People, Yes   (Carl Sandburg, 1936)
The American writer's poem affirms his faith in the American people and in democracy. Hence its affirmative title.

901   The Petrified Forest   (Robert E. Sherwood, 1935)
The play by the American playwright brings together representatives of a decadent civilization in a gasoline station in the Arizona desert. One of them is Alan Squier, an unsuccessful New England author. Another is Duke Mantee, leader of a gang of hunted criminals. The title relates to Squier's description of Mantee as "the last great apostle of individualism" in the "Petrified Forest [...] of outmoded ideas."

902   The Phoenix and the Carpet   (E. Nesbit, 1904)
The British writer's second fantasy novel for children, the sequel to The Five Children and It, tells how the children acquire a nursery carpet in which is wrapped a mysterious egg. When the egg falls into the fire, the Phoenix hatches out of it. He tells the children he can take them wherever they wish by flying on the carpet.

903   The Piano Lesson   (August Wilson, 1987)
The play by the black American playwright concerns the conflict between a brother and sister over an inherited piano. The brother wants to sell the piano and buy the land on which their forebears were slaves. The sister wants to keep it for the family history carved on it. Which is the right "lesson"? The play (and its title) was inspired by a painting of Romare Bearden called *The Piano Lesson*.

904   Picture Palace   (Paul Theroux, 1978)
The American writer's ninth novel is cast as the autobiography of Maude Pratt, a pioneer photographer, famous for her uncompromising portraits. The title overtly refers to this but also to the memories ("the picture palace of my mind") evoked when she unearths some old prints.

905   Pictures from an Institution   (Randall Jarrell, 1954)

The only adult novel by the American children's writer is a campus comedy, describing events and incidents in a progressive women's college in the 1950s. The title alludes to that of Mussorgsky's piano suite *Pictures from an Exhibition* (1874).

906   Picturing Will   (Ann Beattie, 1990)

The American writer's fourth novel, with its punning title, has as its theme the responsibilities incurred by human *will* when balancing career and parenthood, the latter here involving a boy named *Will*.

907   The Pilgrim Hawk   (Glenway Westcott, 1940)

The American writer's third novel is set on a single afternoon in the 1920s in a house and garden in France, when a number of people meet up and share their reminiscences and relationships. One couple, the Cullens, bring a pilgrim hawk, which is mostly hooded and quiet by contrast with its owners, who are eccentric and prey on each other and the world. Cullen gets drunk and tries to free the hawk, which is recaptured. The bird is thus a symbol of the paradox of love: freedom from love is dependence, but captivity in love is liberty.

908   Pincher Martin   (William Golding, 1956)

The title of the British writer's third novel is the name (and nickname) of its central figure, a drowning sailor. In the British armed forces and elsewhere, "Pincher" has been a nickname for anyone surnamed Martin since the mid-19th century, when Admiral Sir William F. Martin was notorious for "pinching" (arresting) sailors for even trivial offences. In the United States, the novel was published as *The Two Deaths of Christopher Martin*. It is possible the choice of title was influenced by that of *Pincher Martin, O.D.* (1915), an early volume of stories and sketches of life in the Royal Navy by the naval officer and writer "Taffrail" (Captain Henry Taprell Dorling) (1883–1968). Golding himself served in the Royal Navy in World War II.

909   Pioneers! O Pioneers!   (Walt Whitman, 1865)

The American poet's work is in 26 quatrains, each ending with the refrain that gives the title. The poem is a celebration of the men and women who were America's earliest explorers and settlers and whose frontier spirit manifested itself in optimism for the future and a revolt against their European past.

910   The Pit and the Pendulum   (Edgar Allan Poe, 1845)

The American writer's story centers on a prisoner of the Spanish Inquisition in Toledo, who describes his terrible tortures. He is confined in a cell between two fearful fates: above, a pendulum with a sharp blade that slowly descends as it swings; below, a deep pit. He is freed at the last moment from this double horror, and from the closing heated metal walls of his cell, when the city is captured by the French.

911   A Place Without Twilight   (Peter S. Feibleman, 1958)

The American writer's first novel, set in New Orleans, has as its central character a "twilight" girl, not quite black yet not quite white, and deals with her search for self-realization. The novel was dramatized as *Tiger Tiger Burning Bright* (1963), a title taken from the well-known opening words of William Blake's poem.

912 Places Where They Sing (Simon Raven, 1970)
The British writer's sixth novel in the ten-volume sequence entitled **Alms for Oblivion** concerns student revolt in Cambridge in 1967. A university college cannot agree how to spend the proceeds of a land sale amounting to £250,000. In the heat of debate, the students revolt and, in a spectacular protest, march into the college chapel during an annual celebratory service. The title at one level obviously refers to the chapel choir, since the choir school has a claim to some of the money. But perhaps "sing" is here intended to imply "singing out," or making one's feelings known in vociferous fashion. The title actually quotes a prayerbook rubric: "In Quires and Places where they sing, here followeth the Anthem."

913 Plagued by the Nightingale (Kay Boyle, 1930)
The American author's first novel tells the story of a young American woman encountering the tired and corrupt Old World for the first time. She meets and marries a Frenchman, who is suffering from a hereditary bone disease, but becomes embroiled with other members of his family, one of whom asks her to go away with him to Indo-China. She remains faithful to her husband, however, partly in order to have a child, and partly to rescue him from his family, whom he hates because of its association with his illness. The nightingale of the title is a caged pet. It is silent because it is caged, and "plagues" because of its silence, symbolizing a family that is gradually stifling itself.

914 Play It Again Sam (Woody Allen, 1969)
The play by the American writer and actor concerns a film critic who is abandoned by his wife and obtains the aid of Humphrey Bogart's "shade." The title is the famous request supposedly made by Bogart in the film *Casablanca* (1942). However, what he actually says is: "If she can stand it, I can. Play it!" (But earlier Ingrid Bergman says: "Play it, Sam. Play *As Time Goes By*." See **You Must Remember This**.)

915 The Playboy of the Western World (J. M. Synge, 1907)
The "playboy" of the Irish dramatist's title is its central character, Christy Mahon, a weakling who comes to be regarded as a hero because he believes he has killed his tyrannical father. Mahon is loved by Pegeen Mike, who tells him: "You're the walking playboy of the western world" (Act II, line 51). The name of Ireland itself is popularly regarded as meaning "western land."

916 The Plough and the Stars (Sean O'Casey, 1926)
The play by the Irish writer is an antiheroic account of the Easter Rising of 1916 in Dublin, set in that city's slums. The title refers to the banner of the Irish Citizen Army, to which O'Casey had at one time belonged.

917 The Plumed Serpent (D. H. Lawrence, 1926)
The British writer's novel is set in Mexico, and tells how its central character, Don Ramón Carrasco, has the task of disposing of Christianity and reviving the old gods

of Mexico, himself representing Quetzalcoatl, the god of the Aztecs whose name translates as "plumed serpent."

918   Plus   (Joseph Prince, 1977)
The American writer's fifth novel is an abstract science fiction work with a title intended to negate its negators. It directly refers to the novel's central character, distilled from a disembodied human brain and called IMP PLUS, where IMP stands for "Interplanetary Monitoring Platform."

919   Point Counter Point   (Aldous Huxley, 1928)
The British writer's long and involved novel is a satire on London intellectuals and members of English upper-class society during the 1920s. It is also a novel within a novel, and one of the main characters, Philip Quarles, is himself planning a novel that echoes or "counterpoints" the events going on around him. The construction of the main novel is said to be based on Bach's *Suite No. 2 in B Minor*, which itself involves counterpoint (the simultaneous sounding of two or more melodies). The fact that the title has "counterpoint" in two words, not one, suggests that it may have been intended to echo (even counterpoint) a phrase from Shakespeare's *Macbeth*:

> Bellona's bridegroom, lapped in proof,
> Confronted him with self-comparisons,
> Point against point, rebellious arm 'gainst arm,
> Curbing his lavish spirit. [I.ii.55]

920   The Polyglots   (William Gerhardie, 1925)
The Russian-born author, who settled in England, was himself a polyglot, and his second novel is a parody of the linguistic limitations that can lead to human confusion. The story is narrated by Georges Hamlet Alexander Diabologh, born in Japan of English parents but raised in Russia, and tells of the consequences of his infatuation with the name and person of his Belgian cousin, Sylvia Ninon Thérèse Anastathia Vanderflint.

921   Pomes Penyeach   (James Joyce, 1927)
The Irish writer's second book of poems was priced at one shilling and contained 13 pieces. Hence its title, with the twelve pennies actually buying a baker's dozen rather than a round dozen.

922   Poor Cow   (Nell Dunn, 1967)
The British writer's first novel centers on a young woman, ironically named Joy, who becomes a "poor cow" through the constant erosion of her life. At the end of the novel she clings to her son, Jonny, and comments on her youth:

> "To think that when I was a kid I planned to conquer the world and if anyone saw me now they'd say, 'She's had a rough night, poor cow.'"

923   The Poor Little Rich Girl   (Eleanor Gates, 1912)
The American writer's novel for children tells the story of a seven-year-old girl, the daughter of a rich society family, who lives a lonely life away from her parents. She

is thus "poor" or to be pitied, as well as literally rich. The title (which may not have been original) caught on to be used as a nickname for any rich woman who suffers misfortune, such as Barbara Hutton (1912–1979), the Woolworth heiress. The title was also that of a popular song of 1924 by Noël Coward. Gates's book was made into a Broadway play in 1916 and a film in 1917, further popularizing the phrase.

924   Porgy   (DuBose Heyward, 1925)
The title of the American writer's novel is the name of its central character, the crippled beggar Porgy. He lives in a black tenement section of the Charleston waterfront, known as Catfish Row, and his name (that of various kinds of sea fish) matches this maritime location. Captain Porgy was a character in various novels by the Charleston author William Gilmore Simms (1806–1870), and no doubt Heyward adopted his name for his own hero. The name was popularized by Gershwin's opera based on the novel, *Porgy and Bess* (1935).

925   Porterhouse Blue   (Tom Sharpe, 1973)
The British writer's third novel, a satire on Cambridge university life, has a title that works on several levels. One of the characters in the story is the priggish college *porter* (caretaker), Skullion, while "blue" refers both to the university sporting award and to the "blue" central episode of the story in which the court is filled with thousands of inflated condoms. At the same time, "Porterhouse" suggests the name of a real Cambridge college, *Peterhouse*, while the name as a whole also hints at "porterhouse steak." Sharpe himself was a Cambridge student, although at Pembroke College, not Peterhouse.

926   Portnoy's Complaint   (Philip Roth, 1969)
The American writer's third novel tells the life story of its central character, Alex Portnoy, as he relates it to his psychiatrist. His main "complaint" is against his domineering Jewish mother, who refuses to let him live his own life. At a secondary (or more physical) level, his complaint is his compulsive masturbation, which results from this repression.

927   A Portrait of the Artist as a Young Dog   (Dylan Thomas, 1940)
The Welsh writer's collection of autobiographical short stories has a title that was probably based on James Joyce's own autobiographical account, *Portrait of the Artist as a Young Man* (1914–15). This in turn adopted a formula familiar from genuine self-portraits, such as Van Gogh's *Portrait of the Artist with Severed Ear*.

928   Possessing the Secret of Joy   (Alice Walker, 1992)
The American writer's novel tells of the decision of a young African woman, Tashi, to undergo the tribal initiation ceremony of female circumcision. The title quotes words from a book by "a colonial author" that she reads: "Black people are natural, they possess the secret of joy."

929   A Postillion Struck by Lightning   (Dirk Bogarde, 1977)
The British movie actor took the title of his first volume of autobiography from an unidentified early foreign language phrasebook, as he explains in the third volume, *An Orderly Man* (1983):

My sister-in-law Cilla, on a wet camping holiday somewhere in northern France [...] once sent me a postcard on which she said [...] she had been forced to learn a little more French than the phrase "Help! My postillion has been struck by lightning!" I took the old phrase for the title of my book.

930   The Power and the Glory   (Graham Greene, 1940)

The British writer's novel concerns a lapsed priest, guilty of drunkenness and lechery, who is pursued across a state in Mexico, in which the Church is outlawed, by a non-religious, humanist police lieutenant. The title comes from the final words of the Lord's Prayer, "For thine is the kingdom, the power, and the glory," these being the attributes of God. At first sight the title appears to be ironic, but at the end of the novel, when the priest is executed with Christlike implications, it can be taken to mean what it says, and to refer to the triumphant survival of the Church in the face of religious intolerance.

931   The Power of the Dog   (Thomas Savage, 1967)

The American writer's novel, about two brothers and closet homosexuality, takes its title from the Bible: "Deliver my soul from the sword; my darling from the power of the dog" (Psalm 22:20).

932   PrairyErth (a deep map)   (William Least Heat–Moon, 1992)

The American writer's lengthy and idiosyncratic book is a close examination of a single region: Chase County, Kansas. By a "deep map" he seems to mean both an "in depth" or detailed one and a comprehensive geographical study that extends downwards from the sky and the clouds to the soil and the rock, taking in the hills and pastures and farmhouses on the way.

933   Prancing Nigger   (Ronald Firbank, 1924)

The British writer's penultimate novel was originally published (at his own expense) in the United States under the above title. (It was issued in Britain as *Sorrow in Sunlight*, Firbank's preferred but eventually discarded title.) As with his earlier novels, the story is of the destruction of "innocents abroad." It was the culmination of the author's negrophilia and is set on the fictional West Indian island of Tacarigua. The plot centers on Ahmadou Mouth, who is tired of living in the provinces and wants to move to the city of Cuna-Cuna. She persuades her pious husband (the "prancing nigger" of the title) to do so, and the whole family makes the move, with colorful consequences.

934   Praxis   (Fay Weldon, 1978)

The British writer's sixth novel has the inequality of the sexes as its theme. Its central character is Praxis Duveen, self-confessed "bastard, adulteress, whore, committer of incest, murderess," who considers sex to be her main talent. She gains a place at university because her name is taken to be a man's, and there meets the slovenly and sexually unsatisfiable Willy. She leaves him, however, in favor of another man, Philip, whom she has always loved and whom she marries. This relationship also founders, and she instead devotes herself to the feminist cause. The main narrative recounts the incidents that lie behind her self-addressed epithets. Her significant forename is actually the Greek word for "deed," "action."

935 Precious Bane (Mary Webb, 1924)
The British novelist's story of harsh rustic life takes its title from Milton's *Paradise Lost* (1667):

> Let none admire
> That riches grow in hell; that soil may best
> Deserve the precious bane. [Book I, line 690]

"Bane" here has the sense "ruin," "poison." See also **Cold Comfort Farm.**

936 Present Laughter (Noël Coward, 1942)
The title of the British writer's comedy is a quotation from one of the Clown's songs in Shakespeare's *Twelfth Night*:

> What is love? 'tis not hereafter;
> Present mirth hath present laughter. [II.iii.48]

937 Prick Up Your Ears (John Lahr, 1978)
The British writer's biography of the gay British playwright Joe Orton has a title that puns on the slang sense of *prick*. In his edition of *The Orton Diaries* (1986), Lahr noted that the title was a triple pun, since "ears" is an anagram of "arse." Orton had himself considered the title earlier for a film on the Beatles, in the event one that never materialized.

938 Pride (William Wharton [pseudonym], 1985)
The American writer's fifth novel is set in the final years of the Depression, with the young narrator's father threatened by union-breakers. The family travels to the sea while the father stays behind to consider his next move. While they are there a lion escapes from a sideshow and kills a man who has tortured him. The title plays on the two senses of *pride* to compare the lion's condition with that of the father: the lion's pride (honor) has been destroyed and he must be killed; the father gathers his pride (family) and embarks on a new course of action.

939 Pride and Prejudice (Jane Austen, 1813)
The "pride" of the title is epitomized by Fitzwilliam Darcy, who courts Elizabeth Bennet. She however is prejudiced against him, not only by his arrogant manner but because of the stories she hears about him. (A handsome young officer has been unjustly treated by him.) In the end, however, pride and prejudice are reconciled, and the two marry. The title originally planned for the novel was *First Impressions*. The present title probably comes from the closing sentences of Fanny Burney's novel *Cecilia* (1787), where the phrase "Pride and Prejudice" (with upper case Ps) occurs three times, e.g., "'The whole of this unfortunate business,' said Dr. Lyster, 'has been the result of Pride and Prejudice.'"

940 The Public Burning (Robert Coover, 1977)
The American writer explained the gist of his novel (which he first conceived as a play) thus:

It is the story of June 19, 1953. On that day, the Rosenbergs are burned in Times Square and all the members of the tribe are drawn to the scene. All that has has happened that day happens there, in a way; everything is condensed into one big circus event.

The novel is actually about much more than this however, and attempts to tell the story of the whole of America on that single crucial day in its history. The novel's narrator and central character is none other than Richard M. Nixon. The title thus alludes not only to the "public burning" of the Rosenbergs (who were actually executed for treason at Sing Sing Prison), but to the moral immolation of the American people, as personified by the chicanery and hypocrisy of their vice president.

941   Puck of Pook's Hill   (Rudyard Kipling, 1906)

The British writer's book of short stories for children, based freely on English history, takes its title from the fairy, Puck, who appears in Shakespeare's *A Midsummer Night's Dream*, and who is summoned by two children, Dan and Una, from his home in "Pook's Hill" when they are acting a scene from this play. The children live in Sussex, where Kipling himself lived, and "Pook's Hill" was actually *Perch Hill*, near the author's house at Burwash. *Pook* has been popularly associated with *Puck*, although where it occurs in other Sussex placenames, such as Pooks Farm and Pook's Wood, it usually derives from the surname *Pooke*. There is a genuine *Pookhill* at the eastern end of the South Downs, however, some miles south of Burwash, where the name almost certainly means "goblin's hill," from the Old English word, *pūca*, that gave the name of Puck himself.

942   Pull Down Vanity   (Leslie A. Fiedler, 1962)

The title of the American writer's first collection of short stories announces his intention, since most of the stories involve characters whose self-importance is punctured by actions of exposure and embarrassment, in one case by being forced to play a game of croquet in the nude. The title is itself an adaptation of a line from Ezra Pound's *Cantos (LXXXI)*:

> The ant's a centaur in his dragon world.
> Pull down thy vanity, it is not man
> Made courage, or made order, or made grace,
>   Pull down thy vanity, I say pull down.

943   The Pumpkin Eater   (Penelope Mortimer, 1962)

The British writer's fifth novel concerns a woman "obsessed" with pregnancy (she is the mother of eight children), which she believes gives her power and purpose. She learns of her third husband's affairs, but is persuaded by him to have an abortion and be sterilized. The title quotes from a nursery rhyme:

> Peter, Peter, pumpkin eater,
> Had a wife and couldn't keep her,
> He put her in a pumpkin shell,
> And there he kept her very well.

A contemporary reviewer wrote:

Jake is the pumpkin eater of the title; he tries to put his wife in a pumpkin shell to keep her very well, as the old rhyme says, and it is this that precipitates the crisis. [*Punch*, October 31, 1962]

944   Put Out More Flags   (Evelyn Waugh, 1942)

According to the British author, the title of his novel about English upper-class life in the 1930s derives from a Chinese saying: "A drunk military man should order gallons and and put out more flags in order to increase his military splendor."

945   Pygmalion   (G. B. Shaw, 1913)

The Irish writer's play concerns a phonetician, Professor Higgins, who creates an elegant lady out of a Cockney flowerseller, Eliza Doolittle. In doing so, he resembles the Pygmalion of classical legend, a sculptor who made a statue of a beautiful woman that was brought to life by Aphrodite, and whom he then married. In Shaw's play, however, Eliza Doolittle does not marry her creator, although she does fall in love with him.

946   QB VII   (Leon Uris, 1970)

The American writer's novel recounts the trial of an American novelist in Queen's Bench 7 for libeling a Polish surgeon. The title is the official abbreviation of the court's designation in the Queen's Bench Division of the British High Court of Justice.

947   The Quare Fellow   (Brendan Behan, 1956)

The play by the Irish playwright, a study of life in a prison on the eve of a hanging, was originally written in Irish. Its English title is an Irish pronunciation of "The Queer Fellow," an traditional phrase referring to a person's unorthodox "alter ego." The following illustrates the sense:

When I am "making up" a story [...] I am never my normal self, the man that other people know. Nor dare my normal self return for a moment in the hope of catching the other one, The Queer Fellow, as they say in Ireland, at work. [John Brophy, *The Queer Fellow*, 1939]

948   Quartet   (Jean Rhys, 1928)

The British writer's first novel was originally published under the title *Postures*. The present title was given when it was reissued in 1969. The novel deals with the plight of a single girl who is at the mercy of a cruel world. The four characters who form the "quartet" of the title are the girl herself, chorus girl Marya, her husband, Stephan, who takes her to Paris, and the corrupt couple with whom she becomes involved in his absence, Lois Heidler and her husband "H.J.," with whom she has an affair.

949   Quartet in Autumn   (Barbara Pym, 1977)

The British writer's novel, regarded by many as her best, portrays the appoach of old age ("autumn") through the interwoven lives of four people ("quartet"), two

women and two men, about to retire from a London office. The author had originally planned to call the book *Four Point Turn*, but was dissuaded from using this
since it suggested some kind of automobile maneuver. (The poet Philip Larkin jok-
ingly suggested she might as well call it *Last Exit to Brookwood*, alluding to the famous motor-racing track.)

950   The Quincunx   (Charles Palliser, 1989)
The American-Irish writer's first novel is set in 19th-century London and tells the
story of John Huffam, a young man who may have a claim to a large estate. Five
families compete for the claim. Hence the title, as the term for a group of five objects arranged in the shape of a rectangle with one at each of the four corners and
a fifth (Huffam) in the center. (The main character, John Huffam, has Charles
Dickens's middle names.)

951   Rabbit, Run   (John Updike, 1960)
The first in a series of four novels by the American writer takes its title from the
nickname, Rabbit, of its central character, Harry Angstrom, who came to be so
called from his high school days as a basketball champion. Frustrated by his alcoholic wife, three-year-old child, and boring job, he decides to run away. The title is
thus a pun on "rabbit run" as a track made by rabbits. (There was also a popular
British song of 1939, "Run, rabbit, run.") The second novel, *Rabbit Redux* (1971),
depicts the household ten years later, after Harry's return. "Redux" means "brought
back," with the title modeled on an earlier work such as Dryden's *Astraea Redux*
(1672) or Trollope's *Phineas Redux* (1873). The third novel, another ten years on, is
Rabbit Is Rich (1981). The fourth, and presumably final, is *Rabbit at Rest* (1990).

952   Racing Demon   (David Hare, 1990)
The British dramatist's play about the Church of England takes its title from the
name of a "patience" card game played by several players, with each player having
his own pack of cards.

953   The Radiant Way   (Margaret Drabble, 1987)
The British writer's novel is set in the first half of the 1980s and tells the story of
two women, Liz Headleand and Alix Bowen, who are both "upwardly mobile" at a
time of social and political upheaval in Britain. The title alludes to the optimism
that ultimately shines through the stresses and strains of the women's personal lives.
In the novel itself, the title is also that of an acclaimed television documentary about
education that Liz Headleand's husband has made.

954   Radical Chic & Mau-Mauing the Flak Catchers   (Tom Wolfe, 1970)
The American writer's fourth book centers on the mutual relationship that developed between the white intellectual elite of New York and the Black Panthers, as
typified by the description of a fund-raising party for this militant black party at the
home of Leonard Bernstein. Race relations in California also figure. The term "radical chic" entered the language thanks to Wolfe, who applied it to the vogue among
fashionable people for socializing with radicals. As he puts it in the book: "Radical

Chic, after all, is only radical in style; in its heart it is part of Society and its tradi-
tions." *Mau-Mauing the Flak Catchers* is the accompanying piece. Its title refers to
the way in which individuals or institutions dealing with criticism ("flak") from the
public can be pressured ("mau-maued") by minority groups to grant material con-
cessions or benefits.

955   Rage to Live   (John O'Hara, 1949)
The American writer's fourth novel, set in the small Pennsylvania town of Fort
Penn (based on Harrisburg), concerns the torments of a faithless wife and ends with
the death of her husband and son from polio. The title comes from Pope's *Moral
Essays*, "Epistle II: To Mrs. M. Blount" (1735):

> You purchase pain with all that joy can give,
> And die of nothing but a rage to live.

956   The Ragged Trousered Philanthropists   (Robert Tressell [Robert
Noonan], 1918)
The posthumous novel by the British writer of Irish extraction draws on the author's experiences while working a painter and decorator. The action takes place
during one year in the lives of a group of working men, and is a bitter attack on the
greed, dishonesty, and gullibility of workers and employers alike. The ironically
named "philanthropists" of the title are the exploited workers, who for pitiful wages
"toil and sweat at their noble and unselfish task of making money" for their employers.

957   The Railway Children   (E. Nesbit, 1906)
The British writer's novel for children concerns three children who move from
London to the country and spend much of their time watching trains on the local
railroad. They enlist the help of a regular passenger, "The Old Gentleman," to treat
their sick mother, and prevent an accident when a landslip blocks the line.

958   Rain   (W. Somerset Maugham, 1921)
The British author's best known short story was originally titled *Miss Thompson*,
after the name of the prostitute, Sadie Thompson, who is one of its two main characters. In 1922 it was dramatized (not by Maugham) under its present title, which
alludes to the tropical rain that provides an appropriately steamy and sultry backdrop to the scenes of passion and spiritual torment that it describes.

959   The Rainbow   (D. H. Lawrence, 1915)
The British writer's novel chronicles the lives of the three generations of the Brangwen family. The title refers to the rainbow seen by Ursula Brangwen, of the third
generation, when convalescing after appearing to suffer a miscarriage:

> She saw in the rainbow the earth's new architecture, the old, brittle corruption of
> houses and factories swept away, the world, built up in a living fabric of Truth, fit-
> ting to the over-arching heaven.

960   Raintree County   (Ross Lockridge, 1948)
The American writer's only novel takes its title from the small fictional Indiana county in which its action is set, on July 4, 1892, Independence Day.

961   A Raisin in the Sun   (Lorraine Hansberry, 1959)
The American dramatist's play was the first by a black woman to be produced on Broadway. It is a comedy about a family of black Chicagoans who plan to move into a white neighborhood. The title quotes a line from the black writer Langston Hughes's poem *Harlem* (1951):

> What happens to a dream deferred?
> Does it dry up
> like a raisin in the sun?

962   Random Harvest   (James Hilton, 1941)
The British writer's novel, about a man suffering from amnesia, takes its title from a propaganda error in World War II when the Germans claimed to have attacked a town called "Random." Their claim was based on a British news report that "bombs were dropped at random."

963   Rates of Exchange   (Malcolm Bradbury, 1983)
The British writer's fourth novel concerns the experiences of a university lecturer in an imaginary foreign country (somewhere in Eastern Europe) with an imaginary language. The author's aim was to illustrate the plight of a writer who uses a language (English) that has been radically changed by its use as a lingua franca. The "exchanges" of the title are thus linguistic rather than economic, although foreign travel involves an exchange of currency.

964   The Razor's Edge   (W. Somerset Maugham, 1945)
The title of the British writer's novel refers to the mode of life which its central character, Larry, comes to adopt after his search for a *tao* or spiritual way. Materially, he must live on the "razor edge" between poverty and minimal subsistence in order to cultivate the life of the spirit. The direct source of the title is the Katha-Upanishad: "The sharp edge of a razor is difficult to pass over; thus the wise say the path to Salvation is hard."

965   Reader, I Married Him   (Patricia Beer, 1974)
The British writer's study of female characters in the works of four women novelists (Jane Austen, Charlotte Brontë, Elizabeth Gaskell, George Eliot), takes its title from the opening words of the final chapter of *Jane Eyre*, in which the central character finally marries the man whom she had nearly married much earlier.

966   Rebel Without a Cause   (Robert M. Lindner, 1944)
This title, famously that of the 1955 movie starring James Dean, was originally that of a work by the named American psychologist, subtitled *The Hypnoanalysis of a Criminal Psychopath*. Lindner appears to have originated the phrase himself. The movie had an adolescent troublemaker as its central character, but he was hardly a

"criminal psychopath," and the film's director, Nicholas Ray, presumably seized on the title for its suggestion of mindless revolt and its audience appeal. The screenplay credit was actually given to Stewart Stern.

967   Reckless Eyeballing   (Ishmael Reed, 1986)
The black American writer's seventh novel, on the theme of racism, takes as its title the colloquial phrase for the ogling of white women by black men. In this instance the specific reference was to one of the charges leveled at lynching victim Emmett Till.

968   The Recognitions   (William Gaddis, 1955)
The American writer's first novel has over fifty characters whose paths cross and who contrast and parallel one another. There are "recognitions" at every turn, and the novel itself is thus a "recognition" of the unity of all living and nonliving things.

969   Red, Black, Blond, and Olive   (Edmund Wilson, 1956)
The American writer's study of four civilizations has a title that alludes to each of them, respectively Zuñi, Haitian, Russian, and Israeli.

970   The Red Badge of Courage   (Stephen Crane, 1895)
The American writer's novel has the factual subtitle, *An Episode of the American Civil War*. It is a psychological study of a soldier's reactions in battle. The central character, Henry Fleming, is thrust into his first battle. At first he swaggers to keep up his spirits, but then is suddenly overcome with fear and runs from the field. He is ashamed when he joins the wounded, for unlike them, he has not earned their bloody wound, or "red badge of courage." He later redeems himself when he is genuinely wounded and seizes the regiment's colors in a gallant charge.

971   Red Cotton Night-Cap Country   (Robert Browning, 1873)
The poem in blank verse by the English poet has an ironic title referring to the description by his friend, Anne Thackeray, of a district in Normandy as "white cotton night-cap country." Browning sought to show that the "red" of passion and violence should replace the tamer, gentler "white." The subtitle of the work is *Turf and Towers*.

972   Red Shift   (Alan Garner, 1973)
The British writer's sixth novel for children is a complex story of two teenage lovers and the crisis in their relationship. Events proceed at three parallel levels at different points in time. The reader thus has a constant shift of level yet a continuous story. The title alludes to this arrangement, and represents the astronomical term for a shift in the lines of a stellar spectrum toward one end of the visible range.

973   Red Wine of Youth   (Arthur Stringer, 1946)
The Canadian-born American writer's biography of the English poet Rupert Brooke has a title quoting words from Brooke's own poem *The Dead* (1914):

These laid the world away; poured out the red
Sweet wine of youth.

974   Regeneration   (Pat Barker, 1991)

The British writer's novel is set in a Scottish military hospital during World War I,
and patients are being encouraged to recall and face the battle traumas that brought
them there, so that they can be rehabilitated. The title comes from the report of a
medical experiment carried out before the war by two doctors, William Rivers and
Henry Head, who are two of the real people that the author includes among the
characters. This read, in part: "The nerve supplying Head's forearm had been severed and sutured, and then over a period of five years they had traced the process of
regeneration." The author thus links this process with the "regeneration" of the hospital patients.

975   The Reivers   (William Faulkner, 1962)

The American writer's humorous novel concerns an 11-year old, Lucius Priest, and
his two adult companions, who are "reivers," or robbers. They steal the boy's grandfather's new motorcar and set off for Memphis.

976   The Remains of the Day   (Kazuo Ishiguro, 1989)

The novel by the Japanese-born British writer, set in England's West Country in
1956, centers on the motoring trip of an ageing butler, itself representing a journey
into his past. The title indicates an episode in the evening of a person's life, as well
as the story of a "relic" from a bygone age, of someone who has "had his day." In the
final chapter, the butler reflects that "the evening's the best part of the day":

> Perhaps [...] I should adopt a more positive outloook and try to make the best of
> what remains of my day.

977   Remembrance of Things Past   (Marcel Proust, 1913–27)

The original French title of the well-known long novel was *À la recherche du temps
perdu*. When G. K. Scott-Moncrieff started publishing the first famous English
translation of the work, in 1922, the year of Proust's death, he gave it an evocative
but not entirely accurate title taken from Shakespeare's *Sonnets*:

> When to the sessions of sweet silent thought
> I summon up remembrance of things past.   [XXX]

The title was in keeping with the florid tone of his translation, and its poetic resonance doubtless helped to sell his work. However, Proust was not writing about idle
remembrance but about arduous search (*recherche*), as he himself exemplified in the
twelve years of illness and solitude that he spent writing the novel. When a freshly
revised translation of the work was published in 1992, therefore, it was given a title
much closer to the intention of the original: *In Search of Lost Time*.

978   Restoration   (Rose Tremain, 1989)

The British writer's fifth novel is a historical one, set against the background of the
early years of the reign of Charles II, the Restoration. The title partly refers to this.

It also alludes to the re-ordering of his broken world on the part of the central character and narrator, Robert Merivel, whose career as King's Fool has collapsed.

979   The Return of the Soldier   (Rebecca West, 1918)

The British writer's first novel opens with the reflection by its narrator, Jenny: "Like most Englishwomen of my time I was waiting for the return of a soldier." The story is thus topical, and concerns the devastation of war from a woman's perspective. The title echoes similar "returns," such as Thomas Hardy's *The Return of the Native* (1878).

980   Revolt into Style   (George Melly, 1970)

The British writer and jazz musician's book on the pop arts in Britain takes its title from a line in the English poet Thom Gunn's poem *Elvis Presley* (1957): "He turns revolt into a style." Melly explains in his book:

> "He turns revolt into a style," wrote Gunn and this is what happens in pop; what starts as revolt finishes as style—as mannerism. [...] I hope to be able to establish how each pop movement in its turn has more or less conformed to this pattern.

981   Rewards and Fairies   (Rudyard Kipling, 1910)

The British writer's collection of short stories for children, a sequel to **Puck of Pook's Hill**, takes its title from the poem "The Fairies' Farewell" by Richard Corbet (1582–1635) which Kipling had first read in F. E. Paget's novel *The Hope of the Katzekopfs* (1844), where it is quoted. The words occur in the first line of the poem:

> Farewell, rewards and Fairies,
> Good housewives now may say,
> For now foul sluts in dairies
> Do fare as well as they.

982   Riceyman Steps   (Arnold Bennett, 1923)

The title of the British writer's novel is the name of the short stone-stepped passage in Clerkenwell, London, where the central character, Henry Earlforward, has an antiquarian bookshop. The street itself is named for Earlforward's uncle, T. T. Riceyman, from whom he had inherited the shop. The original passage, which led into Granville Square, was said to have been nicknamed "Plum Pudding Steps."

983   The Riddle of the Sands   (Erskine Childers, 1903)

The British writer's spy story is set among the sandbanks of the Frisian Islands, where two Englishmen discover that the Germans are rehearsing plans to invade England. The latter is the "riddle" that they unravel, in the process unmasking an apparently German yacht owner, Dollmann, as an Englishman and former Royal Navy officer.

984   Riddley Walker   (Russell Hoban, 1980)

The American-born British writer's fourth novel is set two thousand years after the nuclear holocaust, when some sort of organic life is possible again. The story centers on a group of gatherers digging up long buried scrap metal. They speak a contrived language which bears a basic resemblance to English. The title is the name of the 12-year-old narrator, already a man, which itself hints at the two aspects of his adventures, mental and physical. He explains his name thus: "Walker is my name and I am the same. Riddley Walker. Walking my riddels where ever they've took me and walking them now on this paper the same." Hoban appears to have based the name on that of the *Rideal-Walker* test, used for determining the germicidal effectiveness of disinfectants, and itself named for two British chemists.

985   Riders of the Purple Sage   (Zane Grey, 1912)

The American writer's famous western novel takes its title from the purple sage that is a distinctive feature of the landscape in which it is set, and that is introduced in the story's opening lines:

> A sharp clip-clop of iron-shod hoofs deadened and died away, and clouds of yellow dust drifted from under the cottonwoods out over the sage. Jane Withersteen gazed down the wide purple slope with dreamy and troubled eyes.

986   Riders to the Sea   (J. M. Synge, 1904)

The grim play by the Irish playwright is set on one of the Aran Islands, off the west coast of Ireland. The central character, the old mother, Maurya, laments the loss at sea of her husband and four sons, with a fifth son missing. The youngest son remains, but is drowned when he takes a mare and pony to the horse fair at Connemara. All these male characters are thus "riders to the sea."

987   The Right Stuff   (Tom Wolfe, 1979)

The American writer's seventh book concerns the selection, training, and daily routines of the first American astronauts, who needed to be the "right (sort of) stuff," or people who had the appropriate qualities for their unique task. As the book itself puts it:

> The idea was to prove at every foot of the way up that you were one of the elected and anointed ones who had *the right stuff* and could move higher and higher and even—ultimately, God willing, one day—that you might be able to join that special few at the very top, that elite who had the capacity to bring tears to men's eyes, the very Brotherhood of the Right Stuff itself.   [Chapter 2]

988   The Ring and the Book   (Robert Browning, 1868–9)

The poem in blank verse, in 12 books, was the work that established the English poet's reputation. The "Ring" of the title represents the "pure gold" of fact found in historical documents, which is shaped and given living form by the "pure alloy" of the poet's imagination. The "Book" is "the Old Yellow Book" (as Browning calls it), a collection of documents relating to the late 17th-century Italian murder trial on which the poem is based. (Browning found a copy on a bookstall in Florence.)

989   Ring of Bright Water   (Gavin Maxwell, 1960)

The British author's account of his life on the remote west coast of Scotland and of his relationship with two semitame otters is usually thought to take its title from the shining stream that circled his cottage. This is only partly so, however, and it actually has a deeper meaning. It comes from a line by the poet Kathleen Raine, who had fallen for Maxwell and who wrote the poem as a declaration of love for the wilderness both in Maxwell himself and in the place where he lived. The poem begins:

> He has married me with a ring, a ring of bright water
> Whose ripples travel from the heart of the sea.

990   Ring Round the Moon   (Christopher Fry, 1950)

The title is that of the British playwright's adaptation of the French dramatist Anouilh's play *L'Invitation au Château* (1947). It quotes the first half of the proverb, "Ring round the moon, brings a storm soon."

991   Rites of Passage   (William Golding, 1980)

The British writer's eighth novel is the opening book in what would be a trilogy about a mixed cargo of passengers on a voyage to 18th-century Australia, the others being *Close Quarters* (1987) and **Fire Down Below** (1989). It is a study of a young aristocrat and a clergyman, each torn by strong emotions, with the clergyman dying of shame after sexual involvement with sailors. The title, a set phrase used for a person's key change in status, as when passing from childhood to adultood, or celibacy to marriage, here more specifically refers both to the clergyman's "passage" from honor to shame (and also life to death) as well as to the actual passage of the ship itself. A third implicit reference is to the change in moods and morals that occurs as the 18th century gives way to the 19th.

992   The Road Not Taken   (Robert Frost, 1916)

The American poet's well-known poem tells how the course of his life was decided by two roads that he came on:

> Two roads diverged in a wood, and I—
> I took the one less traveled by
> And that has made all the difference.

993   The Road to Xanadu   (John Livingston Lowes, 1927)

The American writer's critical study of Coleridge and of the workings of the imagination has a title that primarily relates to Xanadu, the exotic place where Kubla Khan decreed "a stately pleasure-dome" in Coleridge's famous poem of 1798. The first part of the title alludes to an exchange of dialogue between Faust and Mephistopheles in Goethe's *Faust* (1808):

> *Faust*   Wohin der Weg? [Whither the way?]
> *Mephistopheles*   Kein Weg! Ins Unbetretene. [No way! Into the unexplored.]

994   The Robber Bridegroom   (Eudora Welty, 1942)

The American author's first novel is based on the Brothers Grimm folktale of the same name (1812). It uses the traditional characters of a fairy story, complete with wicked stepmother and good-hearted bandit, but explores the personality of the characters in a way that the original did not.

995   The Robe   (Lloyd C. Douglas, 1942)

The novel was the response of the American author, a clergyman and writer, to a questioner who asked him what became of the robe of Jesus for which the Roman soldiers cast lots when they crucified him.

996   The Rock Pool   (Cyril Connolly, 1936)

The English writer's only novel (he was mainly a journalist and critic) is a satirical extravaganza describing the adventures of a young literary stockbroker at the decaying French resort of Trou-sur-Mer ("Hole-on-Sea"), where there is an artistic expatriate colony. The title is taken from the "little monograph" that he intends to write about the place, which he sees as "a microcosm cut off from the ocean by the retreating economic tide."

997   Rogue Male   (Geoffrey Household, 1939)

The British writer's second and most popular novel, originally serialized in *Atlantic Monthly*, centers on the efforts of an English gentleman abroad to assassinate a dictator. The title at first appears to suggest that his motives are those of the sportsman, out to track down and shoot a rogue animal (such as an elephant). However, the narrative itself, which is in diary form, makes it clear that it is not the dictator who is the "rogue male" but the narrator, as an epigraph also establishes:

> The behaviour of a rogue may fairly be described as individual separation from its fellows appearing to increase both cunning and ferocity. These solitary beasts, exasperated by chronic pain or widowerhood, are occasionally found among all the large carnivores and graminivores.

998   The Room   (Hubert Selby, Jr., 1971)

The American writer's second novel centers on the mind of a paranoid schizophrenic. The "room" of the title is both his cell and his disconnected consciousness. He is locked within each.

999   Room at the Top   (John Braine, 1957)

The British writer's story of a young clerk with ruthless ambition takes its title from a comment attributed to the 19th-century American politician Daniel Webster, who when advised against joining the overcrowded legal profession is said to have remarked: "There is always room at the top." The novel's central character, accountant Joe Lampton, is told at one point: "You're the sort of young man we want. There's always room at the top." On completing his accountancy exams he actually moves from a poor part of the town where he lives to a more affluent quarter known locally as "T' Top."

1000   A Room of One's Own   (Virginia Woolf, 1929)

The essay, a classic feminist statement, is based on the British writer's thesis that "a woman must have money and a room of her own if she is to write fiction," that is, that she must have her independence.

1001 Room Temperature (Nicholson Baker, 1990)
The book by the American writer details twenty minutes of thoughts as the author bottlefeeds his daughter, known as "The Bug."

1002 A Room with a View (E. M. Forster, 1908)
The title of the British writer's novel relates to the rooms "with a view" that the central character, Lucy Honeychurch, together with her chaperone, are unable to obtain in a Florence hotel. Instead, the women are given rooms which look onto a courtyard. The elderly Mr. Emerson offers to exchange the rooms that he and his son George occupy for those allocated to the two ladies. It is George Emerson whom Lucy eventually marries when back in England. The title was subsequently taken up by Noël Coward for a popular song (1928).

1003 Rootabaga Stories (Carl Sandburg, 1922)
The American poet's nonsense stories for children are set in the "big, big, Rootabaga country," the capital of which is Liver and Onions. *Rootabaga* is an earlier spelling of *rutabaga*, as an alternate name for the Swedish turnip.

1004 Roots (Alex Haley, 1976)
The book is an account of the black American author's origins, tracing his family back to his "roots" in an African ancestor, a slave named Kunte Kinte.

1005 The Rose Tattoo (Tennessee Williams, 1951)
The play by the American playwright is set in a Sicilian community on the Gulf Coast and concerns a dressmaker, Serafina Delle Rose, whose truckdriver husband, Rosario, has just been killed. She finally meets another truckdriver who, like her late husband, has a rose tattoo on his chest.

1006 Rosencrantz and Guildenstern Are Dead (Tom Stoppard, 1967)
The play by the British dramatist is one in which the two named characters from Shakespeare's *Hamlet* meditate on their own identities and on their relationship to the events that occur in the earlier play. In this, they are insignificant courtiers who are friends of Hamlet himself. He arranges for their deaths, however, on learning that they were agents (set up to kill *him*) of his uncle Claudius. The title itself represents words in *Hamlet* spoken by one of the English ambassadors after the killings:

> The ears are senseless that should give us hearing,
> To tell him his commandment is fulfilled,
> That Rosencrantz and Guildenstern are dead. [V.ii.383]

1007 The Rotten Elements (Edward Upward, 1969)
The British writer's novel, subtitled *A Novel of Fact*, is the second in a trilogy entitled *The Spiral Ascent*, whose general theme is the struggle by its central character, a Marxist poet and teacher, to reconcile his literary ambition with his political beliefs. In Communist parlance, the "rotten elements" of the title were "members who deviated seriously from the correct party line." The story thus depicts the isolation

that Upward himself experienced when he left the Communist Party after World War II because he felt it had abandoned its Marxist principles. (He had originally planned to call the novel *The Deviators* but realized that this "might raise the wrong kind of expectation.")

1008   The Rubyfruit Jungle   (Rita Mae Brown, 1973)
The American writer's first novel recounts the "coming out" of its lesbian central character, Molly Bolt. The title has an implicit sexual reference that she spells out:

> When I make love to women I think of their genitals as a, as a ruby fruit jungle. [...] Women are thick and rich and full of hidden treasures and besides that, they taste good.

1009   Rudder Grange   (Frank Stockton, 1879)
The American writer's humorous novel concerns a newly married couple whose search for a suitably modest home leads them to an anchored canal houseboat, which they name with the words of the title.

1010   Ruggles of Red Gap   (Harry Leon Wilson, 1915)
The American writer's comic novel tells how Ruggles, an English butler, is taken across the Atlantic by a rancher to the western town of Red Gap.

1011   Rumble Fish   (S. E. Hinton, 1975)
The American writer's novel concerns a teenager who survives a number of "rumbles" (gang fights) and who while working in a petshop recognizes himself in the actions of a fish that fights its own reflection in a mirror.

1012   Runner Mack   (Barry Beckham, 1972)
The black American author's second novel concerns a poor black Mississippi baseball player who comes to New York for a tryout, knowing baseball to be the American national sport, but instead encounters another national sport, that of "keeping this nigger running." The title refers partly to this, partly to the Mack truck by which he is hit one day, but more obviously to the character that he meets: the black hipster, Runnington ("Runner") Mack, who becomes his mentor in a plot to bomb the White House.

1013   Russet Mantle   (Lynn Riggs, 1936)
The comedy by the American playwright concerns a young woman who falls in love with her aunt's hired man, an aspiring young poet. When she becomes pregnant, her family are outraged, but the two prepare to leave "to live in a world that's *our time.*" The title is a phrase from Shakespeare's *Hamlet*:

> But, look, the morn in russet mantle clad,
> Walks o'er the dew of yon high eastern hill.   [I.i.166]

Cf. **But Look, the Morn.**

1014   Sacred Cows   (Fay Weldon, 1989)
The British novelist's pamphlet denounces Muslim customs and argues that immigration to Britain should follow the "unicultural policy of the United States," with

children attending schools where "one flag is saluted and one God worshipped." The title does not consider the sensibilities of Muslims, however, since it puns on the fact that for them the cow is a sacred animal.

1015   The Sacred Fount   (Henry James, 1901)
The American writer's novelette deals with the relationships among the guests at an English house party. The title refers to the theory of the narrator that, in an unequal marriage or relationship, the older or weaker partner is refreshed at the "sacred fount" of the younger or stronger, which in turn becomes depleted.

1016   Sacred Hunger   (Barry Unsworth, 1992)
The British writer's tenth novel tells the story of Matthew Paris, an 18th-century ship's surgeon who organizes a mutiny on a slaver. Twelve years later, the surviving crew and slaves have set up an egalitarian community in Florida, inspired by the freethinking Frenchman Delblanc, who had been with them on board. Paris is eventually taken prisoner, and explains his reasons for the mutiny thus:

> It was impossible not to see that we had taken everything from them and only for the sake of profit—that sacred hunger, as Delblanc once called it, which justifies everything, sanctifies all purposes.

1017   Sanctuary   (William Faulkner, 1931)
The ironic title of the American writer's novel refers to the shelter that the lawyer Horace Benbow attempts to give to the common-law wife and infant son of Lee Goodwin, who is wrongly accused of murder.

1018   Sartoris   (William Faulkner, 1929)
The title of the American writer's novel is the surname of the family whose story it tells. (The title originally planned for it was *Flags in the Dust*.) Members of the Sartoris family also appear in other Faulkner novels and stories, notably *The Unvanquished* (1938).

1019   Sassafras   (Jack Matthews, 1983)
The title of the American author's sixth novel puns on the natural "sass" of its protagonist, the innocent young phrenologist, Thad Burke, who takes his show from village to village, "reading" the heads of everyone he meets.

1020   The Satanic Verses   (Salman Rushdie, 1988)
The Bombay-born British writer's controversial fourth novel led Ayatollah Khomeini of Iran to serve a death sentence on its author. It takes its title from an apocryphal incident in which the Prophet Muhammad was tricked by Satan into inserting into the Koran two verses that were diabolically, not divinely, inspired. These "satanic verses" were later removed from the Koran, but the incident forms the basis of the novel. (Rushdie also refers to Muhammad throughout by the derogatory name Mahound, and in one section has a number of whores assuming the identity of one of Muhammad's wives.)

1021   The Savage Crows   (Robert Drewe, 1976)
The Australian author's first novel deals with the plight of the Australian Aborigines, a colonial nickname for whom was "savage crows," referring to their "uncivilized" state and their color.

1022   The Scarlet Letter   (Nathaniel Hawthorne, 1850)
The American novelist's romance is a story of conscience and the tragic consequences of concealed guilt. It concerns an elderly English scholar who sends his young wife, Hester Prynne, to set up their home in Boston. On arriving two years later, he finds her in the pillory with her ilegitimate child in her arms. She refuses to name her lover, and his sentenced to wear a scarlet letter "A," for "Adultress," as a sign of her sin. Hence the title. The color derives from that of the "scarlet woman" or "Mother of Harlots" of the Bible (Revelation 17:1–6).

1023   The Scarlet Pimpernel   (Baroness Orczy, 1905)
The title of the Hungarian-born British writer's popular historical novel alludes to the sign, representing the little English wild flower, the scarlet pimpernel, that the hero of the story, Sir Percy Blakeney, leaves when he and his friends have successfully rescued a victim of the French Revolution and smuggled him back to England. The sign came to be the nickname of the hero himself, as in the book's famous verse:

> We seek him here, we seek him there,
> Those Frenchies seek him everywhere.
> Is he in heaven?—Is he in hell?
> That demmed, elusive Pimpernel?   [Chapter 12]

An updated version of the story (with a professor of archaeology rescuing French refugees) was created in the film *Pimpernel Smith* (1941).

1024   Scarlet Sister Mary   (Julia Peterkin, 1928)
The title of the American writer's novel refers to its central character, the black orphan "Sister" Mary, a Gullah living on a South Carolina plantation, who grows up to be deserted by her husband and to have nine children by as many fathers. As a "scarlet" woman she is thus expelled from the church.

1025   Schindler's Ark   (Thomas Keneally, 1982)
The Australian writer's "novel" (a true story based entirely on research) tells the story of the German industrialist Oskar Schindler (1908–1974), who buys up the business of dispossessed Jews in World War II. The reader eventually discovers that his wheeling and dealing lifestyle is actually a front for his true activity: the saving of thousands of Jews from the Holocaust by employing them in his "ark," an armament factory that does not produce a single shell. The first American edition of the book had the title *Schindler's List*, and this was also adopted for the British edition when the 1994 film of the book was released under that title.

1026   A Scots Quair   (Lewis Grassic Gibbon [James Leslie Mitchell], 1946)
The title, meaning "A Scottish book," is that of the Scottish writer's trilogy, which follows the attempts of a Scotswoman, Chris Guthrie, to resolve her personal conflict:

whether to remain in her native Scotland, and accept its relatively parochial values, or betray her ancestors and launch forth into a wider but alien world. The titles of the three individual volumes are: *Sunset Song* (1932), alluding to the Scottish dead of World War I, who perished in the "sunset" of an old world, *Cloud House* (1933), and *Grey Granite* (1934).

1027   Scratch an Actor   (Sheilah Graham, 1969)
The title of the Hollywood gossip columnist's book quotes from a line by Dorothy Parker: "Scratch an actor and you'll find an actress." (Compare her similar: "Scratch a lover, and find a foe," and the traditional: "Scratch a Russian and you'll find a Tartar.")

1028   The Sea, the Sea   (Iris Murdoch, 1978)
The British writer's nineteenth novel tells the story of an ageing theater director who attempts to escape his past by retiring to a quiet village by the sea, where his past catches up with him in the form of two women and a curiously adult young boy. A sea monster also features. The title is taken from Xenophon's *Anabasis*, and is the exclamation made by his Greek mercenaries when they see the Black Sea on retreating after their defeat in battle (401 BC): "*Thalassa, thalassa*" (The sea, the sea).

1029   The Sea Shall Not Have Them   (John Harris, 1953)
The British writer's novel about air-sea rescue operations in World War II took as its title the motto of the former Coastal Command's Air-Sea Rescue Service.

1030   The Second Sex   (Simone de Beauvoir, 1953)
The French writer's classic feminist statement is an analysis of women's secondary status in society. Hence the title. The original French title was *Le Deuxième Sexe* (1949). The phrase implies that men are the prime sex, and is on a par with existing expressions such as "the weaker sex," "the gentler sex."

1031   The Secret Battle   (A. P. Herbert, 1919)
The British author was experienced in legal matters, and his novel, although based on fact, is a fictional account of the unjust trial and execution of Harry Penrose, who was shot for cowardice in World War I. The title refers to "the secret battle," or inner turmoil, of a man who knows he is a coward but who equally knows he must attempt to overcome his fears.

1032   The Secret History   (Donna Tartt, 1992)
The American writer's first novel is both a campus murder mystery and a literary thriller. It is known from the outset that a murder has been committed and by whom, but the reason for the murder is only slowly revealed, and is the "secret history" that gradually unfolds in the sealed world of academic snobbery to which the reader is given privileged "fly-on-the-wall" access.

1033   Seize the Day   (Saul Bellow, 1956)
The title story in the American writer's first collection recounts events during the "day of reckoning" of its protagonist, Wilhelm Adler, who has lost job, home, and

family and is in the act of losing his last few dollars on the commodities market. This day of drastic losses proves a spiritual turning point in his life. The title quotes from Horace's *Odes* (23 B.C.): "Seize the day, put no trust in the morrow." (In the Latin original: "*Carpe diem, quam minimum credula postero.*")

1034   Self-Portrait in a Convex Mirror   (John Ashbery, 1975)

The American poet's long, meditative poem takes its title and theme from a self-portrait of 1524 by the Italian artist Francesco Mazzola executed on a convex wooden panel. The poem has the lines:

> As Parmigianino did it, the right hand
> Bigger than the head, thrust at the viewer
> And swerving easily away, as though to protect
> What it advertises.

1035   The Sensationist   (Charles Palliser, 1991)

The American-Irish author's second novel concerns a "sensationist," a university lecturer who is apparently devoid of any human feeling, although experiencing a number of sexual encounters. Despite his academic success and easy conquests, he is thus a "hollow man," and an incomplete human being.

1036   Sense and Sensibility   (Jane Austen, 1811)

The title of the English writer's novel refers to each of two sisters, Elinor and Marianne Dashwood, and their respective reactions to the dastardliness of their lovers, as they pursue their search for, and finally attain, a suitable husband.

1037   A Separate Peace   (John Knowles, 1959)

The American writer's first novel is a tale of prep school relationships. Gene Forrester has a love-hate attitude to his close friend Finney, and causes him to suffer a serious injury, while later supposedly causing his death from a second injury. But Gene assuages his guilt by arranging a reconciliation with Finney before his death. Hence the title, from Hemingway's *In Our Time* (1924): "You and me, we've made a separate peace."

1038   Serenissima   (Erica Jong, 1987)

The title of the American writer's fifth novel alludes to *La Serenissima*, "The Serene Highness," the Italian title of the Republic of Venice. It also applies punningly to the central character, Jessica Pruitt, a middle-aged actress, who goes to Venice as a judge for the film festival and to play her namesake in *The Merchant of Venice*. When she falls ill, she uses her prolonged stay to embark on a journey back in time to the 16th century. She fancies herself as Shakespeare's "Dark Lady" and is involved in a number of sexual encounters, including with Shakespeare himself.

1039   Serjeant Musgrave's Dance   (John Arden, 1959)

The title of the British writer's pacifist play refers to the macabre dance of vengeance enacted by its central character, Serjeant Musgrave, when one of his men is accidentally killed.

1040   A Servant to Servants   (Robert Frost, 1914)

The American poet's blank-verse dramatic monologue centers on a lonely, over-worked New England farm wife, who though craving liberty, love, and beauty is weighed down with innumerable menial tasks, including the feeding of the farmhands, whose "servant" she has thus become. The title has a biblical ring, as in: "A servant of servants shall he be unto his brethren" (Genesis 9:25).

1041   Set on Edge   (Bernice Rubens, 1960)

The British writer's first novel has as its theme the claustrophobic closeness of Jew-ish family life, as typified by the Jewish matriarch, with her greedy and ambitious mother love. This is personified by the central character, Mrs. Sperber, who burdens her daughter Gladys with guilt. At the end of the novel Gladys has herself taken on her mother's role. The title is biblical in origin: "The fathers have eaten sour grapes, and the children's teeth are set on edge" (Ezekiel 18:2).

1042   The Seven Lamps of Architecture   (John Ruskin, 1849)

The title of the treatise on architecture by the English art critic and social reformer refers to the seven lamps (spirits) that illuminate the seven ideals to which archi-tects should aspire. According to Ruskin, these are Sacrifice, Truth, Power, Mem-ory, Beauty, Obedience, and Life.

1043   The Seven Per Cent Solution   (Nicholas Meyer, 1974)

The American author's novel tells how Sherlock Holmes is treated for a persecu-tion complex and cocaine addiction by Sigmund Freud. Its title, not surprisingly, is from Conan Doyle himself, and is from the opening chapter of *The Sign of Four* (1889), where Holmes addresses Dr. Watson: "'It is cocaine,' he said, 'a seven-per-cent solution. Would you care to try it?'"

1044   The Seven Pillars of Wisdom   (T. E. Lawrence, 1926)

The book is a full account of the British author's experiences as a leader in Arabia in World War I. The title derives from the Bible: "Wisdom hath builded her house, she hath hewn out her seven pillars" (Proverbs 9:1).

1045   The Seven Year Itch   (George Axelrod, 1952)

The American writer's Broadway comedy, in which a married man has a fling with the girl upstairs, has a title referring to the urge to be unfaithful that a husband or wife is said to have after a certain length of marriage (conventionally, seven years).

1046   Seventeen   (Booth Tarkington, 1916)

The American writer's novel tells the story of William Sylvanus Baxter ("Silly Billy"), a 17-year-old youth in the throes of his first love affair.

1047   A Severed Head   (Iris Murdoch, 1961)

The British writer's fifth novel involves the affairs that three men have with three women. Through his own affair, the central character comes to value his instincts, from the heart, rather than the conventions of behaviour that come from the head, which has thus been "severed."

1048   Shadow of a Sun   (A. S. Byatt, 1964)

The British writer's first novel concerns the creative arrangements that a woman needs to combine marriage and career, as experienced by the central character, Anna Severell, a novelist's daughter dominated by her overpowering father. The title comes from Sir Walter Ralegh's poem *Farewell False Love* (1588):

> A maze wherein affection finds no end,
> A ranging cloud that runs before the wind,
> A substance like the shadow of the sun,
> A goal of grief for which the wisest run.

1049   Shadows on the Rock   (Willa Cather, 1931)

The "rock" in the title of the American writer's novel, set in the 17th century, is the one on which the city of Quebec stands in the St. Lawrence. The "shadows" are the interconnecting lives of some of its lowly citizens.

1050   Shame   (Salman Rushdie, 1983)

The Bombay-born British writer's third novel is a part actual, part dreamlike history of Pakistan (here disguised as "Peccavistan," punning on Latin *peccavi*, "I have sinned," and Sind, one of its provinces), a country established in 1947, the year of Rushdie's birth. The title refers to the shameful contrast between the country's elitist class and its poor, and one of the main characters is allegorized into Shame itself.

1051   The Sheltering Sky   (Paul Bowles, 1949)

The American writer's first novel introduced the theme that has sounded throughout his work: the elemental clash between the primitive and the civilized. It concerns an American couple, Kit and Port Moresby, who arrive in North Africa and make their way across the Sahara through a series of grotesque adventures, protected only by the "sheltering sky."

1052   Ship of Fools   (Katherine Anne Porter, 1962)

The American writer's only novel is an allegory, as the title implies: it is ultimately that of Sebastian Brant's *Narrenschiff* (1497), whose own theme is the shipping of fools of all kinds from their native land to the Land of Fools. For Porter, as for others before her, the "ship of fools" is the world, with the passengers cruising to disaster. In this particular instance, the ship is sailing from Vera Cruz to Bremerhaven in 1931 with a cargo of passengers of different races. At first they are determined to be friendly, but soon divisions of race, class, and politics surface and the eventual outcome is war.

1053   The Shock of Recognition   (Edmund Wilson, 1943)

The American writer's anthology, subtitled *The Development of Literature in the United States Recorded by the Men Who Made It*, is a collection of articles about

American authors by their contemporaries from 1845 to the date of publication. The title quotes from Herman Melville's *Hawthorne and His Mosses* (1850): "Genius all over the world stands hand in hand, and one shock of recognition runs the whole circle round."

1054　Shoeless Joe　(W. P. Kinsella, 1982)
The Canadian writer's first novel is a hymn to baseball, which for its central character, the Iowa farmer Ray Kinsella, is a religion. He hears a voice telling him that if he builds a baseball stadium on his farm, "he" will come, "he" being Shoeless Joe Jackson, a member of the infamous Chicago Black Sox team that rigged the World Series in 1919. He does so, complete with bleachers and lights, and the Chicago team does come. But it can only be seen by those who believe in magic and truly love the game.

1055　The Shrimp and the Anemone　(L. P. Hartley, 1944)
The British writer's novel is the first of a trilogy tracing the lives of Eustace and his sister Hilda from childhood to adulthood. The other two titles are *The Sixth Heaven* (1946) and *Eustace and Hilda* (1947). The title of the first novel is a symbolic foretaste of the complex relationship that will develop between the boy (the shrimp) and his elder sister (the anemone). The opening paragraph describes the incident at the seaside that lies behind the title. Eustace sees an anemone devouring a shrimp in a rock pool. The children try to rescue the shrimp, but the anemone has already killed it and in their bid the children destroy the anemone too.

1056　Shrinking　(Alan Lelchuk, 1978)
Subtitled *The Beginning of My Own Ending*, the American writer's third novel chronicles the breakdown of its central character, Lionel Solomon. The title plays on the colloquial term for a psychiatrist, and the novel actually includes a foreword and afterword from Solomon's own "shrink."

1057　The Silence of the Lambs　(Thomas Harris, 1988)
The plot of the American writer's thriller concerns an investigation into a series of sickening murders by a killer nicknamed "Buffalo Bill" because he strips large sections of skin from his victims. These victims are the "lambs" of the title, their silence not revealing the identity of their murderer.

1058　Silences　(Tillie Olsen, 1978)
The American author's collection of essays and lectures delivered at colleges concerns writers who have been silenced because of their sex, their class, or their jobs. Willa Cather, for instance, sent her first published stories to Henry James, whom she greatly admired, only to be met with a lordly silence. Her output over the next five years dwindled in consequence. Katherine Mansfield had her writing interrupted by her husband, John Middleton Murry, calling "Isn't there going to be tea, Tig?" Kafka and Melville were exhausted by daytime jobs that prevented them from writing. The book has hundreds of examples of "silences" of this type.

1059   The Silent Gondoliers   (S. Morgenstern [William Goldman], 1984)
The American writer's novel has innocence and loss as its theme. The story is based
on the fantasy that the gondoliers in Venice no longer sing because even they have
lost their innocence in a world from which there is no escape.

1060   The Silmarillion   (J. R. R. Tolkien, 1977)
The British writer's "prequel" to **The Hobbit** and **The Lord of the Rings**, published
four years posthumously, has a title that in Elvish was interpreted as meaning "The-
Book-of-the-Silmarils." The Silmarils were the three Great Jewels wrought by
Fëanor of the Noldor during the Elder Days (the First Age of Middle-earth), as
the mightiest works of craft ever made. Their own name means "jewels-of-*silima*,"
the latter being a mysterious crystalline substance.

1061   The Silver Cord   (Sidney Howard, 1926)
The play by the American playwright is a psychological study of the dominant
mother of two sons. One remains faithful to her, even though it means breaking off
his engagement. The other is able to break the "silver cord" of a mother fixation only
with the help of his wife.

1062   The Silver Tassie   (Sean O'Casey, 1929)
The central theme of the Irish playwright's tragicomedy is the futility of war, expressed through an Irish football team who are led to victory and who win the cov-
eted trophy: the "silver tassie" (silver cup) of the title.

1063   The Single Hound   (Emily Dickinson, 1914)
The American poet's collection of 146 brief poems, published 28 years posthumously, takes its title from the first poem, written in about 1864:

> Adventure most unto itself
> The Soul condemned to be;
> Attended by a Single Hound—
> Its own identity.

1064   The Sinking of the Odradek Stadium   (Harry Mathews, 1975)
The American writer's third novel is in epistolary form and has an extraordinary
plot that although superficially a love story in fact centers on a search for the where-
abouts of an Italian treasure trove. The many strange clues and incidents eventually
lead to the discovery of the treasure aboard a Panamanian cargo ship, the "Odradek
Stadion" (*sic*), where it is bound for the gold markets of Rangoon. The title inti-
mates that although it has now been discovered, it is soon to be consigned to a wa-
tery grave.

1065   Sitting Pretty   (Al Young, 1976)
The American author's third novel chronicles a year in the life of its black protagonist, Sidney J. Prettymoon, known as "Sitting Pretty" (hence the title) or simply
"Sit," the equivalent of Langston Hughes's Jesse B. Semple, aka "Simple." "Sit"'s
philosophy actually consists in "sitting pretty," or in improvising a way through life

that on the one hand is not harmful to others and on the other does not compromise his sense of values.

1066   Sixty-Four, Ninety-Four!   (R. H. Mottram, 1925)

The British writers's part-fictional, part-autobiographical novel is the second volume in *The Spanish Farm Trilogy*, and is set in World War I. Its theme is the futility of armed conflict, in which so many men's lives are wasted. Its title comes from the army song:

> Sixty-four, ninety-four—
> He'll never go sick no more,
> The poor beggar's dead.

1067   The Skin Game   (John Galsworthy, 1920)

The play by the British playwright is a critique of jealously guarded privilege and social snobbery. In it, one character swindles another in a property deal. She thus uses "skin game" tactics, or deceit. The phrase occurs in the play itself:

> She wants to sell, an' she'll get her price, whatever it is.
> HILCRIST (*With deep anger*) If that isn't a skin game [...] I don't know what is.

1068   The Skull Beneath the Skin   (P. D. James, 1982)

The thriller by one of Britain's foremost crime writers took as its title a quotation from T. S. Eliot's *The Waste Land* (1922):

> Webster was much possessed by death
> And saw the skull beneath the skin.

1069   Slaughterhouse Five   (Kurt Vonnegut, 1969)

The American writer's sixth and best-known novel concerns the bombing of Dresden in World War II by the Allies, an event which Vonnegut had personally experienced, and is a commentary on the wholesale destruction that 20th-century technology can cause. Its title refers to the disused slaughterhouse in Dresden where American prisoners were held, with Vonnegut among their number. The novel's subtitle is *The Children's Crusade*, obliquely referring to the crusade undertaken by European children in the 14th century to recapture Jerusalem. The novel spells out the allusion:

> We had forgotten that wars were fought by babies. When I saw those freshly shaved faces, it was a shock. "My God, my God—" I said to myself, "it's the Children's Crusade." [Chapter 5]

1070   The Slaves of Solitude   (Patrick Hamilton, 1947)

The "slaves of solitude" of the British writer's novel are the inhabitants of the Rosamund Tea Rooms, a depressing boarding house in the wartime fictional town of Thames Lockenden (meant for Henley-on-Thames). The pattern of their lonely lives is disturbed when two American servicemen call one afternoon to take tea. The narrative is pervaded by an atmosphere of gloom and oppression, and admirably evokes wartime England, with its petty restrictions and major frustrations.

1071   The Sleep of Reason   (C. P. Snow, 1968)
The British writer's penultimate novel in the sequence of 11 entitled **Strangers and Brothers** has as its theme the conflict between generations and the sexual revolution of the 1960s, as personalized in the experiences and attitudes of the central character, Lewis Eliot, who is drawn into a murder case as a legal advisor. It takes its title from a Goya etching called "The Sleep of Reason Brings Forth Monsters" (in the original Spanish, "El sueño de la razón produce monstruos"), Plate 43 of *Los Caprichos* (1799). This shows the artist asleep or resting, his head in his arms, on a desk inscribed with the Spanish words. Behind him hover monstrous owls, bats, and a huge cat. Goya's text for the etching runs (in translation): "Imagination abandoned by Reason produces impossible monsters: united with her, she is the mother of the arts and the source of their wonders."

1072   Slouching Towards Bethlehem   (Joan Didion, 1968)
The American writer's collection of essays is arranged in three groups: "Life Styles in the Golden Land" (on California), "Personals" (about the author herself), and "Seven Places of the Mind" (about places that have been meaningful to her). The overall title is based on a line from Yeats's poem *The Second Coming* (1921):

> And what rough beast, its hour come round at last,
> Slouches towards Bethlehem to be born?

1073   Slouching Towards Kalamazoo   (Peter De Vries, 1983)
The American writer's novel is an extravagant account of the arrival of the sexual revolution in a small Midwestern town in the early 1960s. Its plot plays on that of Nathaniel Hawthorne's *The Scarlet Letter*, and its title is an adaption of a phrase in Yeats's poem *The Second Coming* (1921), quoted above for Joan Didion's **Slouching Towards Bethlehem**.

1074   The Small Back Room   (Nigel Balchin, 1943)
The British writer's novel is about the work of "back-room boys" or boffins, that is, the scientists who were engaged on secret research work in World War II. Their laboratory was conventionally a "back room," hidden at the rear of a building.

1075   Small Is Beautiful   (E. F. Schumacher, 1973)
The American writer's influential book was published at a time when cheap oil suddenly became expensive. It expounds the author's thesis that the consequences of squandering irreplaceable fossil fuels would lead to disaster, and that what is needed is a new morality in which "small is beautiful": economic growth must cease as it is simply an end in itself, large corporations must be disbanded because they dehumanize, and western policies in the developing world should be rejected in favor of "intermediate technology." The book is subtitled *A Study of Economics as If People Mattered*.

1076   A Smuggler's Bible   (Joseph McElroy, 1966)
The American writer's first novel tells the story of David Brooke, who on board ship from New York to London is trying to bring coherence to seven autobiographical

manuscripts that he has written himself. At a literal level, the title refers to a hollowed-out copy of a Bible used for smuggling contraband in former times. Metaphorically it alludes to the ways in which humans smuggle meanings under a number of different guises.

1077   The Snake Pit   (Mary J. Ward, 1946)
The American writer's best-known work is the story of a young wife's years in a mental hospital and her struggle to regain her sanity and freedom. The metaphor is that of the pit containing poisonous snakes into which, in some countries formerly, victims were thrown as a method of execution or as a test of endurance. Ward's use of the term caused its adoption to mean "mental hospital."

1078   The Snow Ball   (Brigid Brophy, 1964)
The British writer's novel is an erotic comedy of manners, set at a New Year's Eve costume ball, given by the central character, Anne, who is obsessed by the color white. For this ball, however, she dresses in gold lamé, and it is a guest's daughter, Ruth, who is dressed in white (as the pageboy Cherubino in Mozart's opera *The Marriage of Figaro*), while her boyfriend, Edward, is her opposite (or negative) image, dressed in black (as Casanova). The ball disintegrates into a pairing off for the purpose of sex, and everybody, including Anne and her husband, disperses to various parts of the house. Ruth and Edward lose their virginity to each other and go outside to play in the newly fallen snow. Hence the punning title, with its various allusions.

1079   So Red the Rose   (Stark Young, 1934)
The American writer's novel of life in Mississippi in the Civil War takes its title from Edward Fitzgerald's *The Rubáiyát of Omar Khayyám* (1879):

> I sometimes think that never blows so red
> The Rose as where some buried Caesar bled.

1080   The Soft Machine   (William S. Burroughs, 1961)
The American writer's experimental third novel, based (as were others) on material remaining from **Naked Lunch,** has a title that refers allusively to the human body.

1081   The Soldier's Art   (Anthony Powell, 1966)
The British author's eighth novel in the series **A Dance to the Music of Time** has war as its theme. It is frequently suggested in the narrative that war is play-acting. (When, as the novel opens, the central character orders an army greatcoat, the tailor assumes it is for a stage production.) Hence the title, which alludes to the soldier in Shakespeare's "All the world's a stage" speech in *As You Like It.*

1082   Sombrero Fallout   (Richard Brautigan, 1976)
The American writer's comic-surreal novel, subtitled "A Japanese Novel," tells the story of an American humorist. Grieving over the loss of his Japanese girlfriend, Yukiko, he begins to write a story about a sombrero falling out of the sky to land in

a small town. In frustration, he tears the story up, but repieces the fragments in a narrative that runs in parallel with his thoughts about Yukiko. The title refers not only to the sombrero falling from the sky but to the falling-out of the narrator and Yukiko and perhaps also to the literal fallout that resulted from the atomic bombs dropped on Hiroshima and Nagasaki.

1083   Some Tame Gazelle   (Barbara Pym, 1950)

The British author's gentle comedy of manners is about two middle-aged sisters whose parochial, old-fashioned way of life centers on the local church. The book was originally written in 1934, and at first had the title *Some Sad Turtle*. After rejection by publishers and revision, it was given the present title, from a poem called *Something to Love* by the minor English poet Thomas Haynes Bayly (1797–1839):

> Some tame gazelle, or some gentle dove:
> Something to love, oh, something to love!

1084   Something to Remember Me By   (Saul Bellow, 1992)

The American writer's collection of short stories, published in his 77th year, takes its title from its main story, dedicated "To My Children and Grandchildren," which has relations with parents as its theme.

1085   Son of the Morning   (Joyce Carol Oates, 1978)

The American writer's ninth novel concerns a Pentecostal preacher, Nathanael Vickery, who witnesses seven visitations from the Lord, each more terrifying than the last. The final one shows him that God has abandoned him and left him to sink into oblivion and write a book about himself. The title, appropriately, quotes biblical words: "How art thou fallen from heaven, O Lucifer, son of the morning!" (Isaiah 13:11).

1086   The Song of the Lark   (Willa Cather, 1915)

The "lark" of the title is the central character of the American writer's novel. She is Thea Kronborg, a Swedish minister's daughter in Colorado, who develops an obsessive interest in music. She first makes a living by singing in a church choir and goes on to become a famous Wagnerian soprano in the Metropolitan Opera. Her "song" is the expression of her personal life, which is bound up with her career. The prototype for the singer as child and adolescent was Cather herself. The model for the adult singer was the Wagnerian soprano Olive Fremstad.

1087   The Songlines   (Bruce Chatwin, 1987)

The British writer's novel is about a white man (Chatwin himself) who travels across Australia to investigate the Aboriginal "songlines," the vast network of tracks which crisscross the continent, each charted by a song passed down from the "Dreamtime" when the Aborigines hold that the world was born.

1088   Sonnets from the Portuguese   (Elizabeth Barrett Browning, 1850)

The sequence of sonets by the English poet describes the growth and development of her love for her husband. The title suggests a translation, but it was a private reference: "the Portuguese" was Robert Browning's nickname for his wife, based on her poem *Catarina to Camoens*, portraying a Portuguese woman's devotion to her poet lover.

1089   Sophie's Choice   (William Styron, 1979)

The two main characters of the American writer's fifth novel are Ringo, an American Jewish novelist who comes to New York in 1947, and the woman he meets there, Sophie, a Polish Catholic immigrant recently released from Auschwitz. Her "choice," revealed only at the end of the book, had been whether to let her son or her daughter go to the gas chamber while she was in Auschwitz.

1090   The Sot-Weed Factor   (John Barth, 1960)

The American writer's novel is a fictional biography of Ebenezer Cook, writer of a poem of the same title, published in 1708. This is a satire telling how an Englishman came to Maryland as a factor, or agent, of a British merchant dealing in tobacco, the "sot-weed," so called as it is a weed (plant) that besots the mind.

1091   The Sound and the Fury   (William Faulkner, 1929)

The American writer's novel is in four sections, three of which are interior monologues of the three Compson brothers, who with their mother and their vanished sister Caddy are the sole surviving members of a decaying aristocratic family in Mississippi. The first section is seen through the eyes of the idiot Benjy, and is literally "a tale told by an idiot, full of sound and fury." These words, from Shakespeare's *Macbeth* (V.v.16), gave the title of the novel overall.

1092   Sounder   (William H. Armstrong, 1969)

The American writer's first novel for children, about a black family living in the South in the last part of the 19th century, takes its title from the family's large hunting dog, so named because it "sounds" out its prey. Unusually, the boy who is the novel's central character remains unnamed.

1093   South Riding   (Winifred Holtby, 1936)

The British author's last and posthumously published novel is also her best-known, and is set in her native Yorkshire. The title was designed to match (or complete) the former administrative divisions of Yorkshire: North Riding, East Riding, and West Riding.

1094   South Wind   (Norman Douglas, 1917)

The title of the Scottish writer's novel refers to the sirocco, the hot southerly wind that has a degenerative effect on the moral standards of the inhabitants of the imaginary Mediterranean island of Nepenthe, where the story is set. The island is based on Capri, where the author was living at the time. Capri lies in the path of the sirocco, which brings rain and fog.

1095   Spaces of the Dark   (Nicholas Mosley, 1951)

The British writer's first novel tells the story of Paul Shaun, racked by guilt and angst as the result of an incident in World War II in which he had killed a fellow officer and close friend. The title alludes to lines from T. S. Eliot's *East Coker* (1940):

> O dark dark dark. They all go into the dark,
> the vacant interstellar spaces, the vacant into the vacant.

1096   Speedboat   (Renata Adler, 1976)

As the title of the American author's first novel suggests, the theme of the book is motion: not just the literal motion of travelers or tourists, but the motion of a fictional narrative. The characters in the novel work but never achieve anything, they travel but never reach any final destination or any stopping point among the whirl of transatlantic flights, hired cars, and (as the title implies) speedboats.

1097   Spider   (Patrick McGrath, 1990)

The British-born Canadian writer's second novel tells the story of Denis Cleg, alias Spider, who is recording in a journal his lonely childhood in the East End of London. The narrative is complex, and periodically throws out clues regarding its future direction. It is, in effect, the web that Spider weaves about his childhood. Hence the double sense of the title.

1098   A Sport of Nature   (Nadine Gordimer, 1987)

The South African writer's ninth novel tells the story of rich, white Hillela, whose life is dominated by politics and sex. She gradually comes to identify with the black revolutionary movement, but has constant doubts about her unlikely allegiance: is she the "sport of nature" of the title? "Sport of nature" was earlier the literal English rendering of the Latin phrase *lusus naturae*, meaning a freak.

1099   The Spy Who Came In from the Cold   (John Le Carré, 1963)

The British author's third novel, a bestseller, is the story of an English secret agent, Alex Leamas, who in his last assignment in East Berlin is brutally used and destroyed by his superiors. The title alludes essentially to the Cold War then prevailing, when espionage of this kind was at its height. At the same time Leamas, having been "out in the cold," or operating on his own, "came in" to a sort of hell, where things were hotter and more uncomfortable.

1100   Square's Progress   (Wilfrid Sheed, 1965)

The American writer's third novel is the story of the middle-class couple, Fred and Alison Cope, who try to escape the restraints of their "square" educations and marriage for the freedom of a beat or bohemian life. They discover, however, that the "hip" life is just as empty as their own. The title is clearly based on that of Bunyan's *Pilgrim's Progress* (1678, 1684), though at the same time it is ironic, since the Copes (who couldn't cope) made no "progress" at all.

1101   The Squaw Man   (Edwin Milton Royle, 1905)

The romantic drama by the American playwright tells the story of an English aristocrat who marries an Indian girl after she saves his life. She bears him a son, but commits suicide in order not to impede his social career when he becomes heir to an English title. He is thus the "squaw man" of the title.

1102   Stand We at Last   (Zoë Fairbairns, 1983)

The British author's fourth novel, in her own words "a family saga with a feminist background," traces the lives of a succession of women, starting in 1855. The title quotes from Cicely Hamilton's *The March of the Women*:

> Long, long, we in the past,
> Cowered in dread from the light of Heaven.
> Strong, strong, stand we at last,
> Fearless in faith and with sight new given.

1103   Staring at the Sun   (Julian Barnes, 1986)

The British writer's fourth novel concerns a woman who lives from the 1930s to the 2020s. She is offered three main choices in her life, and after twice making the wrong decision, learns to fly and sets off to see the seven wonders of the modern world. The title quotes from the opening line of a poem by Hilaire Belloc written in 1938:

> Believing Truth is staring at the sun
> Which but destroys the power that could perceive.

1104   Stations   (Burt Blechman, 1963)

The "stations" of the title are both those of the subway and the Stations of the Cross in the American author's third novel, which is a science-fiction-style parody of Catholicism.

1105   Staying On   (Paul Scott, 1977)

The British writer intended this prizewinning novel, his last, to be a postscript or coda to *The Raj Quartet*. It depicts the lives of two minor characters from that sequence, a husband and wife, who stay on in India (hence the title) after most of their compatriots have left. The novel poignantly illustrates the truth that "staying on" in an undertaking or relationship can be a melancholy and degrading business. Scott himself was mortally ill when he wrote it, and died the following year.

1106   The Steagle   (Irvin Faust, 1966)

The American writer's first novel concerns the multiple personality that an English professor develops during the Cuban missile crisis. The title indicates such blurring of identity, and is a composite name formed from two football teams, the Steelers and the Eagles.

1107   Stig of the Dump   (Clive King, 1963)

The British writer's third novel for children tells how the young boy Barney discovers a Stone Age man named Stig living in a rubbish dump (garbage tip) in an old chalk pit. The two become friends, since Barney, at eight years of age, is at about the Stone Age state of development.

1108   Story of My Life   (Jay McInerney, 1988)

The American writer's third novel is the autobiographical narrative of the central character, the "postmodern girl" and aspiring actress Allison Poole, caught in the sex and drugs scene of the 1980s. The title works on two levels, as the narrator's own words indicate:

> The first year I was in New York I didn't do anything but guys and blow. Staying out all night at the Surf Club and the Zulu, waking up at five in the afternoon with plugged sinuses and sticky hair. Some kind of white stuff in every opening. Story of my life.

McInerney may have adopted the autobiographical side of the title from that of Helen Keller's autobiography, *The Story of My Life* (1903). (The phrase is too early, and Keller too honest, to have used the title ironically. Today, however, a blind or deaf person, as Keller was, could perhaps be tempted to use the phrase in a self-deprecatory or wry manner.)

1109   Straight   (Dick Francis, 1989)
The English thriller writer, a former jockey, takes the metaphor of "the straight," the final stretch of a race, to show a jockey facing the end of his career. In a broader way, the title also alludes to the human concept of being "straight," or honest.

1110   Strange Interlude   (Eugene O'Neill, 1928)
The play by the American dramatist, a lengthy tragedy of frustrated desires, ends with the bitter conclusion of the central character, Nina Leeds:

> Strange interlude! Yes, our lives are merely strange dark interludes in the electrical display of God the Father!

1111   Strange Meeting   (Susan Hill, 1971)
The British writer's sixth novel is set in the trenches of Flanders during World War I and recounts the doomed friendship of two young officers, drawn together in the common horrors of war but each having a different family background and each of different temperament. The title was borrowed from that of Wilfred Owen's poem, written in 1918 but published posthumously.

1112   Stranger in a Strange Land   (Robert A. Heinlein, 1961)
The American science fiction writer's bestseller tells the story of a human brought to Earth after being raised by Martians. The title, referring to his predicament, is biblical: "I have been a stranger in a strange land" (Exodus 2:22).

1113   Strangers and Brothers   (C. P. Snow, 1940–70)
The title is that of the British writer's series of 11 novels telling of the fame and fortune of their central character, Lewis Eliot. It was also originally the title of the first novel in the series, later retitled *George Passant* (1940). The title indicates the divided world which Eliot enters: he and his brother and two friends who have an almost fraternal relationship with him are the "brothers," while other people are the "strangers."

1114   The Strangers Are All Gone   (Anthony Powell, 1982)
The fourth volume of the British writer's autobiography, overall entitled *To Keep the Ball Rolling*, comes from the Nurse's words (I.v.148) in Shakespeare's *Romeo and Juliet* following the feast in which the young couple fall in love.

1115   A Streetcar Named Desire   (Tennessee Williams, 1947)
The action of the American writer's play hinges on the visit of the central character, Blanche Du Bois, to her sister Stella, who lives with her husband Jack in the
French Quarter of New Orleans near the stop of two streetcars that run on the
same track. One is named "Desire," the other "Cemetery," in each case for their destination. The names are taken symbolically in the play: Blanche contends that
Stella's marriage is a product of lust, as aimless as the "streetcar named Desire"
which shuttles through the narrow streets. See also **The Comfort of Strangers.**

1116   A Stricken Field   (Martha Gellhorn, 1940)
The novel by the American war correspondent centers on Mary Douglas, an American foreign correspondent in refugee-filled Prague in 1938. Gellhorn wrote the
book to "show what history is like for people who have no choice except to live
through it or die from it." The title is taken, she says, from "a Medieval Chronicle"
describing a battle scene. Some young knights "who had never been present at a
stricken field" avert their gaze from a massacre of prisoners and are castigated by a
veteran: "Are ye maidens with your downcast eyes? Look well upon it. See all of it.
Close your eyes to nothing. For a battle is fought to be won. And it is this that happens when you lose."

1117   Such Counsels You Gave to Me   (Robinson Jeffers, 1937)
The title poem of the American writer's free-verse narrative, dealing with incest
and suicide, is based on the old Scottish ballad *Edward, Edward,* which has the
lines:

> "The curse of hell frae me sall ye bear,
> Sic counsels ye give to me, O!"

1118   Such Is My Beloved   (Morley Callaghan, 1934)
The Canadian-born American writer's novel concerns an idealistic priest who attempts to love and care for two prostitutes as an expression of the divine love found
in the biblical Song of Songs (Song of Solomon). The title thus reflects the language of this book, in which there are many mentions of "my beloved."

1119   The Sudden Guest   (Christopher La Farge, 1946)
The American writer's novel centers on a selfish and domineering New England
spinster who, in the hurricane of 1944, recalls the destruction wreaked by the "sudden guest," the hurricane of 1938. Hence the title. The book was an indirect comment on American international relations.

1120   The Sugar Mother   (Elizabeth Jolley, 1988)
The title of the British-born Australian writer's eighth novel refers to the surrogate
mother that one of the characters uses. The title puns on the better-known "sugar
daddy" as a surrogate father figure.

1121   A Suitable Boy   (Vikram Seth, 1993)
The Calcutta-born British writer's lengthy novel, set in the imaginary north Indian
city of Brahmpur, centers on the search for "a suitable boy" for the central character,
Lata Mehra, to marry.

1122   The Summer of My German Soldier   (Bette Greene, 1973)
The American writer's first novel for children tells how a 12-year-old Arkansas girl harbors an escaped German prisoner-of-war in World War II.

1123   The Summer of the Seventeenth Doll   (Ray Lawler, 1955)
The play by the Australian writer concerns two sugarcane cutters who work half the year and return each summer to their waiting women, always bringing a kewpie doll among their gifts. They fail to notice the needs of the women, and are not ready for the discovery that the 17th summer is not the same as its predecessors. The altered circumstances lead to a fight between the two men, and one of them (symbolically) breaks the 17th doll.

1124   The Sun Also Rises   (Ernest Hemingway, 1926)
The American writer's novel is set in the period just after World War I, and the biblical quotation that is its title comes from the pessimistic opening verses of Ecclesiastes. This accords with the sense of disillusionment and frustration that immediately followed the war:

> The sun also ariseth, and the sun goeth down, and hasteth to his place where he arose.   [Ecclesiastes 1:5]

In England the novel was published under the title *Fiesta*, referring primarily to the fiesta at Pamplona that many of the characters visit on an excursion to Spain. The title implies that for much of the time, despite the prevalent air of gloom, they are genuinely enjoying themselves.

1125   Surfacing   (Margaret Atwood, 1972)
The Canadian author's second novel concerns the search made by the (unnamed) narrator for her missing father and also her quest for her own past, particularly its repressed aspects. She comes to terms with these when she dives into a lake and discovers her father's drowned body, "surfacing" afterwards with a new awareness.

1126   Swallows and Amazons   (Arthur Ransome, 1930)
The British writer's first novel for children concerns the adventures of various groups of children on a sailing holiday. The title alludes to two such groups, who respectively crew the sailboats *Swallow* and *Amazon*, name themselves collectively for their craft, and engage in friendly rivalry.

1127   A Swarm in May   (William Mayne, 1955)
The British writer's third novel for children is set in a cathedral choir school where one of the choirboys is awarded the ceremonious title of Beekeeper, as a relic of the days when the cathedral kept its own bees. He discovers that the holder of this title has to sing a special solo and make a Latin speech, and in trepidation persuades a friend to be Beekeeper in his place. He and his schoolmates then stumble on one of the cathedral's secrets. The title alludes both to the appointment and to the "swarm" of events that follow, and derives from the old rhyme:

> A swarm of bees in May
> Is worth a load of hay.

1128   Sweet Desserts   (Lucy Ellmann, 1988)
The first novel by the American-born British writer has the destructiveness of consumerism as its theme and recounts the life of a young woman who is overshadowed by her father, a successful academic. The title puns on *dessert*, "sweet course," and *desert*, "reward or punishment."

1129   Swiftie the Magician   (Herbert Gold, 1975)
The American author's novel recounts the involvement of a writer with three women: an East Coast innocent, a West Coast "experienced" young woman, and the tough title character, Swiftie, a "magician" who knows what's what in a rough world.

1130   The Sword in the Stone   (T. H. White, 1938)
The British writer's novel is based on the story of King Arthur, who was able to draw a sword from the stone in which it was fixed. The author later rewrote the book and used it as the first part of his tetralogy, **The Once and Future King**.

1131   Tai-Pan   (James Clavell, 1966)
The second novel by the British-born American writer is set in Hong Kong. It concerns a Scot, Dirk Struan, who joins forces with a Chinese to secure English rights to Hong Kong. In the process, Struan becomes "Tai-Pan" ("big-shot"), borrowing vast sums of money to corner markets, smash the Triads, and undertake other grand projects. Clavell was a prisoner of war in the Far East in World War II.

1132   Take a Girl Like You   (Kingsley Amis, 1960)
The British writer's fourth novel tells the story of Patrick Standish, a young man able to "take" (seduce) girls at random. Although the title puns on its other meaning, "Let's consider a girl like you," it was actually adopted by Amis from the Josh White song, "Take a Gal Like You." The novel's sequel was **Difficulties with Girls**.

1133   Take This Man   (Frederick Busch, 1981)
The American writer's fifth novel tells the story of a young boy, Gus, who has two fathers. Aged ten, he goes to the biological one, with his mother following suit. The three form a family, but the two adults never marry. Hence the punning title, with its echoes of the marriage service.

1134   A Tale of Two Cities   (Charles Dickens, 1859)
The "two cities" of the title are London and Paris, with the novel set at the time of the French Revolution.

1135   Tales of My Landlord   (Walter Scott, 1816–31)
The title is the overall one for four series of novels (seven novels in total), purporting to be compiled by the assistant of one Jedediah Cleishbotham, schoolmaster and parish clerk, and sold by the latter to a publisher. As Scott himself admitted, the title is a misnomer, since the tales were not told by the landlord, and the landlord had absolutely no part in them.

1136   Tales of the Grotesque and Arabesque   (Edgar Allan Poe, 1839)
The American writer's first collection of stories, published in two volumes, has a title suggested by an essay of Sir Walter Scott.

1137   Talking It Over   (Julian Barnes, 1991)
The "it" of the title of the British writer's sixth novel is love. The story concerns the love triangle between a dull banker, Stuart, an English teacher, Oliver, and a social worker-turned-picture restorer, Gillian. The title as a whole hints at another theme explored by the novel: the tendency of language to turn one thing into another.

1138   Tamar and Other Poems   (Robinson Jeffers, 1924)
The American poet's collection of five poems begins with the title piece, a free-verse narrative centering on the incestuous love of Tamar Cauldwell for her brother Lee. The piece and its title were based on the biblical story of Amnon and Tamar in 2 Samuel 13, which opens: "And it came to pass after this, that Absalom the son of David had a fair sister, whose name was Tamar; and Amnon the son of David loved her."

1139   Tea and Sympathy   (Robert Woodruff Anderson, 1953)
The play by the American writer is about an unhappy American preparatory school boy accused of homosexuality. The title is extracted from Act I: "All you're supposed to do is every once in a while give the boys a little tea and sympathy." The phrase is a near-proverbial one for advice given to a distressed person, and is found earlier in similar wording, for example Keats' reference to "tea & comfortable advice" in a letter of October 8, 1818, to James Hessey.

1140   The Teahouse of the August Moon   (John Patrick, 1953)
The play by the American playwright, an adaptation of a novel by Vern Schneider, is a comic fantasy about American soldiers who build a teahouse to please the inhabitants of Okinawa during their occupation of that Japanese island.

1141   Tell England   (Ernest Raymond, 1922)
The English writer's novel tells the story of a group of public school boys from school to the battlefields of Gallipoli. It comes from a Boer War memorial at Wagon Hill, Ladysmith, South Africa:

> Tell England, ye who pass this monument,
> We, who died serving her, rest here content.

This occurs in slightly different form in the story itself, in the closing lines of Chapter XII:

> We had walked right on to the grave of our friend. His name stood on a cross with those of six other officers, and beneath was written in pencil the famous epitaph:
>
> > "Tell England, ye who pass this monument,
> > We died for her, and here we rest content."

The perfect words went straight to Doe's heart.
"Roop," he said, "if I'm killed you can put those lines over me."
I fear I could not think of anything very helpful to reply.
"They are rather swish," I murmured.

1142   Tempest-Tost   (Robertson Davies, 1951)

The Canadian writer's first novel is also the first of the three that came to be known as *The Salterton Trilogy*. It describes the misadventures of an amateur theatrical group who are attempting to stage a performance of Shakespeare's *The Tempest*. The title thus punningly alludes to this, but actually comes from *Macbeth*:

> Though his bark cannot be lost,
> Yet it shall be tempest-tost.

1143   Temporary Kings   (Anthony Powell, 1973)

The eleventh volume in the British writer's sequence **A Dance to the Music of Time** opens with one of the characters being recommended to make a trip to Venice. There, he is told, he can have the time of his life as long as his visits lasts, like one of the "temporary kings" described (in the chapter so headed) in Sir James Frazer's *The Golden Bough*, who reign for a brief spell and are then killed. Three of the novel's characters die before the end (one a musician, another an art enthusiast), and the message seems to be that though artists are "temporary kings," their art endures.

1144   Tender Is the Night   (F. Scott Fitzgerald, 1934)

The American writer's novel, set in the decadent period following World War I, is a compassionate account of the love that develops between Nicole Warren, a wealthy mental patient, and Dick Diver, her psychiatrist. The title quotes a phrase from Keats' *Ode to a Nightingale* (1820): "Already with thee! tender is the night."

1145   The Tenth Month   (Laura Z. Hobson, 1971)

The American writer's novel centers on unmarried mothers, who in the "tenth month" (the month following their delivery at nine months) are obliged to face their families and society in general.

1146   The Terrible Twos   (Ishmael Reed, 1982)

The American author's sixth novel is a satire on greed, racism, and inhumanity. Reed sees the United States of the 1980s as a greedy two-year-old (hence the title), draining the world of resources and hiding behind a false veneer of charity and concern.

1147   Textures of Life   (Hortense Calisher, 1963)

The American writer's novel centers on the married couple David and Elizabeth, who realize the importance of "things," whether tangible possessions, such as the baby they have, or abstract concepts, what they call "the kind of stuff they pretend isn't there." They are both artists: Elizabeth is a sculptor, and David a photographer and moviemaker. It is he who wishes to make a film about "the textures of life" itself, whether of life as it is now (in New York at the time when the novel was written) or as it was in the 15th century. Hence the title.

1148   That Damn Y   (Katherine Mayo, 1920)
The book by the American newspaperwoman, famous for her militant writing against social injustice, is an examination of the workings of the YMCA abroad during World War I, and this organization is the "Y" of the title.

1149   That Hideous Strength   (C. S. Lewis, 1945)
The third volume of science fiction by the British author takes its title from Sir David Lindsay's poem *The Monarchie* (1554), itself a description of the Tower of Babel:

> The Shadow of that hyddeous strength
> Sax myle and more it is of length.

1150   That Was Then, This Is Now   (S. E. Hinton, 1971)
The American writer's novel concerns a group of urban youths reluctantly making the transition from "then" (boyhood) to "now" (manhood).

1151   them   (Joyce Carol Oates, 1969)
The American writer's fourth novel is the last of a trilogy about people from different social strata. The events of the story take place between the Depression and the riots of 1967, as experienced by Maureen Wendall, a night school student, and her working-class family. The lowercase initial of the title emphasizes the low status of "them."

1152   There Shall Be No Night   (Robert E. Sherwood, 1940)
The American writer's play is about a Finnish pacifist who decides to fight against the Nazis but who loses his life in so doing. The title is biblical in origin:

> And there shall be no night there; and they need no candle, neither light of the sun; for the Lord God giveth them light.   [Revelation 22:5]

1153   These Enchanted Woods   (Allan Massie, 1993)
The Scottish writer's "comedy of morals" tells the story of a woman who marries into the sombre world of the Scottish gentry and who chances to meet a former lover, with whom she resumes her relationship. The title quotes from George Meredith's poem *The Woods of Westermain* (1883):

> Enter these enchanted woods
> You who dare.

1154   They Call Me Carpenter   (Upton Sinclair, 1922)
The narrator of the American writer's novel falls unconscious in a church in Western City and dreams that Jesus steps down from a stained glass window to enter public life under the name of Mr. Carpenter (a reference to the occupation of Joseph, Jesus's father, and of Jesus himself). Hence the title.

1155   They Knew What They Wanted   (Sidney Howard, 1925)
The play by the Americn playwright tells of the marriage that an ageing wine grower cunningly arranges with a young waitress, and of the wife's affair with the

grower's son. She becomes pregnant by him, and the two, though not in love, decide to elope. Learning the truth, the husband asks his wife to stay with him and offers to accept her child as his own. The title thus indicates the roundabout route by which the characters achieve their desires.

1156   They Might Be Giants   (James Goldman, 1970)

The American writer's play, about a man who thinks he is Sherlock Holmes, includes a dialogue that clarifies the title. When the female Dr. Watson, recruited by Holmes, tells him that he is like Don Quixote, thinking that everything is always something else, he replies:

> "He had a point—of course, he carried it a bit too far, that's all. He thought that every windmill was a giant. [...] If we never looked at things and thought what they *might* be we'd still all be in the tall grass with the apes."

1157   They Shoot Horses, Don't They?   (Horace McCoy, 1935)

The American writer's first novel is the story told on the eve of his execution by a man who had, at her request, killed his marathon-dance partner. The title quotes from the narrative itself:

> "Why did you kill her?" the policeman in the rear seat asked. [...] "They shoot horses, don't they?" I said.

1158   Things Fall Apart   (Chinua Achebe, 1958)

The Nigerian writer's first novel, selling millions of copies on the African continent, tells how the tribal life of the Ibo people in a particular village begins to "fall apart" after the arrival of the first white missionaries. The title comes from Yeats's poem *The Second Coming* (1921):

> Things fall apart; the centre cannot hold;
> Mere anarchy is loosed upon the world.

For another title from the same work, *cf.* **Innocence Is Drowned.**

1159   The Thirty-Nine Steps   (John Buchan, 1915)

The Scottish writer's classic thriller tells how Richard Hannay pursues German spies round Britain, from north to south. The story ends with the search for the "house at the head of the thirty-nine steps," which is found on the English Channel coast. The site is a genuine one in Kent, on the low cliffs not far from Broadstairs (whose own name means "broad steps").

1160   This Island Now   (Peter Abrahams, 1966)

The black South African writer's seventh novel, published in a revised edition in 1985, concerns racial tensions and internal power struggles in a small, black-ruled Caribbean island state. The title comes from the first line of W. H. Auden's poem of 1936: "Look, stranger, at this island now." *Cf.* **Look, Stranger!**

1161   This Rough Magic   (Mary Stewart, 1964)

The British writer's novel concerns a girl who, holidaying on Corfu, becomes involved not only with sorcery but in a gun-running conspiracy between Greece and

Albania. The title quotes words from a speech by Prospero in Shakespeare's *The Tempest* (1611), with the "isle that is full of noises" in that play taken to be Corfu (although Shakespeare's sources related to the Bermudas):

> Graves at my command
> Have waked their sleepers, oped, and let 'em forth
> By my so potent art. But this rough magic
> I abjure. [V.i.48]

1162 Those Barren Leaves (Aldous Huxley, 1925)
The British writer's novel, set in Italy, takes its title from William Wordsworth's poem *The Tables Turned* (1798):

> Enough of science and of art;
>   Close up these barren leaves;
> Come forth, and bring with you a heart
>   That watches and receives.

1163 Three Birds Alighting on a Field (Timberlake Wertenbaker, 1991)
At first sight the play by the Anglo-French-American dramatist, about the modern art market, appears to have an arbitrary title, like that borne by a typical modern painting. The playwright in fact took it from an interview with the British artist Francis Bacon when he described his process of painting. He said he started drawing a figure, but that the figure itself gradually became less and less important, so that the painting finished by being about "three birds alighting on a field." In Wertenbaker's play, this process is reversed. A painter falls in love with a woman and says, "I started off painting this picture about three birds alighting on a field but you've taken over the canvas."

1164 The Three Black Pennys (Joseph Hergesheimer, 1917)
The American writer's three-part novel tells of the "black sheep" in three generations of the Penny family, with gaps of two generations between each part.

1165 Three Men on the Bummel (Jerome K. Jerome, 1900)
The British writer's novel is a sequel to the popular *Three Men in a Boat* (1889), about an accident-prone rowing holiday on the Thames. In the present book the same three characters go on a tour of Germany. "Bummel" is not the name of a river, as sometimes supposed, but a German word for a leisurely stroll or journey. (American slang *bum* as a term for a loafer or hobo is related.)

1166 Three Soldiers (John Dos Passos, 1921)
The American writer's novel is set in the last year of World War I and centers on the experiences of three privates, who together represent a cross-section of American society. Hence the title, which echoes Rudyard Kipling's *Soldiers Three* (1890), which is also about three privates.

1167 Three Times Table (Sara Maitland, 1990)
The British writer's novel, like others before it, is a mixture of lively narrative on the one hand and a blend of naturalism and magic on the other. Set over a time of only

a few days, it tells the story of three women: Rachel, her daughter Phoebe, and her teenage granddaughter Maggie. The title alludes not only to this trinity but to the synchronicity with which each woman faces and masters a personal crisis.

1168   Through Dooms of Love   (Maxine Kumin, 1965)

The American writer's first novel is a semiautobiographical story of conflict between a Radcliffe girl and her pawnbroker father. Its title quotes from E. E. Cummings's poem *my father moved through dooms of love* (1940):

> my father moved through dooms of love
> through sames of am through haves of give,
> singing each morning out of each night
> my father moved through depths of height

1169   A Tiger for Malgudi   (R. K. Narayan, 1983)

The novel by the Indian writer is one of several set in the South Indian community of Malgudi. In this instance the villagers are confronted by Raja, a tiger, who is the central character and narrator. The story is based on Hindu doctrines of reincarnation and recounts how Raja's "potential of violence" is overcome.

1170   The Time of the Crack   (Emma Tennant, 1973)

The British author's second novel is a futuristic fable about a gradually widening crack in the riverbed of the Thames, leading to the partial destruction of London and eventually to the complete severance of the whole of the south of England.

1171   The Time of Your Life   (William Saroyan, 1939)

The play by the American playwright is a poetic fantasy set in a waterfront saloon. The title punningly indicates its theme: that everyone should make the most of life, be compassionate to the weak, and oppose the enemies of life, with force if necessary.

1172   A Time to Dance   (Melvyn Bragg, 1990)

The British author's fourteenth novel concerns a middle-aged bank manager's obsessive passion for a young woman. The title is biblical:

> A time to weep, and a time to laugh; a time to mourn, and a time to dance.   [Ecclesiastes 3:4]

1173   Time's Arrow   (Martin Amis, 1991)

The British writer's seventh novel centers on a German doctor who had participated in atrocities in the Nazi eras. His story is told backwards, from the doctor's death to his birth, in such a way that the killings and torturings seem to be restorations to health. Amis had considered the title for his earlier novel **London Fields**. He adopted it from a term introduced by the British astrophysicist Sir Arthur Eddington in *The Nature of the Physical World* (1928):

> I shall use the phrase "time's arrow" to express this one-way property of time which has no analogue in space.

The novel's subtitle, which Amis had originally planned as its main title, is *The Nature of the Offence*. This was a phrase of Primo Levi's, used by Amis to refer to Levi's suicide in 1987. Levi had himself been sent to Auschwitz concentration camp and recounted his experiences in his now famous novels.

1174   Tirra Lirra by the River   (Jessica Anderson, 1978)

The Australian writer's fourth novel concerns the life of a woman born early in the 20th century. The title quotes from Tennyson's poem *The Lady of Shallott* (1834), to which there are many parallels in the book:

> From the bank and from the river
> He flash'd into the crystal mirror,
> 'Tirra lirra,' by the river
>   Sang Sir Lancelot.

1175   To Be a Pilgrim   (Joyce Cary, 1942)

The British writer's novel is the second of a trilogy (*see* **Herself Surprised**). Its central character is the aged Tom Willcher, who reflects on his life as a "pilgrim" over more than half a century. The title comes from John Bunyan's famous hymn in *The Pilgrim's Progress* (1684):

> Who would true valour see,
> Let him come hither;
> One here will constant be,
> Come wind, come weather.
> There's no discouragement
> Shall make him once relent
> His first avowed intent
> To be a pilgrim.

1176   To Have and Have Not   (Ernest Hemingway, 1937)

The American writer's novel tells how Harry Morgan, a native of Key West, striving to keep himself and his family on the upper edge of the "have-nots," is forced by the Depression to turn to smuggling. He helps four Cuban revolutionaries escape, though realizes that unless he kills them, they will kill him. He does so, but one of them fatally wounds him. His final fumbling words are:

> "A man ... ain't got no hasn't got any can't really isn't any way out ... no chance."

1177   To Kill a Mockingbird   (Harper Lee, 1960)

The American author's first (and only) novel, set in a small Alabama town, tells how a white lawyer, Atticus Finch, defends a black man, Tom Robinson, falsely accused of raping a young white woman. The story is told from the viewpoint of Finch's eight-year-old daughter, Scout. The title comes from Finch's advice to Scout's elder brother, Jem, on giving him an air rifle:

> "I'd rather you shot at tin cans in the back yard, but I know you'll go after birds. Shoot all the bluejays you want, if you can hit 'em, but remember it's a sin to kill a mockingbird."

A family neighbor, Miss Maudie, explains further to Jem:

> "Mockingbirds don't do one thing but make music for us to enjoy. They don't eat up people's gardens, don't nest in corncribs, they don't do one thing but sing their hearts out for us. That's why it's a sin to kill a mockingbird."

The story's real "mockingbird" is the innocent Tom Robinson, shot dead by prison guards when trying to escape. Reporting the event, the local paper's editor compares Tom's death to "the senseless slaughter of songbirds by hunters and children."

1178   To Serve Them All My Days   (R.F. Delderfield, 1972)

The British writer's novel, about a World War I shattered idealist who takes a job in a private school, has a title that evokes, without precisely quoting, a number of religious references. These include: "To serve him truly all the days of my life," from the Prayer Book, "To serve thee all my happy days," from the hymn, "Gentle Jesus, meek and mild," "To serve him all our days" from the Devon carol, "We'll bring him hearts that love him," and "And serve him all my days," from the Sunday school hymn, "I must like a Christian."

1179   To the Chapel Perilous   (Naomi Mitchison, 1955)

The Scottish-born writer was the author of a number of historical novels. This one is based on the many myths that surround King Arthur, the Knights of the Round Table, and the Quest for the Holy Grail. The title refers to the chapel in which the Grail (in this anachronistic version of the story) is said to be preserved and which is sought by several knights.

1180   To the Finland Station   (Edmund Wilson, 1940)

The American writer's study of the European thinkers who laid the ground for the Russian Revolution takes its title from the railroad station in St. Petersburg (then called Petrograd) to which Lenin returned from exile in Switzerland in 1917.

1181   To the Lighthouse   (Virginia Woolf, 1927)

The "stream of consciousness" novel by the British writer centers on the conflict that arises from the desire of the young child, James Ramsay, to visit a lighthouse off the west coast of Scotland, where the scene is set, and the thwarting of this desire by his philosopher father. The visit to the lighthouse eventually takes place many years later at the end of the book. The lighthouse itself symbolizes different things to the book's different characters.

1182   Tobacco Road   (Erskine Caldwell, 1932)

The American writer's novel takes its title from the name of the road on which live the central character, Jeeter Lester, a penniless Georgian farmer and his family. The novel, and so its title, was popularized by the dramatization made of it the following year by Jack Kirkland, and as a stage play it had one of the longest runs in the American theater.

1183   Tobit Transplanted   (Stella Benson, 1930)
The British writer's novel stems from her stay in Manchuria in the 1920s, when she saw a parallel between the plight of the White Russians exiled from the Soviet Union after the Revolution and the story of the exiled Jew Tobit in the Apocrypha. The plot of her book thus broadly follows that of the Book of Tobit, with old Sergei Malinin representing Tobit himself, his son Seryozha as Tobias, and the Christian Chinese barrister Wilfred Chew as the angel Raphael. "The young man's dog" in the original also features as Seryozha's dog. Benson's novel was first published in the United States under the title *The Faraway Bride*, the allusion being to Tanya Osta-penko, the beautiful Russian girl whom Seryozha marries.

1184   Tongues of Angels   (Reynolds Price, 1990)
The American writer's ninth novel is a story of adolescent initiation and adult re-alization in a Smoky Mountain summer camp. It explores the spiritual origins of art and its religious significance as rendered by the artist. The title is biblical in ori-gin: "Though I speak with the tongues of men and of angels, and have not charity, I am become as sounding brass, or a tinkling cymbal" (1 Corinthians 13:1).

1185   Tono-Bungay   (H. G. Wells, 1909)
The title of the British writer's novel is the name of the quack medicine manufac-tured and marketed by the uncle of the central character, George Ponderevo. The name itself is almost meaningless, although the first part suggests "tone." The sec-ond part may have been intended to suggest "bungle," alluding to the eventual bankruptcy of the uncle and the failure of George's marriage and his own commer-cial ventures.

1186   Too Late the Phalarope   (Alan Paton, 1953)
The South African writer's second novel deals with the austere and loveless way of life of the Afrikaans-speaking descendants of the Boers (the Dutch settlers in South Africa). The plot concerns the alienation between a young man and his fa-ther. The two meet to discuss the identification of a bird called the *phalarope* in a book of South African birds, and it seems as if they will be reconciled. But, as the title implies, it is now too late. The father later dies on learning of the son's liaison with a black woman.

1187   Tortilla Flat   (John Steinbeck, 1935)
The novel by the American writer has a title that is the name of the uphill district above Monterey, California, where it is set. This is the home of the *paisanos*, who combine "Spanish, Indian, Mexican and assorted Caucasian bloods." The name is that of a typical Mexican district, so called because it suggests a tortilla, a Mexican round flat corn cake.

1188   The Towers of Silence   (Paul Scott, 1971)
The British writer's fourth novel in the sequence of four entitled *The Raj Quartet* is set in 1942 and centers on an isolated British army community in an Indian hill sta-tion, where their regular and orderly lives mirror the turbulence and confusion that

elsewhere is World War II. Although alluding to this, the title actually refers to the Towers of Silence, where the Ranpur parsees offer up their dead. As the book ends, one of the main characters lies dying in hospital, mentally and physically destroyed. Beyond the window she sees the vultures circling endlessly (and symbolically) over the Towers.

1189   The Transit of Venus   (Shirley Hazzard, 1980)

The American writer's fourth novel concerns a young Australian woman, Caroline Bell, who travels to England with her sister. The narrative moves on to tell of her death in an air crash, and the reader also learns that the man she finally realizes she loves, and was on the way to meet, has committed suicide. The story as a whole is thus about love and about truth. It is also about chance, as the title implies. It refers to the transit of the planet Venus across the sun on June 6, 1769 which the Royal Society sent Captain Cook to observe in the Pacific. In so doing, he chanced to discover the so-called "Terra Australis," otherwise Australia. The title also alludes metaphorically to the "passage of love" made by the novel's heroine.

1190   A Traveler from Altruria   (W. D. Howells, 1894)

The American writer's novel tells the story of Mr. Homos, a visitor from the utopian republic of Altruria, who comes to spend his vacation at a fashionable American summer resort. His native country is so named because it was founded on principles of *altruism*, a virtue he is keen to promote among the wealthy Americans he meets.

1191   A Tree Grows in Brooklyn   (Betty Smith, 1943)

The American writer's novel is a sentimental tale about the Nolans, a working-class family in the author's native New York. The title has a symbolic reference, spelled out in the book:

> There's a tree that grows in Brooklyn. Some people call it the Tree of Heaven. No matter where its seed falls, it makes a tree which struggles to reach the sky.

1192   Trent's Last Case   (E. C. Bentley, 1912)

The British writer's classic detective novel tells how Philip Trent, artist, newspaper reporter, and amateur detective, solves his final case, the murder of the American financier, Sigsbee Manderson.

1193   The Trick of It   (Michael Frayn, 1989)

The British writer's sixth novel consists of letters from a young lecturer in English to a friend in Australia. He describes how he has married a novelist, and thinks he can improve her next novel. When he attempts to do so, he finds he does not have "the trick of it," or the ability to write fiction. Hence the title.

1194   The Triumph of the Egg   (Sherwood Anderson, 1912)

The volume by the American writer is a "book of impressions from American life in tales and poems." The title story is a comic study of a chicken farmer whose life is dominated by eggs and who regards himself as a failure when he is unable to perform a simple trick with an egg for a customer.

1195   Tropic of Cancer   (Henry Miller, 1934)

The American writer's notorious novel, first published in Paris, where it is set, and banned in Britain for nearly 30 years, is an account of a surreal and repulsive city which "sprouts out like a human organism diseased in every part." It is thus cancerous, as the title implies. The title also links with that of the novel's companion volume, *Tropic of Capricorn* (1939), which is set in America, and tells of the author's childhood and his preparation to become an artist. As Miller wrote, "Cancer is separated from Capricorn only by an imaginary line."

1196   The Trouble I've Seen   (Martha Gellhorn, 1936)

The American writer's novel is the fictionalized outcome of a report for Harry Hopkins's Federal Emergency Relief agency on the conditions under which people live when on welfare in industrial areas. The title quotes from the well-known spiritual:

> Nobody knows the trouble I've seen,
> Nobody knows but Jesus.

1197   Troubles   (J. G. Farrell, 1969)

The British writer's novel is a historical fantasy set in Northern Ireland during the civil disturbances ("troubles") of the 1920s. The real "troubles" of the title, however, are the personal ones experienced by the main characters, the Protestant Edward Spencer and the army major Brendan Archer. (Archer comes to Ireland to marry Spencer's daughter, Angela, but she falls ill and dies.) Coincidentally, the recent "troubles" in Northern Ireland began while Farrell was still researching the novel.

1198   Truant State   (Nicholas Hasluck, 1987)

The Australian writer's fifth novel is set in Western Australia in the 1920s and 1930s, and is narrated by a young immigrant from England, whose father has high hopes of a new life. The narrative involves the reactionary West Guard secret society which sought secession for Western Australia. The title refers both to the latter, as a "truant state," and more particularly to the lives of the protagonists, who have "played truant" from their native land.

1199   The Trumpet of the Swan   (E. B. White, 1970)

The American writer's third novel for children tells the story of a trumpeter swan who overcomes the problem of losing his voice by learning to play the trumpet.

1200   Trust   (Cynthia Ozick, 1966)

The American author's first novel centers on a wealthy American family who mask greed and duplicity under an elegant surface of manners. The title is thus ironic, in that every relationship, including that with God, is affected by lack of trust. However, the central character finally revives trust by revoking her decayed cultural heritage and reverting to ancient paganism.

1201   The Truth About Them   (Jose Yglesias, 1971)

The American writer's third novel centers on the attempts of the Spanish American, Pini, to make sense of his family past and to pass on its ethos to his son. "They" are thus both Spanish Americans and their many opponents, while the "truth" is the essence and root nature of their lives.

1202   Tuck Everlasting   (Natalie Babbitt, 1975)
The American writer's sixth novel for children has as its theme the place of death in the universe of living things. It tells the story of 11-year-old Winnie, a small-town girl who discovers that a backwoods family, the Tucks, have drunk from a stream that has granted them immortality. The title thus names the family and alludes to their gift, while playing on the biblical phrase "life everlasting."

1203   Tunc   (Lawrence Durrell, 1968)
The British author intended that this novel should be paired with its "Siamese twin," *Nunquam* (1970), and the two were published together under the joint title *The Revolt of Aphrodite* (1974). The novels have as their theme the destruction of love and creativity by social pressures, and center on "The Firm," a huge, dehumanizing multinational enterprise. *Tunc* is Latin for "then" and *Nunquam* Latin for "never." It has been suggested that Durrell also intended *Tunc* to be interpreted anagramatically for its taboo sexual sense.

1204   The 27th Kingdom   (Alice Thomas Ellis, 1982)
The British writer's novel has as its central character the forceful Aunt Irene, of Russian descent. The "27th kingdom" of the title is Britain, the country in which her ancestors finally settled (and in which she herself lives) after fleeing their motherland as Roman Catholic converts and gradually progressing through many other monarchies (such as Lithuania and Austria) on the way.

1205   Twenty-Six Lead Soldiers   (Dan Wooding, 1987)
The British author's novel, on a top Fleet Street journalist and his search for the spiritual truth, takes its title from the old riddle, "With twenty-six soldiers of lead, I can conquer the world," the "twenty-six soldiers of lead" being a printer's 26 letters of the alphabet. The authorship of the original saying is uncertain.

1206   Twice-Told Tales   (Nathaniel Hawthorne, 1837)
The American writer's collection of 39 stories appears to take its title from a line in Shakespeare's *King John*:

> Life is as tedious as twice-told tale,
> Vexing the dull ear of a drowsy man.   [III.iv.108]

1207   Two Cheers for Democracy   (E. M. Forster, 1951)
The title of the British author's collected of essays indicates his qualified approval for the democratic process. His Prefatory Note ends:

> We may still contrive to raise three cheers for democracy, although at present she only deserves two.

1208   Typee   (Herman Melville, 1846)
The American writer's fictional narrative is based on his experiences when he deserted the whaler *Acushnet* in 1842. The title is the tribal name of the peaceful

savages with whom the novel's two central characters take refuge on a Marquesan island.

1209   U and I   (Nicholson Baker, 1991)
The non-fiction work by the American writer is a study of his obsession with the novelist John Updike. Hence the punning title.

1210   Ulalume   (Edgar Allan Poe, 1847)
The title of the American writer's lyrical poem is the name of its subject, and the poem itself is a ballad expressing the writer's grief over her death. The meaning of the name, if any, is unknown.

1211   Ulysses   (James Joyce, 1922)
The Irish writer's novel consists of a number of episodes, each loosely based on an episode in Homer's *Odyssey*. The central character, Leopold Bloom, represents Odysseus (Ulysses) himself, while his unfaithful wife, Molly, is Penelope.

1212   Under Milk Wood   (Dylan Thomas, 1954)
The Welsh writer's radio play, written for the BBC, tells of the inhabitants of the small Welsh town of Llaregyb, lying under the "tiny dingle" of Milk Wood. Milk features in various ways in the lives of the characters: one is Ocky Milkman; another, the young milkmaid, Mae Rose Cottage. The old blind sailor, Captain Cat, sings a song about a baby in a milking pail, and the young mother, Polly Garter, breast-feeds her baby in the garden. When Thomas first drafted the play he called it *The Town Was Mad*. This then became *Llaregyb, a Piece for Radio Perhaps*, and finally *Under Milk Wood, a Play for Voices*. Thomas originally spelled the town's name as Llareggub, basing it loosely on that of his home town of Laugharne. "Auntie" prudishly objected to the reversal that this clearly was, however, so it was duly modified.

1213   Under the Greenwood Tree   (Thomas Hardy, 1872)
The novel, described by the author as "a rural painting of the Dutch school," is a pastoral tale, interweaving a love story with the fortunes and misfortunes of a group of villagers. The title comes from a song in Shakespeare's *As You Like It*:

> Under the greenwood tree
> Who loves to lie with me,
> And turn his merry note
> Unto the sweet bird's throat,
> Come hither, come hither, come hither:
> Here shall he see
> No enemy
> But winter and rough weather.   [II.v.1]

1214   Under the Net   (Iris Murdoch, 1954)
The British writer's first novel concerns a group of rootless characters in and around London who try to develop some kind of individual identities. Many of them manage to escape "under the net" of conventional society in order to achieve this, but at

the price of reducing the range of their lives to little more than an actual identity. The image of the net comes from Wittgenstein, who understood it as the concepts from which we construct reality and from which we cannot escape. Murdoch further explained to the literary critic Frank Kermode:

> "The problem which is mentioned in the title is the problem of how far conceptualizing and theorizing, which from one point of view are absolutely essential, in fact divide you from the thing that is the object of the theoretical attention." [Frank Kermode, *The House of Fiction: Seven Interviews with Seven Novelists*, 1963]

1215   Under the Volcano   (Malcolm Lowry, 1947)

The British writer's visionary and largely autobiographical novel evolved from a short story of the same title that he had written in Mexico in 1936 after a brief spell in New York's Bellevue Hospital, where he had made a vain attempt to cure his alcoholism. The cottage where he stayed had a view of Popocatepetl, and this is the volcano of the title. It is in its shadow, as well as in that of neighboring Ixtacihuatl, that the brooding tragedy unfolds.

1216   Under Western Eyes   (Joseph Conrad, 1911)

The "western eyes" are those of the narrator of the Polish-born British writer's novel, an elderly English teacher of languages in Geneva, who tells the story of the Russian student revolutionary, Razumov, basing his tale on the young man's diary.

1217   Uneasy Money   (P. G. Wodehouse, 1917)

The British author's comic novel has many strands and subplots but basically concerns the events that ensue when its central character, Bill Chalmers, Lord Dawlish, who has a title but no money, is unexpectedly left five million dollars in the will of an eccentric American millionaire whom he had coached in golf. He thus comes into both "easy money" (in the accepted sense, since he did little to earn it) and "uneasy money," since he has to cope with the millionaire's niece and nephew, who were rightfully expecting to be the beneficiaries.

1218   Unhealthful Air   (Elliott Baker, 1988)

The American writer's sixth novel recounts the adventures of a devious Hollywood scriptwriter and gambler, Corey Burdick, who becomes embroiled with a horserace-fixing syndicate, an Ozark nymphet, and her cruel husband. By using his wits, Burdick manages to survive the "unhealthful air" of Los Angeles and even to prosper.

1219   An Unofficial Rose   (Iris Murdoch, 1962)

The British writer's sixth novel is about a group of people who have reached an impasse in their married lives, unable to fulfill their plans or realize their ambitions. It uses the growing of roses as a metaphor and emphasizes the value of "unofficial" forms that can give a rich and "floral" shape to a human being's individual identity. The title comes from Rupert Brooke's poem *The Old Vicarage, Grantchester* (1915):

> Unkempt about those hedges blows
> An English unofficial rose.

1220   Up above the World   (Paul Bowles, 1966)
The American writer's fourth novel has freedom in all its forms as its theme, and relates the adventures of a married couple from the United States as they journey through Central America. The title quotes from the 1806 nursery rhyme by Ann and Jane Taylor:

> Twinkle, twinkle, little star,
> How I wonder what you are,
> Up above the world so high,
> Like a diamond in the sky!

1221   Ushant   (Conrad Aiken, 1952)
The American writer's autobiographical novel takes its title from the name of an island off the coast of Brittany, northwestern France. On this island, with its rocks and reefs, Chateaubriand was wrecked on his return to France from America.

1222   V   (Thomas Pynchon, 1963)
The title initial of the American writer's first novel refers to the "quest for V" pursued by its central character, Henry Stencil. It is the subjet of much plotting, decoding, and recyphering. It may be a woman, such as the British aristocrat Victoria Wren or the German Vera Meroving, or the place called Vheissu, which may or may not be real, or the Maltese town of Valletta, or (at another level) the convergence of two vectors in a point, or the primal symbol of "Woman," or even the stain on a plate in a beerhall. As Stencil's father notes in his journal: "There is more behind and inside V than any of us had suspected. Not who, but what: what is she." At the end of the novel, the riddle is left unsolved, and Stencil is still looking for V.

1223   Vacant Possession   (Hilary Mantel, 1986)
The British writer's second novel tells how Muriel Axon, a woman of feeble intellect, is released from a mental hospital into the community, whereupon she proceeds to "haunt" the people and places she remembers. The title puns on *vacant possession* as a term used by estate agents (realtors) for an unoccupied house, *vacant* in the sense "stupid," "dull," and *possession* in the sense "state of being haunted."

1224   The Valley of Bones   (Anthony Powell, 1964)
The British author's seventh novel in the sequence of 12 entitled **A Dance to the Music of Time** is set in World War II and has war and the routine of war as its theme. The biblical title is taken from Ezekiel 37:1 ("The hand of the Lord [...] set me down in the midst of the valley which was full of bones"), chosen by a military chaplain as the text for his sermon in a service attended by the novel's central character, the young officer Nicholas Jenkins. "Must we not come together, brethren, everyone of us," asks the chaplain, "as did the bones of that ancient valley?" The narrative tells how the "bones" of everyday life are indeed put together, but in a pattern dislocated from the original.

1225   Vandover and the Brute   (Frank Norris, 1914)
The American writer's novel, probably the first he completed, written when he was at Harvard in 1895, was published posthumously. Vandover is the central character, a

young man who decides to become an artist. The novel tells how "the animal in him, the perverse evil brute," leads him into drunkenness, gambling, and debauchery, until "the brute" literally takes over, and he scampers around naked on all fours, howling like a wolf. He finally finds employment as a cleaner, and his humiliation is complete.

1226   Vanity Fair   (W. M. Thackeray, 1847–8)

The novel, generally regarded as one of the greatest in English literature, traces the interwoven destinies of two contrasting heroines, Becky Sharpe and her friend Amelia Sedley, at the time of the Napoleonic Wars. The title is taken from Bunyan's *Pilgrim's Progress* (1678, 1684), in which Vanity, the town with the fair, is so called because it was "lighter than vanity."

1227   Vein of Iron   (Ellen Glasgow, 1935)

The theme of the novel by the American writer is the "vein of iron" in the character of the central character, Ada Fincastle, that sustains her family during the Depression of the 1930s.

1228   Venusberg   (Anthony Powell, 1932)

The British writer's second novel, a love story, is so called after the *Venusberg*, a mountain in central Germany containing caverns in which, according to medieval legend, Venus, the goddess of love, held her court. Powell no doubt also saw the title as punning on *mons veneris*, literally "mound of Venus," a term for the cushion of flesh over the female genitals.

1229   Victory   (Joseph Conrad, 1915)

The novel by the Polish-born British writer is set in Indonesia, and tells how Axel Heyst, a self-exiled wanderer, takes an English girl, Lena, to his island retreat. The manager of the hotel where she had worked desires her, and tells an unscrupulous adventure, Jones, that Heyst has treasure hidden on the island. Jones and his followers invade the island and Lena is killed in an attempt to save Heyst's life. Heyst then commits suicide in despair. The narrative is in effect a meditation on the biblical text 1 Corinthians 15:20–58, St. Paul's affirmation of the reality of the Resurrection. The "victory" of the title is thus that of the famous words of verse 57: "O death, where is thy sting? O grave, where is thy victory?" This is explicitly alluded to in the novel, in which Lena means to get "the very sting of death in her hands," and to "carry off the terrible spoil, the sting of vanquished death." (When Lena dies instead of Heyst, it is "as if fatigued only by the exertions of her tremendous victory, capturing the very sting of death in the service of love.")

1230   Vile Bodies   (Evelyn Waugh, 1930)

The British writer's satirical novel is about the "bright young things" of the 1920s, with their "vile bodies." The title is of biblical origin: "Who shall change our vile body, that it may be fashioned like unto his glorious body" (Philippians 3:21). Possibly, however, Waugh had more in mind the same words (though omitting "fashioned") as part of the burial service in the Book of Common Prayer.

1231   Villette   (Charlotte Brontë, 1853)

The novel is based on the English author's experiences as a teacher in a girls' school in Brussels, which she here renames *Villette*. The placename is a genuine French one, meaning "little town."

1232   The Violent Bear It Away   (Flannery O'Connor, 1960)

The American writer's second novel tells the story of Tarwater, a 14-year-old prophet who alternately rebels against and yields to the religious visions of his uncle. The title seems to be a modification of a biblical text: "The kingdom of heaven suffereth violence, and the violent take it by force" (Matthew 11:12).

1233   The Virgin in the Garden   (A. S. Byatt, 1978)

The British author's third novel is the first in a tetralogy following the lives of a group of people from the 1950s to the 1980s. It concentrates on the three children of an English teacher and the person each of them is involved with. A main strand of the book is the production of a verse play about Queen Elizabeth I, the Virgin Queen, in the garden of an Elizabethan country house. Hence the title, which also alludes to one of the children, Frederica, who remains a virgin until the novel's closing pages.

1234   Virginia   (Ellen Glasgow, 1913)

The American writer's novel is named for its central character, Virginia Dinwiddie, who was herself named for the state in which she was reared in the 1880s.

1235   Vittoria   (George Meredith, 1867)

The British writer's novel, set in Italy in 1848, tells how an opera singer, Sandra Belloni, appears under this symbolic name ("Victory") to signal a revolt against the Austrians.

1236   The Vixens   (Frank Yerby, 1948)

The black American writer's second novel continued his first, **The Foxes of Harrow**, and deals with Reconstruction. Yerby had wanted to call it *Ignoble Victory*, but his editor had requested a title that suggested "more sex."

1237   Vox   (Nicholson Baker, 1992)

The American writer's novel centers on an erotic telephone conversation between a man and a woman. The title represents both the Latin word for "voice" and a casual pronunciation of "fucks."

1238   Waiting for Godot   (Samuel Beckett, 1953)

The Irish-born French writer's tragicomedy, originally written in French with the title *En attendant Godot*, concerns two tramps, Vladimir and Estragon, who are waiting for a mysterious personage named Godot, who sends a boy to them each day to say that he will come the following day, but who never arrives. Godot is thought to symbolize a revelation of the meaning of life, which, like him, never comes. It is not clear whether his name is meant to suggest "God" (though it would not have done in the original French).

1239   Waiting for Lefty   (Clifford Odets, 1930)

The American dramatist's proletarian play deals with a taxi drivers' strike. Lefty, so nicknamed for his left-wing politics, is the committeeman (trade union leader) whom the men await to learn his decision whether they should strike or not. When they hear he has been murdered, they are roused to take decisive action.

1240   The War Between the Tates   (Alison Lurie, 1974)

The American writer's fifth novel concerns the breakdown of the marriage between Brian Tate, a teacher short in stature, fame (although he obtains it later), and genital apparatus, and his wife Erica, as paralleled by the course of the Vietnam War. The title thus alludes to both the couple and the war while simultaneously punning on the "War Between the States" as an alternate name for the Civil War.

1241   War in Heaven   (Charles Williams, 1930)

The British writer's novel, sometimes described as a supernatural thriller, takes its title from the Bible: "And there was war in heaven" (Revelation 12:7). The story is a modern treatment of the Grail legend, with its quasi-realist narrative gradually turning into the tale of a titanic struggle between the forces of good and evil.

1242   The Wasp Factory   (Iain Banks, 1984)

The British author's first novel, which caused a scandal because of its perverse sexuality and violence, has a title that refers to its central subject (or object), the wasp factory created by its main character, the Scottish teenager Frank. He makes it out of an old clock face to which he has added various tunnels and compartments, each with a special significance. From time to time he introduces a live wasp into this, using the route it takes and the fate it suffers as a prediction of the future. If it enters the fire compartments, for example, this means there will be a fire, or if it enters the water compartments, there will be a drowning. The whole device is up to a point symbolic of Frank's own identity, which is eventually revealed to be that of Frances, a girl.

1243   The Waste Land   (T. S. Eliot, 1922)

The Anglo-American writer's poem, which became the author's most influential work, is an exploration of the sterility of Europe after World War I. Its title refers to a dry and desolate land which can be revived by a fertility ritual. In the elaborate footnotes to the work, Eliot acknowledges that he took not only the title but much of the poem's symbolism from Jessie L. Weston's study of the Grail legend, *From Ritual to Romance* (1920).

1244   Water Witch   (J. Fenimore Cooper, 1830)

The American writer's romance, set in New York at the close of the 17th century, has as its title the name of the brigantine owned by the central character, a pirate captain known as "The Skimmer of the Seas," and the story opens with his abduction of a beautiful heiress. The American *Water Witch* is pursued by the English *Coquette*, a sloop of war, and both names add to the general romantic tone of the tale.

1245   The Waters of Kronos   (Conrad Richter, 1960)

The American author's novel, which draws on the history of his family and his career, has its roots in a short story, "Doctor Hanray's Second Chance," which appeared in 1950. It featured a scientist who meets himself as a young boy and is spirited back to the time of his childhood. A similar theme runs through the novel, so that the central character, an old and ailing writer, is transported back to his childhood, where he is not recognized by his father, from whom he had become estranged as a young man. The title thus refers both to Kronos, as the tyrannical father of Greek mythology, and to chronos, as "time."

1246   Watership Down   (Richard Adams, 1972)

The British writer's popular novel about a community of rabbits in Hampshire, England, takes its name from the hill where the story is set. The name is the real one of a hill on the Berkshire Downs near the author's home. (The "-ship" is as in "township," so that the name effectively means "stretch of water.")

1247   The Waterworks   (E. L. Doctorow, 1994)

The American writer's complex novel is set in New York in the years immediately after the Civil War. The story is told by Mr. McIlvaine, city editor of *The New York Telegram*, and concerns one of his reviewers, Martin Pemberton. One day Martin imagines he sees his supposedly dead father, Augustus, who had gotten rich by selling shoddy goods to the Union army and by running slaves. Martin then disappears, and McIlvaine sets out to find him. The title refers to the novel's pervasive symbol: the city waterworks at 42nd Street. McIlvaine recalls its opening in 1842 and wonders "if it were not a reservoir at all, but a baptismal font for the gigantic absolution we require as a people." He then begins to realize that no amount of water can wash this people clean, and that Augustus Pemberton's ill-gotten wealth itself represents the corruption that eats at all of us.

1248   Watt   (Samuel Beckett, 1953)

The Irish-born French writer's experimental novel, set in Ireland, has a protagonist who is the archetypal fall guy, and who finally ends up in lunatic asylum. His road to madness is reflected in his name, which represents his constant questions concerning his quandaries (how do you feed a dog, or name an object?). He is continually given negative answers by the appropriately named Mr. Knott, in whose surreal house he lives.

1249   The Waves   (Virginia Woolf, 1913)

The British writer's experimental novel, tracing the lives of six characters, is interspersed with italicized passages which record the ascent and descent of the sun, the rise and fall of the waves (hence the title), and the passing of the seasons.

1250   The Way of All Flesh   (Samuel Butler, 1903)

The posthumous autobiographical novel by the British writer is a satirical criticism of English middle-class family life, and mirrors much of the author's revolt against his family and the Church of England in Victorian times. The title is a reference to the phrase "to go the way of all flesh," meaning either to die or to share the common experience of life. The phrase itself is generally regarded as biblical in origin, but its nearest equivalent in the Authorized Version is "I go the way of all the earth" (1 Kings 2:2). In the Douay Bible of 1609, however, these same words are rendered as "I enter into the way of all flesh."

1251   The Wayward Bus   (John Steinbeck, 1949)

The American writer's novel describes the sexual misadventures of a group stranded overnight on a bus at a California wayside station. Steinbeck had become obsessed with King Arthur and "Olde England," and had planned to entitle the novel *Whan That Aprille*, from the opening words of the Prologue to Chaucer's *Canterbury Tales*. However, he abandoned it when a friend expressed consternation.

1252   We a BaddDDD People   (Sonia Sanchez, 1970)

The volume of poetry by the black American writer has a title influenced by black chanting. The eccentric spelling of *bad* is meant to indicate its special pronunciation in the slang sense "good." (This sense developed among black jazz musicians in the 1920s: anything that was "bad" from an establishment point of view was "good" to those outside the establishment.)

1253   We Who Are About To...   (Joanna Russ, 1977)

The American writer's fourth novel has a protagonist who fights for, and kills for, the right to die. Hence the title, which alludes to the famous salutation of gladiators to the Roman emperor, as cited by Suetonius in his *Life of Claudius*: "*Ave, Caesar, morituri te salutamus*" ("Hail, Caesar, we who are about to die salute you").

1254   The Web and the Rock   (Thomas Wolfe, 1939)

The title of the American writer's novel refers to the "web" of devotion that the scenic designer Esther Jack gives to the (autobiographical) hero, George Webber (whose own name echoes it), and to the "rock" that is New York City, where George is a struggling writer.

1255   Weir of Hermiston   (R. L. Stevenson, 1896)

The Scottish writer's unfinished novel centers on Archie Weir, the only child of Adam Weir, Lord Hermiston, a formidable judge, and tells of his conflict with his father. Hermiston itself is the remote Lowland village to which Archie is banished by his father after speaking out publicly against him.

1256   The Well of Loneliness   (Radclyffe Hall [Marguerite Radclyffe-Hall], 1928)

The English writer's classic novel of lesbian love has as its heroine the "invert," Stephen Gordon, who is obliged to release her lovers to a conventional world while she herself remains trapped in a "well of loneliness."

1257   What a Carve Up!   (Jonathan Coe, 1994)

The British writer's fourth novel centers on Michael Owen, a struggling author writing the history of the Winshaws, a Yorkshire family who made their original fortune in the slave trade but later participated in the "carve up" of British national assets that took place (as the author sees it) in the 1980s. The title alludes to this at a secondary level, but in the novel directly refers to the 1961 movie *What a Carve Up*, a spooky house farce, that Owen had been taken to see at the age of nine. The film had long haunted him, and the gruesome fate ("carve up") of its characters in a moorland mansion blends with that of the Winshaws in Coe's novel.

1258   What Every Woman Knows   (J. M. Barrie, 1908)

The Scottish writer's comedy centers on the humorless railroader, John Shand, who is caught breaking into the house of Maggie Wylie, a plain girl, in order to read her parents' books. They agree to finance his studies if he marries Maggie. He does so, having been elected to parliament, where he is a witty speaker. He finally realizes "what every woman knows," that he owes his success as an brilliant orator to his wife, who as his typist has added the witty touches to his dull speeches. The title is referred to near the end of the play:

> Every man who is high up loves to think that he has done it all himself; and the wife smiles, and lets it go at that. It's our only joke. Every woman knows that. [Act 4]

1259   What Maisie Knew   (Henry James, 1897)

The American writer's novel centers on Maisie Farange, the young daughter of an idle, spendthrift English couple, who divorce when she is six. She is ordered by the court to live with each of them in turn, and "what she knows" by the end of the story is "everything" about adult behavior and guile, and certainly enough to make her own decision about her future. She finally lives with her old governess.

1260   What Makes Sammy Run?   (Budd Schulberg, 1941)

The American writer's novel tells how a New York youth, Sammy Glick, works his way into a position of power in the movie industry. The title does not imply "run" in the literal sense but effectively means "What makes Sammy tick?"

1261   What Price Glory?   (Maxwell Anderson and Laurence Stallings, 1924)

The play by the two American playwrights concerns two U.S. marines in France in 1917, Captain Flagg and Sergeant Quirt, both involved with the same French girl, Charmaine. Quirt nearly marries her, but the wedding is called off when the men's company is ordered into action. Later, the two resume their argument about Charmaine and are looking forward to promised leave when once more they are called out to the front and so forget their quarrels and Charmaine. Quirt concludes, "What a lot of God damn fools it takes to make a war! Hey, Flagg, wait for baby!" The title was the writers' own, based on phrases beginning "What price...?" as used contemptuously of something.

1262   What the Butler Saw   (Joe Orton, 1969)

The play by the British playwright is set in a psychiatric hospital, where some of the characters divest themselves of their clothing. The title refers to the former traditional title of a penny-in-the-slot peepshow, where the viewer inserted a coin to view an animated (and usually quite tame) striptease. This title in turn refers to the supposed propensity of staid English butlers to peek through the keyhole when their mistress was undressing.

1263   What's Become of Waring?   (Anthony Powell, 1939)
The British writer's fifth novel concerns a travel-writer named Waring who has mysteriously disappeared. Investigations into his past life threaten to undermine his publishers, who had been depending on him. The apparently straightforward title actually quotes from the opening lines of Browning's poem *Waring* (1842), so that Powell gave his character a name to match:

> What's become of Waring
> Since he gave us all the slip?

1264   What's Bred in the Bone   (Robertson Davies, 1985)
The Canadian writer's novel is the second in *The Cornish Trilogy*, an ambitious series that explores the life and influence of Francis Cornish. The title comes from a medieval Latin proverb, *Osse radicatum raro de carne recedit*, "What is bred in the bone will not out of the flesh," a concept that haunts Francis Cornish, whose life story is narrated in this volume by the Lesser Zadkiel, Angel of Biography, and commented on by Cornish's guiding spirit, Daimon Maimas. The preoccupation of all three novels is the nature of disguise and deception, and it is to this that the title of the second alludes, even if obscurely.

1265   When the Kissing Had to Stop   (Constantine FitzGibbon, 1960)
The American-born British writer's most successful book is a futuristic political morality about a possible Soviet takeover of a Britain in decline. Its title comes from Robert Browning's poem *A Toccata of Galuppi's* (1855):

> As for Venice and its people, merely born to bloom and drop,
> Here on earth they bore their fruitage, mirth and folly were the crop,
> What of soul was left, I wonder, when the kissing had to stop?

1266   Where Angels Fear to Tread   (E. M. Forster, 1905)
The British writer's first novel is a tragicomedy telling of the consquences of the marriage between an impulsive young widow and an Italian dentist, whom she meets when touring Italy. The title quotes from Pope's poem *An Essay on Criticism* (1711):

> Nay, fly to altars; there they'll talk you dead;
> For fools rush in where angels fear to tread.

1267   Where Are You Going, Where Have You Been?   (Joyce Carol
         Oates, 1974)
The title short story of the American writer's collection first appeared in *The Wheel of Love* (1970). It has male violence and female passivity as its theme, and is based on the biblical story about the Levite who goes to fetch his concubine when she leaves him and returns to her father. On the return journey with her, he is looking

for somewhere to stay the night when an old man sees him and asks: "Whither goest thou? and whence comest thou?" (Judges 19:17).

1268   Where Has Tommy Flowers Gone?   (Terrence McNally, 1971)
The American playwright's comedy about an innocent adrift in New York has a title that appears to be punningly based on the line from the song by Pete Seeger: "Where have all the flowers gone?" (1961).

1269   Where the Wild Things Are   (Maurice Sendak, 1963)
The children's book by the American writer and illustrator tells how a small boy, Max, sent to bed supperless as a punishment, imagines himself away to the country of the "Wild Things," who make him their king. The Wild Things themselves are grotesque monsters. An early version of the book, drawn in 1955, was titled *Where the Wild Horses Are*, and the present title doubtlessly evolved from this.

1270   Where's the Rest of Me?   (Ronald Reagan, 1965)
The American president's early autobiography, written long before he reached the White House, takes its title from the line "Randy—where's the rest of me?" spoken by Reagan himself in the 1941 movie *King's Row*, in which he plays Drake McHugh, who wakes from an operation at the hands of a sadistic doctor to find that his legs have been amputated. He addresses the painful question to Randy Monaghan, played by Ann Sheridan.

1271   Whistle Down the Wind   (Mary Hayley Bell, 1958)
The British writer's novel, made into an acclaimed movie of the same name (1961), tells the story of some childen who while hiding in a barn stumble on a murderer on the run and think he is Jesus Christ (from his oath to that effect). The title comes from a phrase meaning either to abandon something lightly or cast it off (from the releasing of a hawk downwind), or to talk or argue to no purpose. It is not clear what the relevance of either sense is to the action of the novel.

1272   Whistlejacket   (John Hawkes, 1988)
The first part of the American writer's novel is presented as the autobiography of a young boy, Michael, and contains an account of his first hunt on an unusual horse. His family own a painting of a horse named Whistlejacket (hence the title) by the English painter George Stubbs, and the second half of the novel centers on Stubbs himself.

1273   The White Album   (Joan Didion, 1979)
The Californian writer's collection of essays takes its title from the Beatles album of 1968. The title of one song on the album, "Helter Skelter," was written in blood by the murderers in the Sharon Tate/Leno LaBianca 1969 massacre, and this is cited symbolically in the book.

1274   The White Hotel   (D. M. Thomas, 1981)
The British writer's third novel interweaves "fact" and fiction to tell the story of Lisa Erdman, a former patient of Sigmund Freud in Vienna, who finally perished

in the massacrte of Ukrainian Jews at Babi Yar in 1941. The underlying theme of the novel is the conflict between sex and death, with the former expressed in terms of a Utopia and a regression toward the womb, the "white hotel" of the title.

1275 White-Jacket (Herman Melville, 1850)
The American writer's semiautobiographical novel is based on his service on the man-of-war *United States* over the 14 months from August 1843. The title is the nickname of the narrator, a young seaman, given him after he buys a white pea jacket in Peru during a cruise on the frigate *Neversink*. The jacket itself plays a major role in the narrative, since it protects him in dirty weather, picks him out among the crew, and nearly causes his death when he becomes entangled in it during a storm.

1276 The White Negro (Norman Mailer, 1957)
The American writer's long essay is a sympathetic study of a marginal social type, the "hipster," whom he defines in metaphorical terms as a "white Negro," a white person who sympathizes with blacks. (A "white Negro" is literally an albino black.) As Mailer expatiated in *Dissent* IV (1957): "The hipster had absorbed the existentialist synapses of the Negro, and for practical purposes could be considered a white Negro."

1277 Who Has Seen the Wind (W. O. Mitchell, 1947)
The Canadian author's first novel concerns the development from infancy to maturity of a boy in Saskatchewan. The title quotes the first line of Christina Rossetti's identically named poem of 1872.

1278 Who Will Run the Frog Hospital? (Lorrie Moore, 1994)
The American writer's second novel tells the story of Berie, an American woman on holiday with her unfaithful husband in Paris, unhappily married and doomed to childlessness. Berie recalls her times with her adolescent "emotional business partner," Sils Chaussée, in Canada. Both girls had worked in Storyland, an amusement park based on fairytale themes. One of these was the tale of the frog who turns into a prince, and Sils, inspired by this, had painted two little girls with wounded frogs. Even in their fairytale setting, the girls know that the frogs cannot be saved, let alone turned into princes. Hence the novel's unusual title. Back in Paris, Berie tells a story about a girl who refuses to restore an enchanted prince to form because "at this point I'm actually more interested in a talking frog."

1279 Who's Afraid of Virgina Woolf? (Edward Albee, 1962)
The play by the American playwright takes place on a single night in an American university, when a history professor and his wife, George and Martha, and a young colleague of his and his wife, Nick and Honey, become involved in bitter conflict and a subsequent act of purgation. The title refers to the latter, since all four characters are finally determined to live without illusions, as Virginia Woolf did. The title occurs in the dialogue:

> *George* Who's afraid of Virginia Woolf ...
> *Martha* I ... am ... George ... I am. [The ellipses are in the original.]

Albee is said to have taken the title from a graffito scrawled on the wall of a men's room. It is itself an alteration of "Who's Afraid of the Big Bad Wolf?", the title of a song in the Walt Disney cartoon *Three Little Pigs* (1933).

1280   The Wide, Wide World   (Elizabeth Wetherell [Susan B. Warner], 1850)
The American author's three-volume sentimental novel for juvenile readers recounts the moral development of a young orphan, who learns to love the God who has brought upon her a series of misfortunes, including the death of her mother and that of a close friend. The title was already a stock phrase for the whole earth, here regarded as open to the power of God.

1281   The Wig   (Charles Wright, 1967)
The American writer's second novel, a comedy subtitled *A Mirror Image*, recounts how its black protagonist, Lester Jefferson, curls his Afro hair into a white "wig" that will gain him admittance to white society. When it does not, he realizes that "visibility" does not concern the manufacturing of an outward sign but, on the contrary, the creation of a true inner self.

1282   Wild Swans   (Jung Chang, 1991)
The Chinese author's book tells the life stories of three generations of Chinese women: the author herself, her mother, and her grandmother. When the author was born, the doctor commented that another wild swan had arrived. She was thus originally named Er Hong Chang, from Chinese *èr*, "two," and *hóng*, "swan." When she joined the Communist Party, however, she realized that this name could also mean "faded red," from *ér*, "and also" and *hóng*, "red," so she adopted her present name, meaning "military affairs," from *jūn*, "military."

1283   The Will to Change   (Adrienne Rich, 1971)
The American poet's volume of poems has a title that reflected her attitude at the time to active involvement in the process of political and social change.

1284   Williwaw   (Gore Vidal, 1946)
The American author's first novel is set in the Aleutian Islands and was based on his experiences in World War II. It tells the story of seven men on a ship whose enforced intimacy results in a death. The ship is caught in the middle of a *williwaw*, or sudden storm. Hence the title.

1285   Wilt   (Tom Sharpe, 1976)
The British writer's comic fifth novel takes its name from that of its likeable hero, Henry Wilt, and is designed to reflect his nature, as a henpecked and downtrodden university lecturer. He is involved in a suspected murder, and becomes engaged in a battle of wills with the equally aptly named police officer, Inspector Flint.

1286   The Wind in the Willows   (Kenneth Grahame, 1908)
The British writer's popular children's story was called *The Mole and the Water-Rat* in the author's first draft. It was then retitled *The Wind in the Reeds*, which was itself the original title of the chapter called "The Piper at the Gates of Dawn," in

which Mole and Rat have a vision of Pan. Grahame finally decided in favor of the alliterative title, itself evocative of his earlier lyrical essays on the English countryside.

1287   The Wings of the Dove   (Henry James, 1902)

The American writer's novel concerns a long postponed marriage, which in the end never takes place. The title quotes from Byron's poem *The First Kiss of Love* (1815): "For years fleet away with the wings of the dove." There is no doubt also an allusion to the biblical line: "Oh that I had wings like a dove! for then would I fly away and be at rest" (Psalm 55:6).

1288   Winner Take Nothing   (Ernest Hemingway, 1933)

The 14 stories by the American writer are mainly about people who appear to win but who (according to the author) are actually "losers," such as prostitutes, American tourists, and gamblers. The title is thus the converse of the traditional gambling phrase, "Winner takes all."

1289   With Malice Towards Some   (Margaret Halsey, 1938)

The book by the American writer about the British has a title that plays on words from Abraham Lincoln's Second Inaugural Address (1865), after the Civil War:

> With malice toward none, with charity for all, with firmness in the right as God gives us to see the right, let us strive on to finish the work we are in.

1290   With Shuddering Fall   (Joyce Carol Oates, 1964)

The American writer's first novel, like many to follow, concerns a romantic yet ultimately destructive relationship. It takes its title from George Meredith's poem *The Spirit of Earth in Autumn* (1862):

> Into the breast that gives the rose
> Shall I with shuddering fall!

1291   With the Procession   (H. B. Fuller, 1895)

The American writer's novel centers on a wealthy Chicago merchant whose interests are restricted to his business. When his children strike out for social and romantic success, with varying results, the strain of keeping up "with the procession" is too much for him, so that he sickens and dies.

1292   The Woman of Andros   (Thornton Wilder, 1930)

The American writer's novel is the story of a Greek concubine, based on Terence's Latin comedy *Andria* (a title itself meaning "woman of Andros").

1293   The Women's Room   (Marilyn French, 1977)

The American feminist writer's bestseller, her first novel, tells the composite story of many women who studied together at Harvard. The title obliquely refers to the "women's room" (lavatory) that is a repository of women's intimate conversations in a public, male-dominated place.

1294   A Word Child   (Iris Murdoch, 1975)

The British author's seventeenth novel tells the story of orphan Hilary Burde, whose life progresses from an illiterate, violent, and immoral youth to a literate, caring and moral adulthood. He is thus the "word child" of the title, who is rescued from illiteracy at the age of 14 by a teacher of French and Latin, Mr. Osmond. In a flashback, he reflects on this momentous event in his childhood:

> I also learnt my own language, hitherto something of a foreign tongue. I learnt from Mr. Osmond how to write the best language in the world accurately and clearly and, ultimately, with a hard, careful elegance. I discovered words and words were my salvation. I was not, except in some very broken down sense of that ambiguous term, a love child. I was a word child.

1295   The World According to Garp   (John Irving, 1978)

The American writer's novel is a cautionary tale centering on T. S. Garp, the son of a New England heiress and a brain-damaged aerial gunner who can only shout the meaningless word "Garp." ("T. S." stands for "Technical Sergeant," the gunner's rank.) Garp himself writes a novel titled *The World According to Bensenhaver*, a tale of fearful happenings.

1296   World Enough and Time   (Robert Penn Warren, 1950)

The American writer's novel is an account of the murder in Kentucky of Colonel Solomon P. Sharp by Jeroboam O. Beauchamp, whose trial was the sensation of 1826. The title comes from Andrew Marvell's poem *To His Coy Mistress* (1650–2):

> Had we but world enough, and time,
> This coyness, lady, were no crime.

1297   The World Owes Me a Living   (John Llewellyn Rhys, 1939)

The Welsh writer's novel, about a redundant Royal Flying Corps hero who tries to make a living with a flying circus, takes its title from the familiar saying, "All the world owes me a living," popularized by Walt Disney in his early "Silly Symphony" animated cartoon *Grasshopper and the Ants* (1934), itself based on the Aesop fable about the ant and the grasshopper. In the movie, the grasshopper becomes a fiddler and sings a song (written by Larry Morey to music by Leigh Harline) with the lines:

> Oh! the world owes me a living
> Deedle, diedle, doedle, diedledum.
> Oh! the world owes me a living
> Deedle, diedle, doedle, diedledum.

1298   The Wound and the Bow   (Edmund Wilson, 1941)

The American writer's volume of literary criticism has a title alluding to Sophocles' play *Philoctetes*, in which a warrior is exiled to an island because of his foul-smelling wound, where he is sought by his fellows, who need his magic bow to win the Trojan War. Wilson interprets this as symbolic of the modern writer, who pays for his creative achievements by his psychological vulnerability: on the one hand society makes the writer an "odd man out," on the other it demands the "healing" power of his art.

1299   A Wrinkle in Time   (Madeleine L'Engle, 1962)
The American writer's fourth novel for children tells how a brother and sister and their friend, aided by three strange beings, travel across "a wrinkle in time" to the planet Camazotz to search for the siblings' missing scientist father.

1300   Written on the Body   (Jeanette Winterson, 1992)
The British writer's fifth novel is a study of love, in which a lover of indeterminate sex describes in both anatomical and allegorical terms the various parts of the body of the loved one, who is dying of cancer. The title is extracted from the narrative itself:

> Written on the body is a secret code only visible in certain lights; the accumulations of a lifetime gather there. In places the palimpsest is so heavily worked that the letters feel like braille.

1301   Wuthering Heights   (Emily Brontë, 1847)
The famous novel's title is the name of the moorland house that is the home of its central character, Heathcliff. The narrative itself explains the name:

> Wuthering Heights is the name of Mr. Heathcliff's dwelling. "Wuthering" being a significant provincial adjective, descriptive of the atmospheric tumult to which its station is exposed, in stormy weather. Pure, bracing ventilation they must have up there, at all times, indeed.   [Chapter 1]

The author is said to have based Wuthering Heights on a Yorkshire farmhouse actually named Top Withins. If this is so, *Top* presumably gave *Heights* (itself genuinely found in the name of elevated sites), while *Withins*, which actually means "willows," suggested *Wuthering*.

1302   Xorandor   (Christine Brooke-Rose, 1986)
The writer, daughter of a British father and Swiss-American mother, was born in Switzerland, raised in Belgium, educated in England, and went on to live in France This cosmopolitan background may go some way to explaining the complexity of her novels. Her principal concern is with narrative and language. Here Xorandor, the central character, is a computerized being named from the logic of the program language he uses: exclusive OR (XOR) *and* non-exclusive OR. He is discovered in a stone near a Cornish tinmine by two computer-mad twins, Jip (a boy) and Zab (a girl), and the narrative that ensues is almost as much a dissertation on the necessary requirements for storytelling as it is the telling of an actual story itself.

1303   The Years   (Virginia Woolf, 1937)
The British writer's popular novel presents a portrait of the English middle classes and their changing values and attitudes as described in three generations of a family, spanning the years (hence the title) from 1880 to 1937.

1304   Yonnondio   (Tillie Olsen, 1974)
Subtitled *From the Thirties*, the American author's novel was only published 35 years after she had written it (but abandoned it near the end), in the 1930s. It is

thus set in the Depression, and tells of a child, Mazie, and her mother, Mary Holbrook, the latter gradually dying of exhaustion, childbearing, and malnutrition. The title is taken from the poem of the same name by Walt Whitman, and is itself an Iroquois word for a lament for the aborigines.

1305   You Can't Take It with You   (George S. Kaufman and Moss Hart, 1936)
The popular farce by the American playwrights is about an unconventional but very happy family who enjoy themselves right in the middle of New York City making fireworks, writing plays, practicing ballet, and printing anarchistic leaflets. The title implies "Enjoy yourself while you can," since the money that you have now will be no use to you after you are dead. The proverbial saying dates from at least the 19th century and occurs, for example, in Frederick Marryat's novel for boys, *Masterman Ready* (1841).

1306   You Must Remember This   (Joyce Carol Oates, 1987)
The American writer's eighteenth novel portrays a working-class family in upstate New York in the years between 1944 and 1956, the era of McCarthyism and the Cold War. Its title comes from a line in Herman Hupfeld's song *As Time Goes By* (1931):

> You must remember this, a kiss is still a kiss,
> A sigh is just a sigh,
> The fundamental things apply,
> As time goes by.

1307   The Young in One Another's Arms   (Jane Rule, 1977)
The novel by the American-born Canadian writer is one of many exploring the friendships, kinships, and love that can exist between women. It concerns the residents of a Vancouver boarding house who work together to start up a restaurant on Galiano Island, British Columbia (where Rule herself lives). The title comes from Yeats' poem *The Tower* (*Sailing to Byzantium*) (1928), which opens with the lines:

> That is no country for old men. The young
> In one another's arms, birds in the trees
> —Those dying generations—at their song.

1308   The Young Visiters   (Daisy Ashford, 1919)
The novel of Victorian society was written when the English author was only nine, and contains a number of idiosyncratic spellings and turns of phrase. Hence the spelling of the title. (In the manuscript original this was actually *The Young Viseters*, and it is unclear why this was changed.)

1309   The Zeal of Thy House   (Dorothy Sayers, 1937)
The British writer's first successful play is an exploration of the sin of pride, as depicted in the character of William of Sens, the architect responsible for the rebuilding of Canterbury Cathedral (where it was first performed). The title was appropriately adopted from the Bible:

For the zeal of thine house hath eaten me up; and the reproaches of them that re-
poached thee are fallen upon me.   [Psalm 69:9]

The title was not the author's own, but was suggested by Laurence Irving, the stage
designer, after reading a draft of the first act. Sayers later wrote to a friend: "Though
I sat grinding my teeth with jealousy for two hours, I could not think of anything
half as good."

1310   Zen and the Art of Motorcycle Maintenance   (Robert Pirsig, 1974)

The American writer's cult classic is basically a "road saga," in which a father and
son ride the backroads from Minnesota to California, savoring forgotten America
and discovering themselves in the process. The motorcyle on which they ride represents the human vehicle on its journey through life. The title wittily juxtaposes
the earthly skills of motorcycle maintenance with the otherworldly refined techniques of Zen Buddhism, while at the same time deliberately invoking earlier titles,
such as Eugen Herrigel's *Zen in the Art of Archery*, *Zen in the Art of Flower Arrangement*, by Herrigel's wife, Gustie, and Horst Hammitzsch's *Zen in the Art of the Tea
Ceremony*, all translated into English from the original German. The title may even
have been suggested by Ray Bradbury's essay *Zen and the Art of Writing* (1973).

1311   Zuckerman Unbound   (Philip Roth, 1981)

The American writer's novel is the second in a trilogy about the writer Nathan
Zuckerman, with the title hinting at that of Shelley's drama *Prometheus Unbound*
(1820). When Roth published the three books together as a single work, he gave it
the punning title *Zuckerman Bound* (1985).

SELECT
BIBLIOGRAPHY

There are hundreds of books on modern literature in English, and the bibliography that follows concentrates chiefly on sources that supply information about individual literary titles and their authors on the one hand and origins of quotations and allusions on the other. As mentioned in the Introduction, in order to establish the origin of a literary title it is frequently necessary to marry the former with the latter.

The word "English" in some titles below does not necessarily mean "British." It may refer to writers in English or literature in English, and so comprehend American, Canadian, etc. writers and literature.

The bibliography does not include general biographical accounts, obituaries, or book reviews, such as those appearing respectively in the *Encyclopaedia Britannica*, the volumes of *The Annual Obituary* published by St. James Press, Chicago, and the *Times Literary Supplement*. Nevertheless, such sources were all exploited for information on writers and their works.

Amos, William. *The Originals: Who's Really Who in Fiction*. London: Cape, 1985.

Adair, Gilbert. "Let the title credits roll." *Sunday Times*, June 27, 1993.

Augarde, Tony (ed.). *The Oxford Dictionary of Modern Quotations*. Oxford: Oxford University Press, 1991.

Banham, Martin (ed.). *The Cambridge Guide to Theatre*. Cambridge: Cambridge University Press, 1990.

Barnes, Philip. *A Companion to Post-War British Theatre*. Beckenham: Croom Helm, 1986.

Benét, William Rose. *The Reader's Encyclopedia*. 3rd ed. London: A. & C. Black, 1987.

Bernard, André. *Now All We Need Is a Title: Famous Book Titles and How They Got That Way*. New York: W. W. Norton, 1995.

Blain, Virginia, Patricia Clements, and Isobel Grundy. *The Feminist Companion to Literature in English*. London: Batsford, 1990.

Bradbury, Malcolm. *The Modern British Novel*. London: Secker & Warburg, 1993.

Browning, D. C. *Everyman's Dictionary of Literary Biography: English and American*. Rev. ed. London: Dent, 1969.

Buck, Claire (ed.). *Bloomsbury Guide to Women's Literature*. London: Bloomsbury, 1992.

Burgess, Anthony. *Ninety-Nine Novels*. London: Allison & Busby, 1984.

Carpenter, Humphrey, and Mari Prichard. *The Oxford Companion to Children's Literature*. Oxford: Oxford University Press, 1984.

Chevalier, Tracy (ed.). *Twentieth-Century Children's Writers.* 3rd ed. Chicago: St. James Press, 1989.

Cohen, J. M., and M. J. Cohen. *The Penguin Dictionary of Twentieth-Century Quotations.* London: Viking, 1993.

Conn, Peter. *Literature in America.* Cambridge: Cambridge University Press, 1989.

Drabble, Margaret (ed.). *The Oxford Companion to English Literature.* 5th ed. Oxford: Oxford University Press, 1985.

Eagle, Dorothy, and Hilary Curnell (eds.). *The Oxford Illustrated Literary Guide to Great Britain and Ireland.* Oxford: Oxford University Press, 1981.

Enser, A.G.S. *Filmed Books and Plays: A List of Books and Plays From Which Films Have Been Made, 1975–81.* Aldershot: Gower, 1982.

_____. *Filmed Books and Plays: A List of Books and Plays From Which Films Have Been Made, 1928–1974.* Revised cumulated ed. London: André Deutsch, 1975.

Farrow, Nigel, Brian Last, and Vernon Pratt (eds.). *An English Library.* 6th ed. Aldershot: Gower, 1990.

France, Peter (ed.). *The New Oxford Companion to Literature in French.* Oxford: Clarendon Press, 1995.

Freeman, William. *Everyman's Dictionary of Fictional Characters.* Rev. by Fred Urquhart. 3rd ed. London: Dent, 1973.

Gray, Martin. *A Chronology of English Literature.* Harlow: Longman, 1989.

Grote, David. *Common Knowledge: A Reader's Guide to Literary Allusions.* Westport, CT: Greenwood Press, 1987.

Halliwell, Leslie, with Philip Purser. *Halliwell's Television Companion.* 3rd ed. London: Grafton Books, 1986.

Harrowven, Jean. *The Origins of Rhymes, Songs and Sayings.* London: Kaye & Ward, 1977.

Hart, James D. *The Oxford Companion to American Literature.* 5th ed. New York: Oxford University Press, 1983.

Hartnoll, Phyllis (ed.). *The Oxford Companion to the Theatre.* Oxford: Oxford University Press, 1983.

Harvey, Sir Paul (comp. and ed.). *The Oxford Companion to English Literature.* Rev. by Dorothy Eagle. 4th ed. Oxford: Oxford University Press, 1967.

_____, and J. E. Heseltine. *The Oxford Companion to French Literature.* Oxford: Oxford University Press, 1959.

Henderson, Lesley (ed.). *Contemporary Novelists.* 5th ed. Chicago: St. James Press, 1991.

Holland, Harold E. "Fiction Titles from the Bible." *Oklahoma Librarian* 15 (1965), pp. 116–122.

Howatson, M. C. (ed.). *The Oxford Companion to Classical Literature.* 2nd ed. Oxford: Oxford University Press, 1989.

Jeffrey, David Lyle (ed.). *A Dictionary of Biblical Tradition in English Literature.* Grand Rapids, MI: William B. Eerdmans, 1992.

Kamm, Anthony. *Collins Biographical Dictionary of English Literature.* Glasgow: Harper-Collins, 1993.

Kaplan, Justin (ed.). *Bartlett's Familiar Quotations.* 16th ed. Boston: Little, Brown, 1992.

Kayhoe, Walter (comp.). *Book Titles from the Bible.* Moylan, PA: The Rose Valley Press, 1946.

Keating, H.R.F. *Whodunit? A Guide to Crime, Suspense and Spy Fiction.* London: Windward, 1982.

Kingsley, Hilary, and Geoff Tibballs. *Box of Delights: The Golden Years of Television.* London: Macmillan, 1989.

Lass, Abraham H., David Kiremidjian, and Ruth M. Goldstein. *The Facts on File Dictionary of Classical, Biblical & Literary Allusions.* New York: Facts on File, 1987.

McLeish, Kenneth. *Bloomsbury Good Reading Guide.* Rev. ed. London: Bloomsbury, 1994.

Ousby, Ian (ed.). *The Cambridge Guide to Literature in English.* Cambridge: Cambridge University Press, 1988.

_____. *Literary Britain and Ireland.* 2nd ed. London: A. & C. Black, 1990.

Parker, Peter (ed.). *The Reader's Companion to the Twentieth Century Novel.* London/Oxford: Fourth Estate/Helicon, 1994.

Partington, Angela (ed.). *The Oxford Dictionary of Quotations.* 4th ed. Oxford: Oxford University Press, 1992.

Pattison, Robert B. "Bible Words as Book Titles." *Religion in Life* 7 (1938), pp. 439–450.

Payton, Geoffrey. *The Penguin Dictionary of Proper Names.* Rev. by John Paxton. London: Viking, 1991.

Perkins, George, Barbara Perkins, and Phillip Leininger (eds.). *Benét's Reader's Encyclopedia of American Literature.* Glasgow: HarperCollins, 1992.

Pine, L.G. *A Dictionary of Mottoes.* London: Routledge & Kegan Paul, 1983.

Prebble, Roger (comp. and ed.). *Chambers Fiction File.* Edinburgh: Chambers, 1992.

Pringle, David. *Imaginary People: A Who's Who of Modern Fictional Characters.* London: Grafton Books, 1987.

Rees, Nigel. *Brewer's Quotations: A Phrase and Fable Dictionary.* London: Cassell, 1994.

____. *Dictionary of Popular Phrases.* London: Bloomsbury, 1990.

____. *Dictionary of Phrase & Allusion.* London: Bloomsbury, 1992.

Rintoul, M. C. *Dictionary of Real People and Places in Fiction.* London: Routledge, 1993.

Roberts, Andrew Michael (ed.). *The Novel.* London: Bloomsbury, 1993.

Rogers, James. *A–Z of Quotes and Clichés.* New York: Facts On File, 1985.

Ross, Sir E. Denison. *This English Language.* London: Longmans, Green, 1939.

Seymour-Smith, Martin. *The Dent Dictionary of Fictional Characters.* London: Dent, 1991.

Sharp, R. Farquharson. *A Dictionary of English Authors Biographical and Bibliographical: Being A Compendious Account of the Lives and Writings of Upwards of 800 British and American Writers From the Year 1400 to the Present Time.* London: Kegan Paul, Trench, Trübner, 1904.

Smith, Benjamin E. (ed.). *The Century Cyclopedia of Names.* 11th ed. New York: The Century Co., 1904.

Smith, William George. *The Oxford Dictionary of English Proverbs.* Oxford: Oxford University Press, 1970.

Smith, F. Seymour. *An English Library: A Bookman's Guide.* Rev. ed. London: Deutsch, 1963.

Smith, Eric. *A Dictionary of Classical Reference in English Poetry.* Cambridge: D. S. Brewer, 1984.

Tennant, Emma. *The ABC of Writing.* London: Faber, 1992.

Thomson, Peter, and Gāmini Salgādo. *The Everyman Companion to the Theatre.* London: Dent, 1985.

Todd, Janet (ed.). *Dictionary of British Women Writers.* London: Routledge, 1989.

Walker, John (ed.). *Halliwell's Film Guide.* 11th ed. London: HarperCollins, 1995.

Ward, A. C. *Longman Companion to Twentieth Century Literature.* Rev. by Maurice Hussey. 3rd ed. Harlow: Longman, 1981.

Whitehead, Allison. "Titillating Titles." *Verbatim* Vol. XX, No. 4 (Spring 1994), p. 22.

Zasursky, Ya., G. Zlobin, and Yu. Kovalev (comps. and eds.). *Pisateli SShA [Writers of the USA].* Moscow: Raduga, 1990.

INDEX

All authors are indexed herein. With a few exceptions, the other entries in this index relate to the titles, not to the subjects of the books. Wars and non–Anglo countries and ethnic heritages are the main exceptions. Also cited are all persons or works from which titles are derived, and persons and place-names to which a title alludes.